PREHISTORIC THAILAND

FROM EARLY SETTLEMENT TO SUKHOTHAI

PREHISTORIC THAILAND

FROM EARLY SETTLEMENT TO SUKHOTHAI

Charles Higham and Rachanie Thosarat

RIVER BOOKS

First published and distributed in Thailand by
River Books, 396/1 Maharaj Rd. Tatien, Bangkok 10200
Tel: (66 2) 224-6686, 225-0139, 225-4963
Fax: (66 2) 225-3861, E-mail: riverbkk@samart.co.th

A River Books Production
Copyright text © Charles Higham and Rachanie Thosarat
Collective Work © River Books 1998

British Library Cataloguing-in-Publication Data
A catalogue record for this book is available from the British Library

Editor Narisa Chakrabongse
Production Paisarn Piemmettawat
Design Supadee Ruangsakvichit
Typesetting Wannapa Promjeen

ISBN: 974 8225 30 5

Colour Separation by Kanoksilp (Thailand) Co., Ltd.
Printed and bound in Thailand by Bangkok Printing (1984) Co., Ltd.

Contents

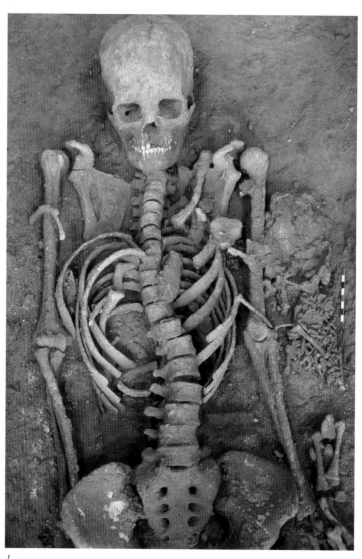

1

Preface

"The transformation of our knowledge of prehistoric Australia and Southeast Asia over the course of the last 30 years has been one of the most exciting developments to have taken place in modern archaeology." Renfrew and Bahn 1996:478

The study of Thailand's past is intertwined with its political history. All its neighbours have been colonised: Myanmar and Malaysia by the British, Vietnam, Cambodia and Laos by the French, Indonesia by the Dutch. The colonial powers introduced their traditional methods for archaeological research. Over a century has elapsed since the discovery of *Homo erectus* on the banks of the Solo River in Java by Eugene Dubois, and the foundation of the French School of Research in Hanoi took place in 1898. Only Thailand stood firmly against the colonial tide, and in consequence, looked to its own resources. This came with royal inspiration. King Rama IV travelled widely as a monk, and soon realised the importance of collecting and safeguarding precious inscriptions and objects for public education and research. King Rama V and his successor continued this tradition, the latter passing the legislation "Proclamation for the survey and protection of ancient objects". The duties of a committee of the Vajirayana Library, to safeguard objects from antiquity, anticipated the establishment of the Archaeological Service of Siam in 1924, the National Museum of Siam in 1926 and the successor to both, the Fine Arts Department in 1933 (FAD 1991). H.R.H. Prince Damrong gave inspirational leadership in a role maintained by his son, H.S.H. Prince Subhadradis Diskul, and now filled by H.R.H. Crown Princess Maha Chakri Sirindhorn.

2

1: *This woman, interred at Khok Phanom Di 3,700 years ago, has a baby next to her left arm.*

2: *One of the richest of prehistoric graves in Thailand is the Princess of Khok Phanom Di, who lived 3,600 years ago, and wore over 120,000 shell beads.*

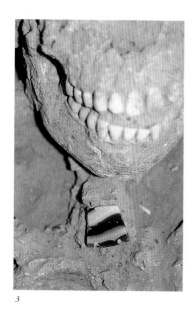

3

3-5: *Prehistoric Iron Age people revelled in exotic jewellery. Here we see agate pendants and carnelian beads.*

Meanwhile, the foundation of the Siam Society, at a meeting held in the Oriental Hotel on 26th February 1904, saw a coming together of Thai and foreign scholars in Bangkok devoted to the study of Thailand's rich cultural heritage. Loofs-Wissowa (1997) has written with refreshing frankness on the subsequent laying of foundations for research into prehistoric Thailand by collaborative fieldwork involving *farangs* (Westerners) and Thais. The first joint venture saw collaboration between Danish and Thai archaeologists in Kanchanaburi, commencing in 1959. There followed teams of Thai and American, Australian, British and New Zealand scholars. This programme began, as Loofs-Wissowa has stressed, in a virtual vacuum of knowledge on the prehistoric period. Research, while advancing on a broad front, often found itself in blind alleys and at controversial crossroads. Anyone reviewing the publications of one of us (C.H.) over the past 25 years will find that at times, the wrong signpost was followed, but we both feel confident that a sufficiently firm pattern has now emerged to justify this book.

We are particularly gratified to be able to write it jointly, since it is symbolic of the past, present and hopefully the future cooperation between *farangs* and Thais. One of the first lessons for any foreign archaeologist in Thailand, is the importance of undertaking research in harmony with Thai colleagues. Since working together at Ban Chiang in 1975, we have co-directed excavations at a series of sites, in programmes designed to contribute their mite to understanding Thailand's past. We spent seven months excavating at Khok Phanom Di in 1984-5, in an attempt to illuminate prehistoric adaptation to the coastal environment of the Gulf of Siam. This was followed by three seasons at Nong Nor, which involved early coastal hunter gatherers and a later Bronze Age cemetery. In 1992, we moved focus to the Mun Valley and in our present research programme, we are trying to find out more of the Iron Age communities which were to develop in time into the Empire of Angkor.

It was during this last period of joint research in Phimai, that we had a chance meeting with Paisarn Piemmettawat. We had for some time been pondering a book on early Thailand, and with his encouragement, we met with Narisa Chakrabongse for further discussions. Out of these, arose a commitment and we thank them both for their constant encouragement. It is particularly pleasing to be associated with River Books, for they have already demonstrated the value of joint publication by Thai and Western scholars in *Palaces of the Gods* and *Ancient Capitals of Thailand*. Nevertheless, it might well be asked why write a book on Thai prehistory and early history now, when we already have available texts by Chin You-di, Srisak Vallibhotama and Pisit Charoenwongsa (Charoenwongsa 1982, You-di 1986, Vallibhotama 1996). The answer is simple. There has been such a deluge of results and new information since their excellent summaries appeared, that we consider it time to present a general synthesis.

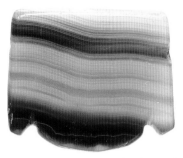

4   *(length 2.5 cm)*

5   *(length of longest bead 3.8 cm)*

Writing this book has brought home to us the gratitude we owe to many people, and while the following list is by no means exhaustive, its length indicates our indebtedness. First, we thank the following Directors General of the Fine Arts Department who have encouraged our work and facilitated the necessary formalities: Captain Sompop Piromp, Dejo Saowananon, Khunying Aree Kultan, Taweesak Sennanarong, Khunying Kullasap Gesmankit, Dr Suvit Rasmibhuti, the late Somkid Chotigavanit and Nikhom Musigakama. The staff of the Archaeology Division have always been a source of strength, and we thank Prachote Sangkhanukit and Janya Manavid. At the National Research Council, we acknowledge the generous assistance of Tuenchai Niyamankoon and her colleagues.

We have been privileged by the support and enthusiasm for our research shown by numerous Thai colleagues and friends. H.S.H. Prince Subhadradis Diskul has always been generous with advice and help. We wish to thank Professor Sanga Sabasri for his hospitality and encouragement, and to M.R. Sarisdiguna Kitiyakara, who never failed to provide assistance when needed, even while preoccupied with the affairs of the Shell Company of Thailand. At the same company, we recall the kindness of Preecha Phonprasert. Sakhon Vanabriksha, former Thai Ambassador to New Zealand, and Sumet Jumsai have provided support at critical moments. We also thank Thiva Supajanya, Sin Sinsakul, Samphan Ratanasupa and Kamolthip Kasipa.

In the field, we have had the pleasure of working alongside a host of friends and colleagues from the Fine Arts Department. We recall the wise counsel of Chin You-di in the early days. He heads a list which includes Anat Bamrungwongse, Pongdhan Bandhom, Chutima Chanted, Chalit Chaikanchit, Pisit Charoenwongsa, Phrapid Choosiri, Sod Daeng-iet, Payao Khemnark, Amphan Kijngam, Nujchanard Kijngam, Aroonsak

Kingmanee, Staporn Kwanyuen, Somsuda Leyavanija, Seehawat
Naenna, Damrongkiadt Noksakul, Suphot Phommanodch,
Pirapon Pisnupong, Anand Poomjam, Niti Saengwan, Samart
Sapyen, Dusit Thummakorn, Metha Wichakana, and Warrachai
and Sirikun Wiriyaromp. Colleagues who have contributed
specialist information to this book through their collaboration
with us in the field or laboratory include William Boyd, Carl
Heron, Thomas Higham, Philip Houghton, Alan Hogg, Lisa
Kealhofer, the late Elizabeth Lyons, Robert Maddin, Bernard
Maloney, Bryan Manly, Graeme Mason, Gerry McDonnell, Ken
McKenzie, Elizabeth Moore, Christine Pailles, the late Hamilton
Parker, the late Jacqui Pilditch, Dolores Piperno, Warankhana
Rajpitak, Tony Reay, Sharma Saitowitz, Nigel Seeley, Nancy
Tayles, Gillian Thompson, Brian Vincent and Barbara West.
In the same breath, we should mention those students at Otago
University who have completed dissertations, or who have
worked with us during excavations. The list spans 28 years, and
includes Lee Aitken, Hallie Buckley, Angela Calder, David
Cassaidy, Nigel Chang, Payom Chantaratiyakarn, James
Chetwin, Rebecca Connelly, Joss Debreceny, Kate Domett, Alan
Grant, Jeremy Habberfield-Short, Diane Hall, Dinah Higham,
Thomas Higham, Carolyn McGill, Michelle Moore, Kirsten
Nelsen, Dougald O'Reilly, the late Jacqui Pilditch, Melanie
Pearson, Helen Pollock, Paul Rivett, Katherine Roy, Nicola
Smith, Sarah Talbot and Judith Voelker.

An excavation programme represents a considerable
commitment of time and energy, and seeking sources of funding
is a preoccupation for any would be archaeologist. We have been
particularly fortunate in the loyalty and generosity of many
funding agencies: the Asian Cultural Council, the Breezewood
Foundation, the British Academy, The Fine Arts Department
of Thailand, the Ford Foundation, the Marsden Fund, the
National Geographic Society, the New Zealand Foundation for
Research in Science and Technology, the Shell Company of
Thailand, the Society of Antiquaries of London, the Universities
of Cambridge and Otago and the Wenner Gren Foundation.
The Center for Field Research organises through Earthwatch,
a research corps of volunteers. Over the years, we have received
the help of over 150 volunteers who join us in the field. Clearly
there are too many to mention all by name, but we are sure that
not one would begrudge us particularly acknowledging Herman
Seibert and Allen Thompson, who return every year, as regularly
as the first swallows of summer, to join our team.

This volume has drawn on the skill of Martin Fisher and Leslie O'Neill, of the Department of Anthropology, University of Otago. Both have brought their experience of many archaeological reports to bear on the maps and drawings which complement our text and we thank them accordingly. We are also most grateful to the Fine Arts Department, Donn Bayard, Sod Daeng-iet, Pisit Charoenwongsa, Michael Freeman, Muang Boran, Paisarn Piemmettawat, Surapol Natapintu, Jean-Pierre Pautreau, Dougald O'Reilly, Vincent Pigott, Vichai Tankitti-korn, Suphot Phommanodch, Marielle Santoni, Per Sørensen and Andrew Weiss for allowing us access to their photographs.

Many of our colleagues have contributed to the study of prehistory in general and unravelling the mysteries of Thai prehistory in particular. Through their research and contributions to the literature, this book has been immeasurably enriched. We particularly thank Donn Bayard, Peter Bellwood, Robert Blust, Pisit Charoenwongsa, Roberto Ciarla, the late Sir Grahame Clark, Ian Glover, the late Chester Gorman, Helmut Loofs-Wissowa, Aude Matringhem, Eiji Nitta, Jean-Pierre Pautreau, Vincent Pigott, Colin Renfrew, Wilhelm Solheim II, Per Sørensen, Matthew Spriggs, Miriam Stark, William Watson, Andrew Weiss, Joyce White, Richard Wilen, Moira Woods and Henry Wright for so many interesting conversations and ideas.

(height 47 cm)

6: A pottery vessel dating to the Iron Age from Ban Chiang.

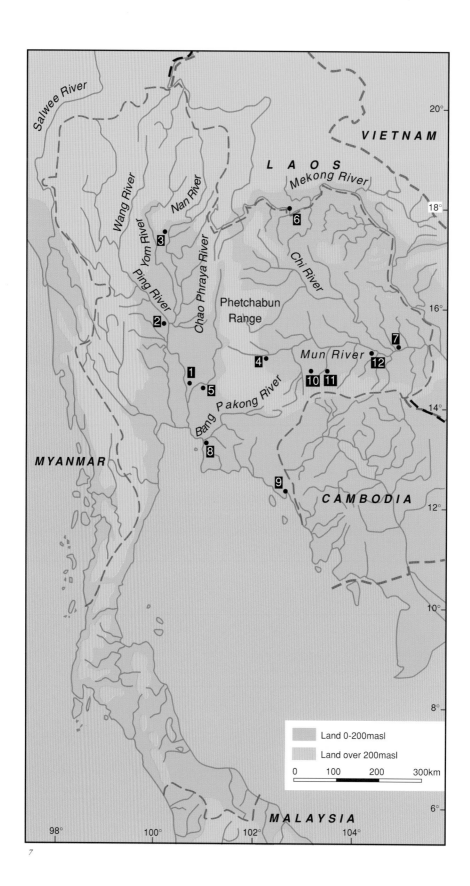

Chapter One
Thailand: An overview

"The art of the present day reflects Thailand's prestigious cultural heritage, merging past, present and future into one."
Srivichit 1991:216

Scratch the surface of Thailand, and you find evidence for change. Nothing, it seems, is immune. Some changes reflect natural processes beyond human control, but the impact of people is seen in every corner of the kingdom. For the visitor reaching Thailand for the first time, probably now by air, the first impression is the heat. The second is the size and bustle of Bangkok, but leave for the countryside, and you find a quite different scene. Central Thailand, called "the heart of the country", is now an immense, flat alluvial plain, criss-crossed by a myriad of waterways natural and artificial, sprinkled with villages now linked by road and rail as well as canal or river. But a century ago, the land behind Bangkok was totally different. It was a seemingly endless marshland, the occasional elevated land being covered by forest. Transport was easy by water, almost impossible by land during the monsoon floods.

9

7: The location of places mentioned in chapter I.
1 Lopburi, 2 Nakhon Sawan, 3 Uttaradit, 4 Nakhon Ratchasima, 5 Saraburi, 6 Vientiane, 7 Ubon Ratchathani, 8 Chonburi, 9 Trat, 10 Buriram, 11 Surin, 12 Sisaket.

8: The Southeastern region of Thailand includes much flat land now under rice. This dry season view looks west from Wat Khao Kirirom in Chonburi Province.

9: Much information about prehistoric people comes from their burials. This man from Noen-U-Loke was buried with beautiful pots, an iron knife still covered in ancient cloth, and a necklace of agate and gold beads.

8

10

11

10: Inselbergs emerge from the Bangkok
Plain in the vicinity of Lopburi.

11: The coast of southeastern Thailand is
gently shelving, and is backed under
natural conditions by thick mangrove
forests.

12: The regions of Thailand.

As canals penetrated laterally across the plain from Bangkok, so human settlement followed, and rice fields began to replace the natural swamps (Hanks 1972). Proceed back 5,000 years, and the land behind Bangkok was a shallow extension of the Gulf of Siam all the way up to Ayutthaya. The Chao Phraya River and its many tributaries have subsequently brought down vast quantities of silt to fill the shallow sea with marine clays which today see the delta advance by up to six metres every year. This process, which extends back for millennia, has resulted in river and marine deposits under Bangkok that extend down several hundred metres. Go back a further 4,000 years, and the Central Plain was of a much larger expanse of low-lying land that extended hundreds of kilometres beyond the present coast, for the sea level was then up to 100 m below its present height.

Central Thailand today comprises a broad plain rising gradually in altitude as one proceeds northward (Donner 1982). A chain of uplands to the west separates Thailand from Myanmar, and the Phetchabun Range to the east divides this heart of the country from the Khorat Plateau. The central region incorporates extensive rice land, but as one travels northward to the vicinity of Lopburi, the occasional limestone outcrop or inselberg can be discerned, and with increasing elevation, rice gives way to crops which do not need the swampy conditions in which rice thrives. Under natural circumstances, much of the coast and tidally influenced land behind it encourages mangrove and nipa forest. Salt flats are often found beyond the high tide mark. Former tidal flats and alluvial soils

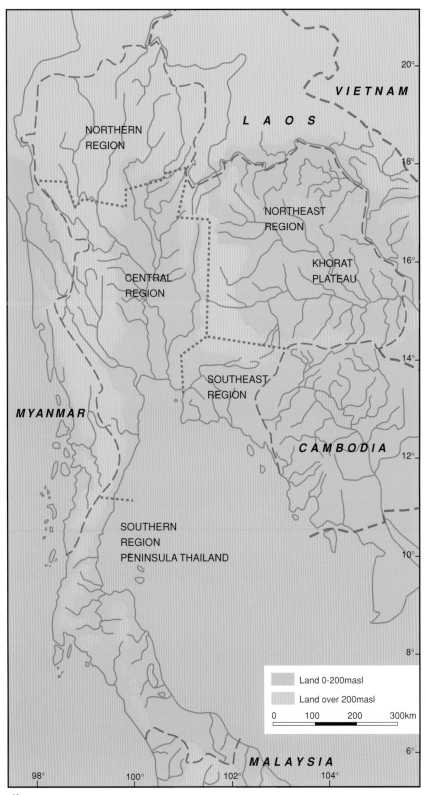

VIETNAM

LAOS

NORTHERN
REGION

NORTHEAST
REGION

KHORAT
PLATEAU

CENTRAL
REGION

SOUTHEAST
REGION

MYANMAR

CAMBODIA

SOUTHERN
REGION
PENINSULA THAILAND

Land 0-200masl

Land over 200masl

0   100   200   300km

MALAYSIA

20°

18°

16°

14°

12°

10°

8°

6°

98°   100°   102°   104°

12

13

14

15

13: *Looking west from the Phetchabun Range over the Pasak Valley, the ground is parched by the end of the dry season.*

14: *The coming of the monsoon brings downpours, and heralds the start of the agricultural year.*

15: *The Mekong at Nong Kai is an immense river. This view looks north to the Laotian bank.*

of the interior are now under extensive rice, but as one climbs in altitude, so one encounters various forest types ranging from dry dipterocarp forest on the lower slopes to tropical evergreen at higher levels.

These encircling uplands also influence rainfall. The Central Region is affected by the distinction between the wet and dry seasons. The bitter Siberian winter builds high pressure systems which drive prevailing winds south to Thailand. By the time they reach the Central Region, they are dry and relatively cool, bringing mean maxima and minima of 32 and 17.5°C to Nakhon Sawan during December and January. During March, the wind direction reverses, and hot, moist air from the southwest heralds the rainy season. April is a month of exhausting heat.

Temperatures rise to their maximum, reaching a mean of 39°C in Uttaradit, and people eagerly anticipate the breaking of the monsoon, when rains will transform the landscape. Then rock-hard soil exposed to sun over the previous dry months gratefully absorbs the rain. Fish and shellfish emerge from their refuges and villagers prepare their ploughs and harrows and plant out the rice in seed beds for later transplanting. Between May and October, an average season sees up to 1400 mm of rainfall, and as rivers rise, so does the risk of flooding.

It is easy now, by road or rail, to travel from Saraburi to Nakhon Ratchasima and so enter the Khorat Plateau. But this masks the former isolation of this northeastern part of Thailand, which accounts for about a third of the area of the Kingdom.

16

17

18

Before the establishment of more efficient means of transport linking it to the Central Region, the Phetchabun Range discouraged communication. Just as the Mun and Chi rivers, which drain the majority of the plateau, flow to the east, so in former times contact with the outside world naturally followed rivers which, in the case of Northeast Thailand, involves the Mekong. This great river originates in the eastern Himalayas, cuts through Yunnan and Laos before girdling the plateau. Having passed the eastern extremity of the Dang Raek Mountains, it flows through Cambodia and southern provinces of Vietnam until it reaches the sea. In 1641, the Dutch merchant Gerard van Wusthof proceeded by boat from the delta to Vientiane, and therefore found the Khorat Plateau on his left hand side as he travelled upstream. His diary brings home to us the dense forest cover and the abundant game which then characterised the countryside, and the importance of the river to trade and the exchange of ideas. During the prehistoric period, this would have been no less significant, as we will stress below.

The Mun and Chi rivers form the two largest catchments on the plateau, involving 185,000 and 82,000 km^2 respectively, compared with the 20,000 km^2 for the Songkhram Basin in the northeast corner. These two rivers converge in the vicinity of Ubon before travelling the short distance to the Mekong, and their eastward flow would have been the natural conduit for goods and ideas to reach the prehistoric communities which appear to have begun to settle in their catchments from about 1400 BC. The contrast between wet and dry seasons is a

16: With the rains, the Khorat Plateau becomes emerald green with young rice plants.

17: This rice seed bed is drying out, and the rice is withering. Taken in Nakhon Ratchasima Province in June 1997, this picture underlines dramatically the problems facing rice farmers living in this unpredictable environment.

18: The Khorat Plateau during the dry season resembles a golden carpet made up of rice stubble.

19

20

19: The Bang Fai festival is designed to bring the rainy season. Here, villagers in Udorn Thani Province put on their finery for the occasion.

20: The Chi River, seen here in the dry season, carries 60 times as much water with the rains.

recurrent theme which dominates life on the plateau, and this is to be seen in the pattern of rainfall and the nature of the rivers. The northeast is surrounded on all sides by uplands which cast rain shadows. The Truong Son Cordillera beyond the Mekong ensures that the northeast winds are dry by the time they reach the plateau, while the southwest monsoon winds drop much rain on the Phetchabun Range, which ensures that Nakhon Ratchasima, with annual rainfall of about 1150 mm, is particularly dry. The transition to the wet season is also hazardous for rice farmers, as their seed beds for rice can dry out if rain is not consistent.

Being more continental and lacking maritime influence, the Khorat Plateau experiences a particularly sharp contrast between the wet and dry seasons. Hardly any rain falls in December, but in May, the local people keenly anticipate the rains with the Bang Fai festival, and by September, flooding is widespread. Indeed, there is sixty times more water in the Chi during October than in March. The swollen rivers cross a gentle gradient, and the water rises and floods extensively. On reaching the mighty Mekong, the main channel is so choked that waters back up and add to the extent of flooding. This reduces forest cover, for most trees dislike waterlogged ground, but once away from the flood plains, the plateau sustains a dry deciduous forest which once supported a diverse fauna. Wild cattle, several varieties of deer and their predators were adapted to the woodlands, but crocodile, rhinoceros and water buffalo occupied the lakes, rivers and their swampy margins.

Deforestation has greatly increased water flows and silt levels since the prehistoric period, but available evidence indicates that flooding occurred then. So the low-lying flood plains of the major rivers would have been an unattractive place in which to settle, at least until technological skills permitted flood control measures. These areas also encourage the growth of a grassy swamp forest which does not encourage agriculture. As one moves away from the larger flood plains onto the lower terraces, however, gentler flood regimes are encountered along the course of stream tributaries, and it is here that most early prehistoric settlements are found, and rice was cultivated.

Traditionally, the Khorat Plateau has received rather a bad press from geographers, who stress its thin soils, harsh and unpredictable rainfall regime and the problems posed by flooding. Yet it sustained prehistoric communities of growing

21: Walking through the forest of Mae Hongson 25 years ago was an invigorating experience.

complexity over a period of at least three millennia before the establishment of the empire of Angkor.

If we now return to the Central Plain and travel north, we enter a third distinct region of Thailand. The nine provinces concerned are Mae Hongson, Chiang Mai, Lamphun, Lampang, Phrae, Chiang Rai, Phayao, Uttaradit and Nan. It is characterised by a series of uplands lying roughly on a north to south axis, drained by the Ping, Wang, Yom and Nan rivers. To the east, there lies part of the Mekong catchment and to the west, the Salween. But most of the drainage trends south to the Chao Phraya. It isn't possible to present a single overview of the climate or vegetation, because of the variability imposed by the mountain ranges. There are humid, relatively wet slopes giving way to small rain shadow areas. In general, rainfall remains seasonal with most concentrating between July and September, while December and January are dry. However, there is sufficient rainfall to sustain an evergreen, canopied forest on higher slopes. Twenty five years ago, walking through this forest in Mae Hongson was an invigorating experience. The air was filled with the sound of chattering monkeys, and it was possible to drink from the crystal clear streams. By night, deer and wild cattle came out of the depths to feed, and the distant cough of the tiger was still to be heard.

These uplands have been devastated by deforestation. Some of the hill tribes practice slash and burn cultivation which leads to severe soil degradation and erosion. The intermontane valleys now have virtually no natural vegetation cover, being under permanent rice fields.

The Bang Pakong is a major river which drains the northern part of the Southeast Region of Thailand. The lowlands through which the river flows were formerly under a dry deciduous forest, but today, the vast majority of this area is under rice. To the south of the Bang Pakong, however, the land rises to form extensive uplands which, exposed to the full effect of the southwest monsoon, experience among the highest rainfall in the country. This sustains under natural conditions, a thick evergreen forest cover. The narrow coastal plain, which extends from Chonburi to Trat, likewise offers a diverse habitat which includes formerly extensive mangrove forests.

The last natural region is often referred to as the south, or Peninsula Thailand. It is long and narrow, and dominated by a central spine of hills with a coastal plain to the east and west. At its narrowest, the peninsula is only 40 km wide. The hills are naturally clothed in an evergreen tropical forest. The long western coast has only a narrow plain, and incorporates thick belts of mangrove. In contrast, the eastern plain is broader, sandier and has few secure anchorages. Small rivers issue from the central range and cross the coastal plains, but none, naturally, attains any size. Nevertheless, those on the eastern side of the central range bear much silt, and have built up substantial deltas.

Being a narrow strip of land surrounded to east and west by the open sea, southern Thailand lacks the continental influences typical of the other four regions. The western coast and hills experience the full force of the southwestern monsoon, which brings heavy rain between May and October. But the opposite side lies in a rain shadow, and most rain falls with the prevailing northeast wind between October and the end of the year.

Economically, southern Thailand sees relatively little rice cultivation, but there are substantial plantations of coconuts, bananas and rubber trees. Tin mining is also a mainstay and formerly, timber production was important. The long coastline also encourages a vigorous fishing industry.

Thailand has a diverse environment involving uplands, long coastlines and many rivers. Its location is also nodal, in the sense that east to west communication is facilitated by sea and the narrow width of the Kra isthmus, while north to south movement is made possible by the Mekong, Salween and Chao Phraya river systems. It is not surprising, therefore, to find a considerable ethnic diversity. The majority of people are Thai, and speak Central Thai or in the northeast, the closely related

Lao dialect. These belong to the Austro-Tai family of languages, which has a distribution extending into Yunnan and across much of southern China. Particularly in border regions in Buriram, Sisaket and Surin provinces, one finds groups of Khmer speakers who have affinities south of the Dang Raek Range in Cambodia. These people, along with the 25 villages of Mon speakers in Khorat, Phetchabun and Chaiyaphum provinces (Nai Pan Hla 1994), have languages belonging to the Austroasiatic family, which is quite different from Thai. Early inscriptions in Mon and Khmer indicate that these languages predate the arrival of the Thai speakers. In northern Thailand, and down the western mountain ranges, there are the so-called hill tribe people which include the Lahu, Lisu, Akha, Karen and Hmong. Many of these communities represent relatively recent migrations into Thailand from the north. In the extreme south, there are surviving forest groups of negrito hunter-gatherers, known as the Semang. In the same region one finds the *Chao Nam,* or sea gipsies, a people who spend much of their time at sea and whose lives reveal extraordinary mobility. All over the kingdom, one finds recently assimilated Chinese, whose ancestors reached Thailand only two or three generations ago. One of the objectives of this book is to identify how these many groups, over the millennia, have been assimilated into one kingdom.

22: The coastline of Chonburi has extensive intertidal flats, and is quickly colonised by mangroves.

23: Mangrove forest was once thought to inhibit human settlement. Khok Phanom Di has tought us otherwise.

22

23

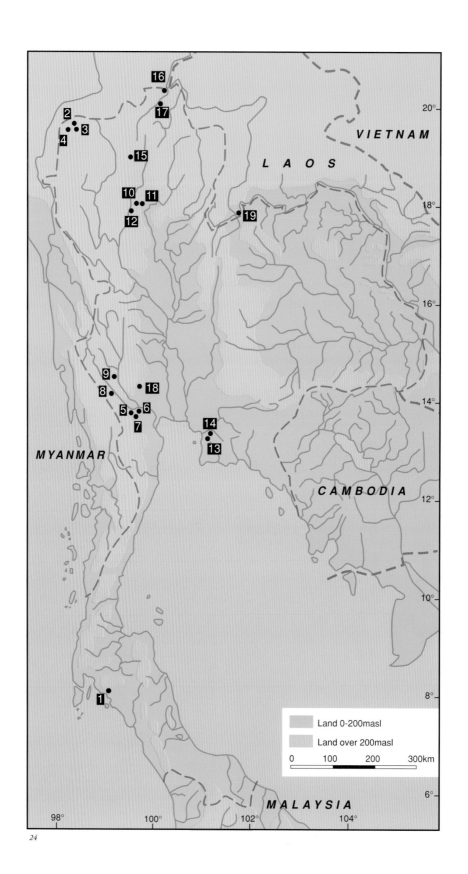

Chapter Two
Hunters and Gatherers

The human species originated in tropical Africa and evolved over many hundreds of thousands of years into a proficient and opportunistic meat eater and tool maker. Only stone implements have survived regularly from the millions of years which are involved, and it is clear that these early humans survived despite being themselves hunted by such predators as leopards and eagles. Living with danger must have encouraged communication, agility and tight social bonding, and early humans survived and prospered. They came to walk upright, their brains increased in size and through language, they were better able to adapt to new surroundings. One result of their evolutionary success is that they expanded out of Africa and by gradual degrees, colonised new lands.

This process of expansion involved a species named *Homo erectus*. The first bones of this type of human were discovered in Java, along the banks of the Solo River over a century ago. But further research has traced the origins of *Homo erectus* to Africa. Dating their intrusion into Southeast Asia is not easy, for most of the few surviving bones have been redeposited from their original resting places. Most authorities, however, agree that people were arriving by at least a million years ago. Thailand would have lain in the path of this pioneer human expansion which was to reach north into China, and south to the present islands of Southeast Asia. Sure in this knowledge, archaeologists have identified the region round Lampang as a likely area to seek traces of *Homo erectus*, or of their activities. As yet, no bones have been found but at Ban Mae Tha and Ban Don Mun, a research team has found ancient river gravels under a basalt

25   (height 8 cm.)

24: The location of hunter-gatherer sites mentioned in chapter II. 1. Lang Rongrien, Moh Khiew, 2. Spirit Cave, 3. Banyan Valley Cave, 4. Steep Cliff Cave, 5. Heap Cave, 6. Khao Talu, 7. Ment Cave, 8. Sai Yok, 9. Ongbah, 10. Ban Mae Tha, 11. Ban Don Mun, 12. Khao Pah Nam, 13. Nong Nor, 14. Khok Phanom Di, 15. Pha Chang, 16. Chiang Saen, 17. Tham Pra, 18. Don Noi, 19 Chiang Khan.

25: This stone projectile point comes from the Hoabinhian of Banyan Valley Cave.

26: These chipped stone tools are over 700,000 years old, and were found at Ban Mae Tha. The largest is 7 cm wide. (Courtesy Pisit Charoenwongsa)

flow. The gravels contain several intriguing stones, each with flakes removed to form a tool. It is possible to date the overlying lava, and it seems that the tools are over 700,000 years old (Pope *et al.* 1986).

Khao Pah Nam is a steep-sided karst tower also in Lampang Province and here, in a limestone cave, further flaked stone implements have been recovered together with the bones of hyaena, hippopotamus, tiger, wild cattle and deer. Some of the hippo bone was charred, and lay near what looks like a hearth. Pope and his associates have suggested that this find is contemporary with the tools from the river gravels. If so, then groups of *Homo erectus* probably occupied a relatively open, deciduous woodland: the faunal remains do not include any of the animals found today in thick rainforest (Pope 1985, Pope *et al.* 1978, 1986). It is surely only a matter of time before further finds are made, and we will discover more about the earliest occupation of Thailand. It would be particularly exciting if the remains of the people themselves could be found, as in Vietnam, China and Indonesia. At present, however, we face a gap of at least half a million years before it is possible to describe further evidence for human settlement.

Lang Rongrien

A great deal must have been happening between settlement by *Homo erectus* and the next evidence for human activity. The stone tools in Lampang were flaked by remote ancestors whose brain was about two thirds the size of ours. They had thick skull bones and a broad face, and stood no higher than 1.6 m. Over the next half million years, these early humans evolved into forms virtually identical with people today, but we are still unsure whether the fully modern looking people of the past 40,000 years represent a further intrusive expansion into Asia from Africa, or whether there was a local evolution. What we do know, however, is that by 40,000 years ago, people living in Southeast Asia were able to construct water craft and cross to Australia. We find traces of occupation by these modern humans at the rock shelter of Lang Rongrien.

This is a large cavern located on a limestone tower that lies between two streams. Its airy shelter has attracted human settlement over a long period, and when excavated from 1983 by Douglas Anderson, the remains of their activities were found.

These included charcoal from hearths dated from at least 38,000 until 27,000 years ago. This time span does not mean that the cave was occupied permanently. Rather, bands of hunters and gatherers sheltered there briefly before moving elsewhere. This part of Thailand attracts much rain, four times that of the dry northeast, and even today, the hills round Lang Rongrien support luxuriant rainforest. Thailand has seen many environmental changes over the years, and even during these three phases of occupation, the coast moved between about 30 and 100 km from the cave. Hence, we find an absence of any marine fish or shellfish and assume that the inhabitants collected and hunted locally available sources of food.

27: The basalt at Ban Mae Tha dates to about 700,000 years ago. (Courtesy Pisit Charoenwongsa)

In the earliest occupation episode, the excavators found two hearth areas, broken and charred animal bone and flaked stone tools. After a period of abandonment that might have lasted for several thousand years, prehistoric hunter gatherers reoccupied the site. More hearths formed, ringed by bones and flaked stone implements. During the last phase, Anderson found seven hearth areas, two of which had been lined with stones. Bones and stone implements clustered round them as if their warmth attracted prehistoric people while they cooked and ate. Perhaps the smoke helped disperse the mosquitoes. These people fashioned scrapers, knives and choppers from the local chert, but few stone artefacts were found, only 45 from all three phases of occupation. There is, however, also a piece of deer antler which had been grooved round the tine to remove it, presumably for later conversion into a tool.

Lang Rongrien is the only site to have provided us with a glimpse of life in Thailand between 38,000 and 27,000 years ago but it is likely that the interior stream valleys were inhabited by other small, scattered groups of hunter gatherers. What was happening on the coast is unknown because the major fluctuations in sea level have covered or destroyed all the evidence. Once again, there is a long period of silence before we can track down groups of hunters and gatherers.

Inland Hunter-Gatherers

From Southern China to Myanmar, archaeologists have found that inland rock shelters were often occupied by prehistoric hunter-gatherers. Their living sites were first recognized in northern Vietnam by a French woman, Madeleine Colani, who

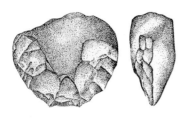

28: These stone tools were found by H.R. van Heekeren when he was a prisoner of war in Kanchanaburi. The largest is 10.5 cm across. (Courtesy Pisit Charoenwongsa)

named them Hoabinhian after the province in which she worked. As research began in Thailand, many similar remains were found, and the name Hoabinhian is often used to describe them. The first clear evidence for this tradition of hunting and gathering came with excavations by Sarasin at Tham Pra near Chiang Rai in 1931. There, he found flaked tools of diabase and green slate, in association with bone implements which he named the Siamian (Sarasin 1933, You-di 1957). Another discovery was made under most unusual circumstances. In 1943, the Dutch archaeologist H.R. van Heekeren was taken prisoner and forced to work on the infamous railway linking Thailand with Myanmar through the valley of the Kwae Noi River. As he worked, he found six flaked pebble tools and resolved that when peace returned, he would enquire further into this area.

Seventeen years later found him working at a series of rock shelters and caves at Sai Yok and in one of these shelters, he found a series of layers extending to a depth of four metres. These included many shellfish collected, it is thought, from the adjacent river, and the bones from wild cattle, pig, deer, rhinoceros, water buffalo and serow. If screening of the cultural deposits through a sieve had been undertaken, he would almost certainly have extracted the remains of small fish and mammals. The living floors yielded many stone tools, formed by removing flakes from a river pebble. These have been called picks, choppers, and axes. None would have been of any use in hunting, they are far too heavy and cumbersome. Perhaps people hunted with wooden implements. Bamboo is a perfect material for fashioning traps, spears or arrows. van Heekeren has suggested that the site was occupied briefly by bands of hunters and gatherers who, to judge by the open sites also containing such stone tools, often camped away from caves or rock shelters (van Heekeren and Knuth 1967). Unfortunately, no charcoal was recovered for radiocarbon dating, but the excavators suggested that initial occupation took place about 8-10,000 BC.

This dating context has received support from excavations at the huge cavern of Ongbah, located 15 km to the northeast. Here, Per Sørensen (1979) found a thick layer containing Hoabinhian stone tools, canarium nuts and hearths which have has been dated to between 9200 and 7400 BC.

Radiocarbon Dating

All the prehistoric societies described in this book have been traced and described by archaeologists over the past 40 years. One of the most important aspects of this study is time. How long ago was a site occupied? When did agriculture begin? How old is the Bronze Age in Thailand? The vital answers are obtained by radiocarbon dating. This technique was developed by an American, Willard Libby, just after the Second World War.

Carbon is ubiquitous in the Earth's biosphere and forms compounds with many different elements. Carbon exists for example in graphite (used in pencil lead) and as lignite and coal used for house fires. The carbon found in these forms is very old indeed and is composed of two different types, or isotopes of carbon; carbon 12 (C12) and carbon 13 (C13). In living things, amongst the C12 and C13 there is another isotope, Carbon 14 (C14), or radiocarbon. This isotope is radioactive, which means it is unstable atomically. Carbon 14 is created in the upper atmosphere through the bombardment of cosmic radiation upon the earth. Soon after its creation it enters the earth's plant and animal lifeways. Living organisms take up C14 as they ingest food and carbon dioxide. As soon as the organism dies, this process stops and the C14 is no longer replenished. The C14 begins to decay and disappear.

Willard Libby and his team found that the radiocarbon decays at a fixed rate. They found that after 5,730 years, half the C14 has decayed. After another 5,730 years, another half of the remaining amount has also decayed. After 10 half lives, or about 60,000 years, all the C14 has decayed and the sample has no C14 remaining.

The role of a radiocarbon laboratory is to produce an accurate estimate of the age of the carbon sample excavated from the archaeological site in question. This is not a straightforward process because C14 is only present in very small amounts proportional to the other isotopes of carbon. Libby's first counter was a modified geiger counter and used solid carbon coated to the inside of counting equipment. All the University of Waikato dates in this book were obtained in New Zealand using a more modern method called Liquid Scintillation Spectrometry. The samples of carbon-bearing material are first pretreated so that any contaminating, non-sample carbon is removed using physical and chemical means. They are then combusted or burnt, to produce carbon dioxide. After three complex chemical reactions, a small amount of the solvent benzene is produced. The benzene is mixed in a small silica (glass) vessel with an organic compound called a 'scintillant'. When C14 decays it emits a beta particle and the scintillant compound traps these particles and emits their energy as a light pulse. Each emission of light, then, is equivalent to a C14 particle decaying. Each light emission, or C14 decay, can be recorded by the laboratory counters and an age calculated by comparing the decays from an unknown archaeological sample, with modern, known aged samples.

Until recently, archaeologists had to obtain 6-8 gm of charcoal in the field for each date. But a new technique known as accelerator mass spectroscopy (AMS) now makes it possible to date tiny samples by actually counting individual 14C atoms. This method incorporates a physical accelerator which uses powerful electromagnets and high voltages to separate the three carbon isotopes and measure their ratios in the space of an hour. A large range of new dating materials has been made available by using this method, including rice grains and seeds, and tiny samples of valuable artefacts like the Dead Sea Scrolls and the Turin Shroud.

Both counting methods, however, face two problems. The first is the standard deviation. Because it is impossible to obtain a precise year, it is necessary to place a degree of variation against each date. This is called the standard deviation of the age, and is represented by a ±, or plus/minus value which describes the statistical confidence which is expressed in the age. Consider a radiocarbon age of 2,500 ± 200 years BP (before present), for instance. In practical terms, this means that the actual age has a 68% chance of falling between 2,300 and 2,700 years ago. Some archaeologists opt for a more conservative two standard deviation value, which means that the true age has a 95% chance of falling between 2,100 and 2,900 years ago.

The second problem is that the amount of radiocarbon in the atmosphere has fluctuated in the past. This means that a radiocarbon date, expressed in years before present, may not actually equate to solar or calendar time. One way of correcting radiocarbon dates is by comparing the date to an absolutely dated material, to check the reliability of the radiocarbon date. The method of calibrating radiocarbon has been to use tree rings. Trees lay down an annual ring, therefore by counting backwards it is possible to build a 'dendrochronology' or tree ring dated sequence. By dating tree rings of known age, it is possible to build a calibration curve which can be used to correct dates for the fluctuation of radiocarbon in the atmosphere. The calibration curves which have been produced using tree rings now extend back over 10,000 years.

Colin Renfrew and Paul Bahn have commented that erroneous dates usually result not so much from mistakes or contamination in the laboratory, but rather misjudgements by archaeologists in the field. In their words, "The stratigraphic context of the sample must be clearly established by the excavator before the material is submitted to the laboratory for dating" (Renfrew and Bahn 1996:136). We only submit for dating, charcoal taken from clearly identified sources, such as hearths or rice grains found within a pottery vessel The results from dating Noen U-Loke are consistent with the sequence of layers there. This is due to careful selection of charcoal in the field, and the experience and skill of scientists in the radiocarbon laboratory.

See Fig. 29.

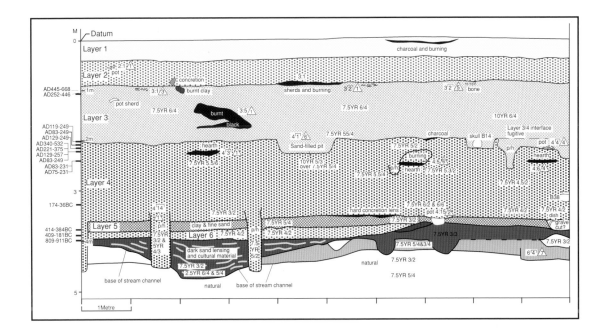

The Spirit Cave Expedition

Chester Gorman opened a new dimension in our understanding of the Hoabinhian in Thailand with his fieldwork in Mae Hongson Province. Beginning in October 1965, he explored the rugged uplands in the extreme northwest of the kingdom, an area of canopied forest laced with streams which empty into the Salween River. Spirit Cave was one of his major finds, and he began excavations in June 1966. The cultural layers were only 75 cm deep, within which he identified four distinct periods of occupation. Radiocarbon dates suggest that the site was occupied between 11,000 and 5500 BC. It is clear that the cave was visited only intermittently over these millennia, and probably only for brief stays. He ascribed the lower three layers to a general Hoabinhian occupation, within which were many stone artefacts similar to those from Sai Yok. The surface of layer 2, however, provided evidence for a significant change in material culture, for he found pottery sherds, a complete and two broken polished stone adzes and two small, slate knives. These novel items were associated with hearths and a continuation of established Hoabinhian chipped stone implements.

The presence of pottery vessels and polished stone tools raised an important issue. In many parts of the world, pottery is associated with farming communities rather than hunter

29: This section through the site of Noen U-Loke shows the stratigraphic buildup and the associated radiocarbon dates. The sequence of dates reveals initial settlement about 850 BC, with occupation continuing at least to about 500 AD.

30

30: The landscape of Spirit Cave is covered in canopied rainforest, laced with clear streams.

31: Looking into Spirit Cave during the excavation reveals a small site and shallow stratigraphy. The bamboo in the foreground is a frame for holding the screens.

gatherers. Polished stone adzes are also found often with farming groups whose first task in settling a new area was to remove the tree cover in creating fields. This conjunction is not always the case. The hunter gatherer Jomon people of Japan, for example, made the earliest known pottery. The reason for this association of pottery with farming is because farmers usually live permanently in one place, while hunters are often mobile. Pottery is of little use if you have to move your occupation regularly because it breaks so easily. One of the problems with these innovations at Spirit Cave is that the potsherds and adzes are only found in the topmost layer, which was between 3 and 8 cm thick. Does the pottery actually belong to this layer, or could it have been left much later, and become incorporated, fortuitously, with the Hoabinhian artefacts? This question must be posed, because the date of 5500 BC for the upper layer would make the pottery and adzes far and away the earliest in Thailand.

Spirit Cave and the Neolithic Revolution

In many general textbooks, particularly those published in the 1970s and 1980s, it is stated that Spirit Cave has provided evidence for early agriculture. These drew upon claims made by Professor W.G. Solheim for the world's earliest transition to plant domestication at this site. The evidence comprised small slate knives, polished stone adzes, pottery sherds and plant remains recovered by Chester Gorman.

Spirit Cave is a small rock shelter, perched on a steep slope some distance above the Khong Stream Valley. It seems a most unlikely place for a transition to agriculture. There is no flat land nearby, nor good soil. But it is excellently placed for hunting and gathering. The cultural layers at Spirit Cave are thin, suggesting that occupation by prehistoric people was of brief duration. There is no botanical evidence that any of the plants were modified by human activity. Nor is there any evidence for animal domestication. The potsherds, slate knives and stone adzes come from the latest occupation layer, which is very thin. They could have been left behind during a later visit to the site than the layer into which they were trampled. Even if the pottery, adzes and knives are as early as Solheim has claimed, there is no reason to accept that their presence means that the occupants of the cave developed agriculture. Knives can be used to harvest wild plants, and as we will see, pottery making and polishing stone adzes were activities associated with coastal hunter gatherers in Thailand.

There are, therefore, no grounds for suggesting that Spirit Cave was linked in any way with the 'Neolithic Revolution', the transition to farming and animal domestication.

See Solheim (1972)

31

32: These Hoabinhian stone implements come from Banyan Valley cave. They are 'Sumatraliths', or unifacial discoids. They were probably used for woodworking. Each is about 6 cm in width.

These alternatives aside, Gorman brought an important new technique to the excavation, for he passed all the cultural material through a fine mesh screen. The result was a series of finds which opens a new image of these hunter gatherers. At Sai Yok, only the bones of large animals were found, but at Spirit Cave, even the tiniest bones were recovered, and we can therefore find out more about hunting, fishing and trapping activities. The cavern is a sharp climb up from the Khong Stream, which bisects the valley below. But fish, crabs and shellfish were collected and brought up to the shelter. The inhabitants hunted or trapped large mammals, but not many. Only the sambar deer is found in all the layers, but we also encounter the bones of pigs and small deer. Monkeys, including the langur, macaque and gibbon were abundant. If you venture into the forest today, one of the first impressions is the din coming from the monkeys in the canopy of branches. Squirrels, palm civets and the marten also live aloft, and a few ground or water dwellers including the otter, jungle cat and badger were represented. The people of Spirit Cave hunted game in many different environments, from the jungle canopy to ground level, and down to the stream and its margins.

The screening recovered plant remains which have survived in the dry cave environment. Canarium seeds were the most abundant, and their fleshy fruit is still eaten in the area today. This plant can also supply resin and gum. The candlenut was also part of the diet, while its oil can be used for lighting. The upper layers included the remains of betel nuts, used today as a mild stimulant. Fragments of gourds were found, which could have been used as containers. Some other plant remains proved hard to identify, but there is a possibility that beans and peas were present. Despite the screening procedure, no rice remains were found (Yen 1977), but plant fragments have opened our eyes to the close relationship between the Hoabinhian people and their forest habitat. They collected a wide range of plants for food and stimulus. Some were useful as a gum, and may have been used to make composite tools or hunting implements and the poison from others could have tipped bamboo arrowheads. It has been suggested that these people may have begun to tend and even domesticate some of the plants, but this remains highly speculative, and given the brief occupation episodes, most unlikely.

Banyan Valley and Steep Cliff Caves

One swallow does not make a summer, and one prehistoric site affords only a limited view of a prehistoric society. Realising this, Gorman extended his fieldwork in Mae Hongson beyond the Khong Stream valley and found many further rock shelters. One lies at the end of the Banyan Valley, where the clear water plunges into a vertical sinkhole in the valley floor, and the limestone cliffs tower upwards, covered in canopied forest. A small test square excavated in early 1972, following in the wake of the recovery of plant remains at Spirit Cave, yielded a small sample of rice which encouraged the hope of tracking down the elusive origins for early domestication. Major excavations across the front part of the cave took place later that year, and in all, 40m² of the site were uncovered.

33: The excavation of Banyan Valley Cave in December 1972, caught during the brief time of day when the sun pierced the tree canopy. It got very cold at night.

The excavators soon learnt about life in the jungle. Miles from the nearest village, all their meat was locally hunted. By night, other hunters were also active, not least the local colony of tigers. The sun rarely penetrated the tree canopy and it was cold by night. The expedition hunter could aim at the monkeys which kept up a steady chorus of sound even while he was eating his evening meal. The climb up to the cave to dig each day was no more than 30 steep paces. Eight squares were laid out, a generator would hum to provide sufficient light for the diggers when the sun dipped low in the sky, and local Shan diligently screened all the excavated material to add to the growing sample of plant and small animal remains which, in earlier excavations, would have been overlooked.

The latest deposits, assigned by Gorman to a general layer 1, were strongly reminiscent of the uppermost layer at Spirit Cave. They contained a few sherds of cord-marked or plain, burnished potsherds, some large flaked pebble tools and flakes derived from a ground and polished adze. A unique flaked stone projectile point was also found, while a pit dug down from this layer contained fragments of rice chaff. Below, there were two thicker general layers – the precise stratigraphy was elusive due to the amount of animal and prehistoric human disturbance. These contained numerous hearths, some of which were lined with stone. A typical Hoabinhian stone tool industry was in place, including river cobbles flaked on one side, a tool known as a sumatralith, short axes and hammers. Some of these tools were probably used to smash and process animal bone, to judge from the fragmented condition in which most bone survived.

34: The animal bones from Steep Cliff
Cave were burnt and butchered. Here
are deer shoulder blades, pictured with
complete modern equivalents.

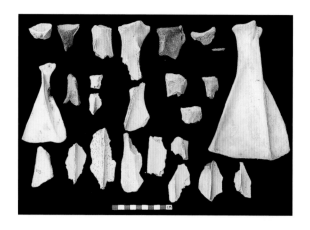

The occupants obtained shellfish and fish from the Banyan
Stream and, during the first two cultural phases, hunted pigs,
cattle and deer. As at Spirit Cave, they showed an interest in a
wide range of animals, for some of the bones come from langurs
and macaques, the bear and badger, porcupines and squirrels
and on one occasion, the rhinoceros. The uppermost occupation
saw fewer species, but included fish, rhinoceros and deer. While
most interest in the assemblage of plant remains centred on the
rice, some of the plants exploited at Spirit Cave were also present
again, such as the canarium nut, gourd and bean.

When the excavation was over, Gorman hired local Shan to
bring in their mules and carry the heavy load of finds back to
where the land rover had been parked, and after a day's hike
along jungle trails, the material was transferred for the journey
back to Mae Hongson. At this point, a burning question was the
date of the deposits. We who had worked there confidently
anticipated that the rice would be about as old as the pottery
fragments from Spirit Cave. If so, it would be strong evidence
for an early centre of rice cultivation. But the results from the
various laboratories came as a surprise and in some respects, a
disappointment. The uppermost cultural horizon was dated to
between 900 BC and 900 AD, while the lower two belong
within the period 3500-2000 BC.

Chester Gorman died tragically nine years after the
excavation, and was never able to bring his analysis of the
material to completion. Based on his notebooks, however,
Reynolds (1992) has published an interpretation of the site in
which he describes the lower two cultural periods as
Hoabinhian, but notes important differences between them and
the material from the last occupation phase, particularly in the
nature of the stone industry and the new elements such as

pottery. This raises a significant issue in relating this upper layer with that of Spirit Cave. Is it possible that six thousand years separates these two contexts, or is the date of the final occupation of Spirit Cave much later than has been suggested? A second surprise followed Yen's (1977) analysis of the rice remains: he found that they are probably from a wild rather than a cultivated variety. So, it seems likely that Banyan Valley Cave was home to hunters and gatherers four to five thousand years ago, and that even a thousand years ago, it was visited by people who hunted and collected in the vicinity.

Tham Pa Chan (Steep Cliff Cave) is the third site excavated by Gorman. Two radiocarbon dates suggest occupation within the period 5500-3500 BC. This site's name reflects its location, and the narrow ledge in which prehistoric remains were found is today two kilometres from the Pai River. This might explain the absence of fish bones, but by the same token, the cave must have been on a thickly forested slope, for the animal bones include the remains of the giant red flying squirrel and the tiny Himalayan striped squirrel. It is, in other respects, a singular site, for the four occupation layers are dominated by a thick, ashy bone midden which contains the remains of at least three wild cattle, two water buffalo, 13 deer and two pigs. The bones have all been systematically smashed and charred. Higham (1989), who studied the animal bones, has suggested that game might have been killed in the vicinity of the cave, dismembered and brought to the site for the meat to be smoked, just as the excavators of Banyan Valley Cave smoked the meat of deer to make it last. Many large flaked stone tools were found at Steep Cliff Cave, and these could then have been used to smash the bone in order to reach the marrow.

36

37

36: *The Pha Chang shelter is located at the foot of the rockface which emerges from the forest in the middle of this view to the north. The Mae Cham Stream flows below the site, which was excavated by Marielle Santoni in 1986. (Photograph by J.C. Liger, by permission of M. Santoni)*

37: *Hunter-gatherers lived at the base of the Ob Luang rock shelter. (Photograph by S. Vacher, by permission of M. Santoni)*

Rachanie Thosarat (Bannanurag 1988) has moved beyond speculation in considering possible uses for these tools, however, by examining 28 flaked implements for signs of use wear. She found that polishing was present on the working surfaces of 17 specimens, while four bore scratch marks, 17 had micro flaking and 10, bruising. By considering both experimental and ethnographic cases of tool use, she concluded that these implements were used for some time and were resharpened when necessary. The steeply-flaked edges and type of polish probably result from working hard wood. It has long been speculated that wood was an important raw material for Hoabinhian hunter gatherers, and Thosarat's work is a step towards confirming this on sound evidence.

Ob Luang

Similar results have been obtained by Jérémie and Vacher (1992) in their study of stone tools from the Pha Chang rock shelter in Ob Luang. This site, and a series of others, lies in the Mae Chaem stream valley, a tributary of the River Ping. A rich artefactual assemblage has been found during excavations by Santoni, including typically Hoabinhian flaked axes and scrapers. According to the animal remains, the environment would have been a stable and luxuriant rain forest, and some at least of the stone tools are thought to have been used in wood working. One of the most intriguing aspects of this site is the presence of paintings on the surface of the cave walls. While most are probably quite recent, some poorly preserved traces of red forms might be prehistoric, particularly given the presence of haematite pieces in undisturbed Hoabinhian layers in the deposits below. These layers, while rich in stone implements, were devoid of any pottery or evidence for edge grinding or polishing (Santoni *et al.* 1986).

Although most research has concentrated in rock shelters, there is no doubt that these Hoabinhian hunter-gatherers moved freely across the landscape. Maleipan (1972), for example, found stone chopping tools at the base of Doi Kam in Chiang Rai, while Phommanodch identified similar implements beside the Mekong River near Chiang Saen (Natapintu and Phommanodch 1990). The latter site is reminiscent of a second river bank site containing Hoabinhian types of stone artefacts near Chiang Khan (Bayard 1980)

The Khwae Noi Valley Sites

In 1977, Surin Pookajorn from Silpakon University, and a large team of Thai specialists, undertook research on the hunter-gatherer occupation of a series of caves about 4.5 km north of the Kwae Noi River in Kanchanaburi (Pookajorn 1981). At the cave of Khao Talu, his team found four successive occupation floors containing the remains of Hoabinhian stone tools, in association with the remains of deer, cattle and pigs. The river was visited by hunter gatherers for its fish, shellfish, crabs and turtles and again, the plant remains come from many species. These floors date within the period from 8000 to 1000 BC. The uppermost layer is particularly interesting, because it contains not only flaked pebble tools matching those from the Mae Hongson sites, but also cord-marked, incised and black burnished potsherds. These are similar to those excavated from a nearby Neolithic cemetery at Ban Kao, and have been dated within the period 2500-1000 BC. As it happens, this span covers the occupation of the Neolithic site, and it seems likely that there was interaction of some sort between local hunters and gatherers, and the new groups of rice farmers. Perhaps the two groups coexisted, and exchanged goods one with the other.

This is supported by the sequence at Heap (Coffin) Cave, where Pookajorn found a sequence of living floors containing typical Hoabinhian stone tools in association with the remains of large mammal bones, fish, shellfish and fragments of gourd and palm seeds. One of these was dated to 6400-4700 BC. The uppermost layer, while also containing this material, included cord-marked, burnished and incised potsherds made of clay identical with that from the lowland Neolithic cemetery at Ban Kao. Clearly the hills behind the Kwae Noi River were regularly visited by hunters and gatherers over a period of thousands of years, because Pookajorn excavated further Hoabinhian layers at Phetch Kuha and Ment Caves.

This Hoabinhian hunting and gathering tradition extended from the extreme north to the southern part of Thailand, for we find occupation layers with stone tools similar to those from the Kanchanaburi caves in the Krabi sites of Moh Khiew and Lang Rongrien. At the former, Pookajorn (1992) has recovered evidence not only for typical Hoabinhian stone tools, but also four inhumation burials, one of which may have been interred in a seated, crouched position. Unfortunately, only part of the upper body has survived. The other three were all extended inhumations on a north to south orientation. Grave goods

38

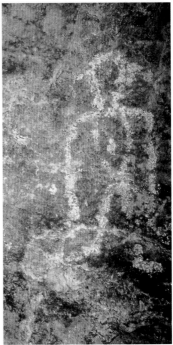

39

38-39: The name Pha Chang means Elephant Shelter after the paintings of elephants on the rock walls. These are probably quite recent, and overlie faint red paintings which might belong to the period when hunter-gatherers occupied the cave. (Photograph by S. Vacher, by permission of M. Santoni)

40

41

42

40: The excavations of Ob Luang, revealing rock falls and prehistoric occupation layers. (Photograph by S. Vacher, by permission of M. Santoni)

41-42: The tools found at Ob Luang are very similar to those from Banyan Valley and Steep Cliff caves. The largest is 10 cm. in width. (Photograph by S. Vacher, by permission of M. Santoni)

comprised flaked stone tools and quartz pebbles. These Hoabinhian contexts underlie two upper layers which contain plain, polished and cord-marked potsherds and polished stone adzes. No radiocarbon dates are available.

It will be recalled that a deposit of limestone overlay the early occupation layers at Lang Rongrien. Above it, there was an accumulation of further cultural remains between one and two metres deep. Anderson has recognised two layers, dated approximately between 8000 and 4000 BC. This is a particularly interesting span in Southeast Asia, for the sea level rose from approximately -38 to +1-2 metres relative to its present level. At Lang Rongrien, this would have seen the shore about 66 km distant at the base of layer 6 but only 8 km towards the end of layer 5. It is not surprising, therefore, to find that while the mammals adapted to the rainforest, such as deer and pig, were regularly represented in the sample of faunal remains, shellfish from mangroves or a muddy shore became increasingly abundant. Did the inhabitants exchange food with coastal groups, or did they venture by river to the shore to exploit its resources?

The stone tools fall within the range for the Hoabinhian hunter gatherer culture, with flaked core tools such as choppers and axes present, but the majority of stone finds, which are dominated by a fine-grained shale, are flakes which were probably removed to sharpen the parent implement. Two small fragments of polished stone hint at the innovations detected far to the north at Spirit Cave, and from the upper part of layer 5, a thumbnail-sized fragment of cord-marked pottery was recovered.

The increasing quantity of marine shellfish as the sea encroached ever nearer to the cave is a timely reminder that pottery is often associated with permanent communities irrespective of whether they were farmers or hunters. From 4000 BC onward, the sea reached a high point and then began to fall back to its present level. The former beaches now lie well inland, and one can trace the old shoreline by following the ancient sand dunes. From time to time, settlements of the prehistoric people who were adapted to marine conditions survive. One such site is Nong Nor, and we will now turn to the evidence found there during three excavation seasons.

Geomorphology and the Ancient Environment

The environment of Thailand has changed dramatically and often in the past. This is due to both natural and human influences. Deforestation, or the natural rise and fall of the sea level, are but two of many variables which have an impact on the landscape. The climate also changes over time.

We have found that it is essential, when excavating prehistoric sites in Thailand, to be sure that we have an expert geomorphologist to work with us. Professor William Boyd, for example, has contributed to our research at Nong Nor, Ban Lum Khao and Noen U-Loke. His skills involve past landforms, river courses, the location of old shorelines, and how prehistoric settlements and their occupants relate to the changing environment. In the field, he excavates under and round the prehistoric sites to obtain samples of naturally deposited sediments, like old river channels, sand dunes, flood plain or marine deposits, and then with the aid of laboratory analyses and aerial photographs, pieces together the sequence of changing habitats seen in landforms, drainage patterns and coastlines. At Nong Nor, he showed us how the phase 1 settlement had been located on the edge of a broad marine embayment. By opening up the flood plain deposits round the inland settlement of Noen U-Loke, he found that the so-called Iron Age moats were old river channels. The latter site had been surrounded by natural swamps and rivers when occupied.

Without such professional colleagues to contribute to fieldwork, we would have only a partial, and often a misleading, impression of what life was like in prehistory.

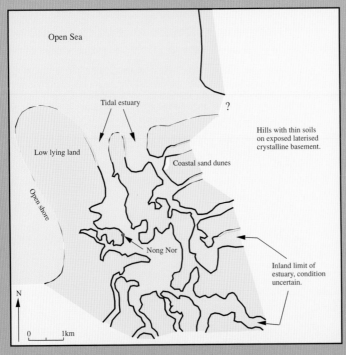

43: The reconstructed coastline in the vicinity of Nong Nor 4,500 years ago.

44

45

44: The coastline nearest to Nong Nor still shows the mangroves colonising the land in the intertidal zone.

45: Excavations at Nong Nor took place out in the rice fields. Four and a half thousand years ago, the site had occupied a dry eminence overlooking an extensive marine embayment.

Nong Nor

Nong Nor lies on the flood plain of the Bang Pakong River in Chonburi Province. This area has undergone major environmental changes over the past 10,000 years, as the rising sea covered much of the region before retreating again. The highest sea level was in place about 4000 years BC and as the rivers entered the sea, so they laid down thick deposits of sediment. Human settlement followed the receding shore, and we can trace prehistoric occupation sites along the former coasts. The tropical shore, and in particular the estuary, is one of the three richest habitats in the world, expressed in terms of biological productivity. Its wealth begins with the mangroves which are often found along the coastal fringe. These trees shed their leaves regularly throughout the year and a host of marine organisms consume them, thus initiating a complex food chain which incorporates crabs, small fish, larger fish and their predators, ending with humans. The mangrove is not a particularly attractive place to settle, with its clouds of mosquitoes, low-lying muddy soils and tidal flows, but it does harbour some food plants. Leaf eating monkeys and pigs live among the landward mangrove trees, and where the forest is pierced by an estuary or marine embayment, one can expect to find evidence for occupation by hunter gatherers.

In 1984, we began a research programme in the Bang Pakong Valley, in order to find out more about this pattern of settlement. In Vietnam, Malaysia and Indonesia, many coastal sites had been excavated, but none in Thailand. The first season was spent armed with a geological map and notebook, walking over the flat landscape looking for traces of prehistoric activity. We asked villagers if they knew of any prehistoric pottery like the examples we showed them, or if they had ever come across

marine shellfish in areas now far inland. We found several low mounds and were taken to rice fields where diggings had exposed such pottery and marine shells. One site was called Nong Nor and in 1990, we began the first of three excavation seasons.

46: At Nong Nor, millions of sharp shellfish made for an uncomfortable excavation.

We found that the site had been occupied on two occasions in prehistory. The earlier involved the deposition of over six million shellfish, nearly all of which came from a species of cockle which lives in sandy to muddy beaches. This shell midden was cut into by graves belonging to the Bronze Age. We took samples of charcoal from hearths found in the shell midden, and the results showed that it was occupied about 2500 BC. We were trying to answer several key questions. How big was the site for example, and how many people might have lived there? What was the environment like, and what did people eat? How long did they stay at this site, and what did they do? What sort of people are involved, are there any burials? We opened an area of about 400m², and found that, far from being simply an accumulation of shellfish, many activities had taken place. By probing the surrounding area, we also found that the site probably covers only about 1200m² in all, and could hardly

47: The shell midden at Nong Nor followed the natural contours of the ground, and included many thin lenses of ash resulting from the local firing of pottery vessels.

have been home to more than a few families. The shell midden was quite thin in part, but reached a depth of just over a metre where shellfish accumulated in natural hollows.

Realising the importance of reconstructing the ancient environment, we invited William Boyd, a geomorphologist, to join us in the field, and he arranged for several pits to be excavated in strategic places in order to examine and interpret the sequence of deposits. He found that the site had been situated on the southern shore of an extensive, sheltered marine embayment. By canoeing out from the site in a westerly direction, people could soon reach the breakers and proceed beyond to the open sea. Once we mapped the ancient shoreline, we found that many other sites we had previously discovered, also lay beside this broad embayment.

As we removed the layers of cockleshells, so we found evidence for a wide range of activities. Shark and dolphin bones show that the inhabitants indeed went out to sea on their fishing and hunting expeditions. The bones of deer, wild cattle and water buffalo were brought back to the settlement, and converted into useful tools, such as fishhooks and awls. One of the unusual aspects of the animal bone assemblage was the high proportion of worked or modified specimens, as if only certain bones were brought back to the site to be converted into artefacts. Despite persistent attempts, however, we were unable to find any evidence for rice, nor implements which might have been used to cultivate the soil. Nor was there any evidence for the domestication of animals.

Yet the people were proficient at making pottery vessels. We found many potsherds, most being impressed with the cordage which would have been wrapped round the wooden paddle used to shape the pots. To this day, such paddles are used in association with clay anvils to form vessels. There were also numerous thick lenses of ash, indicating where pots were fired, and stones bearing faint scratches where they had been in contact with clay when burnishing the surface of the unfired pots. Such smoothing imparts a glossy surface after the pots are fired. Bone fishhooks and awls were also manufactured. There is no good local source of the fine-grained stone, and the polished stone adzes were probably obtained through exchange with inland groups. Sandstone was also brought to the site, and used to sharpen the cutting edge of the adzes. After many repeated sharpenings, the adzes became smaller and smaller, but were used for as long as possible nevertheless.

Dougald O'Reilly (1995), who studied the artefacts from this site, has found that the fishhooks, worked bone, pottery anvils and burnishing stones concentrate in specific parts of the site throughout the period when the midden was accumulating. He has inferred that the same activities were undertaken through what would, in all probability, have been a brief period of occupation, perhaps only lasting a season of the year. One burial was found which probably belongs to this first phase of occupation. The body of the woman was buried in a seated, crouched position, and was then covered in pottery vessels. This way of interment differed radically from the extended position of the later Bronze Age burials, but, interestingly, is duplicated in several sites of coastal hunter gatherers found along the raised beaches of Central and Northern Vietnam. The presence of just the one burial supports the idea of a brief period of occupation, for over a number of years, one would expect more burials to have been present. Likewise, O'Reilly has estimated that 62 pottery vessels are represented within an excavated area of 70 m². By extrapolating from this figure to the total area of the site, and given that one woman can be expected to have a daily output of four pots he has concluded that the site was unlikely to have been occupied for more than six months. This brief period of occupation is supported by Mason's (1998) analysis of the shellfish.

48

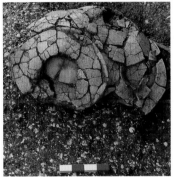

49

48: Pottery vessels are made in Thailand today in just the same way as they were in prehistory, here with a wooden paddle and a clay anvil held within the pot as it is shaped.

49: The only burial of a hunter gatherer from Nong Nor involved the seated and crouching remains of a woman under a group of whole pottery vessels.

(width 15 cm)

(width 13 cm)

(width 10.5 cm)

50: The potters of Khok Phanom Di made their vessels in a wide variety of shapes and with many decorative motifs.

Nong Nor has answered a number of intriguing questions, and has posed more. It is highly likely that there are many other coastal hunter gatherer sites behind the present shore of the Gulf of Siam. Some will almost certainly go back at least 1500 years earlier than Nong Nor, because this site was located on a coast which was formed lower and later than the greatest extension of the sea. But it demonstrates nevertheless, that the coastal hunter gatherers were long adapted to marine fishing and hunting, and lived long enough in one settlement to encourage the manufacture and use of pottery vessels. They exchanged goods with inland groups, and were particularly interested in sources of high quality stone for adze making. They treated the dead with respect, and interred the corpse in a seated position, associated with grave offerings. It would be difficult to envisage any sort of food shortage in this bountiful environment, and the cultivation of plants was not pursued, nor were animals domesticated. What happened to these coastal people? We can find out more by considering another site in the Bang Pakong Valley, known as Khok Phanom Di.

Khok Phanom Di

Lying 14 km north of Nong Nor, Khok Phanom Di lies like a stranded whale on the flood plain of the Bang Pakong River. It covers 5 hectares, and rises 12 metres above the surrounding rice fields. This great mound has attracted much interest among archaeologists. Damrongkiadt Noksakul from the Chachoengsao Teachers College, Pornchai Suchitta from Silpakon University and Pirapon Pisnupong from the Fine Arts Department had all excavated there before we continued and built upon their results with a large excavation in 1985 (Suchitta and Noksakul 1979, Suchitta 1980, Noksakul 1983, Pisnupong 1984). To judge from their work, Khok Phanom Di had been located near or on the sea shore, and had been occupied for a long time. They had encountered many human burials associated with pottery vessels, and samples of rice had been recovered. When we planned our excavation, we anticipated that we would be able to expand on our understanding of when and how rice came to be cultivated, an economic development of profound importance to the early history of Thailand.

In 1984 we laid down plans for the excavation of a single square measuring 10 by 10 metres (Higham and Thosarat 1994). We began in late December of that year, and reached the

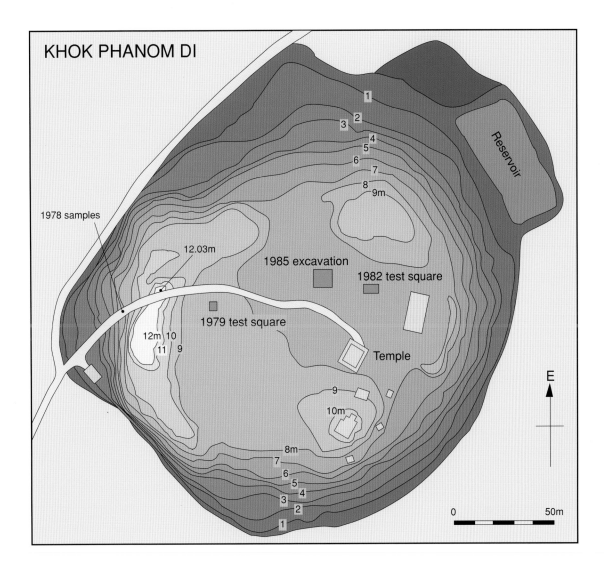

KHOK PHANOM DI

1978 samples

12.03m

1985 excavation

1982 test square

1979 test square

12m 10
11 9

Temple

9

10m

8m
7
6
5
4
3
2
1

Reservoir

E

0   50m

51: *The mound of Khok Phanom Di, showing the areas excavated.*

mudflats upon which the first people settled seven months later, at a depth of nearly seven metres. We found that Khok Phanom Di had been occupied for about five centuries, beginning in the vicinity of 2000 BC. What happened, accorded to Boyd, was that after the abandonment of Nong Nor, the marine embayment gradually filled up as the sea level fell and the sluggish river deposited its burden of silt. Five centuries after the abandonment, a large estuary had formed to the north, and its wealth of food resources attracted human settlement. We have been anxious to track down the relationship between the people of Nong Nor and those who settled at Khok Phanom Di for many reasons, one of which is our discovery of fragments of rice in the lowest layers at the latter. Does the presence of rice indicate local origins of plant domestication, the Neolithic

52

53

52: Khok Phanom Di lies like a stranded whale on the flat floodplain of the Bang Pakong River.

53: The excavations at Khok Phanom Di in 1985 took place under our own roof, which covered a square 10 by 10 metres in extent. During the rainy season, we had to dig a special drain to prevent water from flooding into the excavation.

54   *(width 11 cm)*

Revolution? Was the rice collected wild? Or was Khok Phanom Di, like Nong Nor, the home of hunter gatherers who entered into an exchange relationship with inland agriculturalists, sending perhaps marine shell jewellery to the interior and receiving rice in return?

There are many possible formulations and one way of beginning to consider them is through the sort of implements made at each site, even if they were separated in time by half a thousand years. Take the case of pottery vessels. It is possible to make an almost infinite variety of shapes from the clay before firing, and there are countless permutations as to how the pot can be decorated. Similar forms and styles of decoration at both sites would point to a relationship between the inhabitants. A completely different repertoire would argue for a different group of people. The situation, naturally, is never as clear cut as this. Both groups could have traded their pots from the same third party. Potters could have imitated the styles of people they came into contact with. So it is necessary to look for supporting or contrary evidence. Were the pots locally made, for example? This we can often investigate by examining the minerals found naturally in the clay and sourcing it locally or from some distance away. Is there any evidence for local manufacture in the form of firing areas, or the tools used to make and ornament vessels? Nor is our search limited just to pottery vessels. Do we, for example, find similar bone or stone tools at Nong Nor and Khok Phanom Di?

Before examining the evidence, let us not overlook the fact that five centuries, 20 generations, lie between the occupation of Nong Nor and the pioneer settlement of Khok Phanom Di.

This is a long time span over which to expect similarities in material culture to persist, even if the pace of change then was much slower than we are accustomed to. We must expect changes, but similarities appear all the more significant.

Dougald O'Reilly has considered the artefacts from Nong Nor and basal Khok Phanom Di. He has found that the Nong Nor potters made large vessels, possibly used for cooking, with a simple turned over rim and cord-marked impressions all over the body. We found virtually identical pots at Khok Phanom Di. People at both sites also made their vessels in the same way, by the paddle and anvil technique. Some special pots were then burnished. This involves taking the vessel when leather hard, that is before firing, and rubbing a smooth pebble over the surface. This in effect polishes it, and when fired, the surface takes on a lustrous sheen. These pots, at both sites, were also incised with decorative designs. Even some of the designs survived over five centuries.

The bone tools also reveal similarities. Fishhooks had just the same shape. Awls and shuttles could have come from the same workshop. The stone adzes had a similar shape. At both sites, we find imported sandstone for sharpening adzes. It is difficult to find a better alternative to our conclusion that Khok Phanom Di was settled by people whose remote ancestors had lived at Nong Nor and back even beyond 2500 BC to the trackless time before the sea rose and covered settlements with water to a depth of over 100 metres.

Khok Phanom Di is a complicated site to describe, because it was occupied for so long, and we have so many sources of information. We ensured, for example, that a sample of all the material we removed underwent wet sieving. This involves bubbling water up through a sample of the archaeological deposit, and collecting the organic fraction as it rises and spills over the outlet into a screen. We thus assembled a collection of seeds, tiny shellfish, and charcoal fragments, vital clues to the ancient environment and way of life. Organic material was remarkably well preserved. On occasion, we would encounter leaves, or leaf impressions, and wooden posts still standing in ancient foundations. The most significant find, however, was the fact that the inhabitants buried their dead beside, and with time over each other, in clusters. Again, the preservation not only of bone but also other aspects of the mortuary ritual was unusually good. We found that wood had been used as a plank or bier over which the corpse had been placed. White fabric, made

(width 16 cm)

(width 10 cm)

(width 8 cm)

(width 14 cm)

55   *(width 16 cm)*

54-55: A further selection of the diverse range of pots found at Khok Phanom Di.

56

57

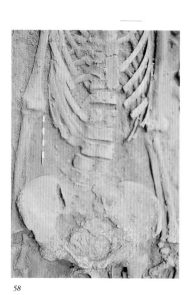

58

56: The white streaks on the skull of this infant are asbestos fibres used as a shroud. Even newly born infants had their own graves.

57: This section from Khok Phanom Di shows how an ash lens has been severed with the cutting of a post hole. The wooden post is still in place.

58: An extraordinary find by Thai archaeologist Metha Wichakana: the remains of partially digested food in the pelvic area of this woman. She had eaten rice with the chaff still present, and the bones and scales of the climbing perch fish.

from beaten bark or sheets of naturally-occurring asbestos had been used to wrap the body. On one occasion, Metha Wichakana, a colleague from the Fine Arts Department staff, uncovered a mass of tiny bones within the pelvic area of a woman. This turned out to be partially digested food, which included fish scales, fish bones and fragments of rice chaff. Another grave had human faeces which on examination, revealed fish bones and rice. When the excavation was nearing completion, we took samples from every stratigraphic context for Ken McKenzie in Australia, an expert on the analysis of ostracodes and forams. These tiny aquatic organisms are many and varied, and each has a preferred habitat. So he was able to trace changes to the environment with the passage of time (McKenzie 1991). We found many animal, fish and bird bones, the remains of turtles and crabs, and hundreds of thousands of shellfish which represent over 200 species. Bit by bit, over the years which have elapsed since we reached the bottom of this site, we and many colleagues have assembled the pieces of the jigsaw puzzle and sought the resulting pattern.

The first settlers lived near the edge of a broad river estuary. It must have been low lying and damp, for high tides would have threatened them with flooding. If the present is any guide to the past, clouds of mosquitoes would have plagued them as dusk approached and to judge from the numerous hearths, the smoke from smouldering mangrove wood might have kept some of the insects at bay. As we uncovered the remains of their

59

60

61

activities, seven metres down in the heart of the mound, we found two small pits dug into the natural substrate. Each contained a hoard of adzes, clay anvils for shaping pots and burnishing stones. The adzes revealed scars of use along their cutting edges (Pisnupong 1993a). They were in all likelihood, the very tools used to cut down the mangrove trees to create living space. And already, the settlers had discovered a good source of clay for making their pots. Thick lenses of ash also indicate where they fired them. This low-lying, damp place might seem inhospitable, but it was possible to slip their boats into the water and sail or paddle into rich fishing grounds, to lay nets or to bring in a catch with hook and line. At low tide, extensive shellfish beds were exposed on the mudflats and at least at initial settlement, the waters were clear enough to sustain shellfish from which desirable ornaments could be fashioned. Even stacks of coral formed offshore.

59: Nearing the bottom: after seven months, the excavation of Khok Phanom Di became a world of its own.

60: The end is nigh at Khok Phanom Di for four of the excavators, from right to left, Charles Higham, Anat Bamrungwongse, Amphan Kijngam, Rachanie Thosarat.

61: At the base of Khok Phanom Di, we found the tools left behind 4,000 years ago by the earliest settlers: stone adzes, clay anvils for shaping pots, and burnishing stones.

62

63

62: Fishhooks from Khok Phanom Di were fashioned from bone, and are only found in early layers at the site. Height 4 cm.

63: Polished stone adzes from Khok Phanom Di are similar to those from Nong Nor. Width of left hand adze, 4.8 cm.

The passage of time inevitably saw the first deaths. Treatment of the dead tells us much about the living. When a community settles permanently in one place, we often find that an invisible umbilical cord links the living to the ancestral burial ground. But if a group regularly moves round its territory, the dead are likewise scattered. The earliest deaths at Khok Phanom Di saw the corpse interred in shallow graves cut into the ashy remains of pottery firing, or the accumulating middens of shellfish. There was, nevertheless, some pattern to this behaviour, for in most cases the body was positioned with its head to the east, and one person was buried with some shell beads. The survival of the human bones in good condition opens a vista on the people themselves.

The study of human remains

Before the adoption of Buddhism and Hinduism in Thailand, the dead were buried in graves cut into the ground or, if very young, placed in pottery vessels. Many cemeteries have been excavated, and the human bones which have survived provide much vital information on the prehistoric people. In many parts of the world, archaeologists are forbidden from excavating and studying human remains. Fortunately, the authorities in Thailand provide permission to do so. We have uncovered in our own excavations, approximately 600 prehistoric graves and without exception, have accorded the prehistoric remains the same respect as we would our own ancestors. We value the investigation of cemeteries for many reasons. The burial ritual represents actions by the living, and how an individual was interred provides us with information on their status in life. A person interred, for example, with many valued exotic artefacts might have been a person of high standing in the community.

The bones are themselves a vital source of information on life in prehistory. Bones are affected by age, sex, activities, diet and some diseases.

By calling on specialists, therefore, it is possible to build up the profile of a population. We find, for example, that few prehistoric people in Thailand had a life expectancy at birth of more than about 30 years, and to survive to 50 was exceptional. So leaders in the communities we study were young by modern standards. We also find that there was usually a high death rate among infants. Most, if not all people were well fed, which is hardly surprising when you consider the richness of the natural environment, the abundance of fish, game animals, and the responsiveness of rice to cultivation. There is also widespread evidence for some illnesses, particularly anaemia.

One of the most difficult areas of study is the question of race, because bones respond to the environment in which people live. Most of the prehistoric Neolithic, Bronze and Iron Age people however, probably looked similar to modern Thais, who are themselves described as southern Mongoloid.

The study of bone is also entering a new and exciting period of research, because new techniques now permit DNA from prehistoric bone to be sequenced. No research has yet been applied in detail to Thai prehistoric people, but that time will come, and when it does we will be able to examine the relationships between individuals and groups in much more detail.

See Houghton and Wiriyaromp 1984, Pietrusewsky 1997 and Tayles 1998.

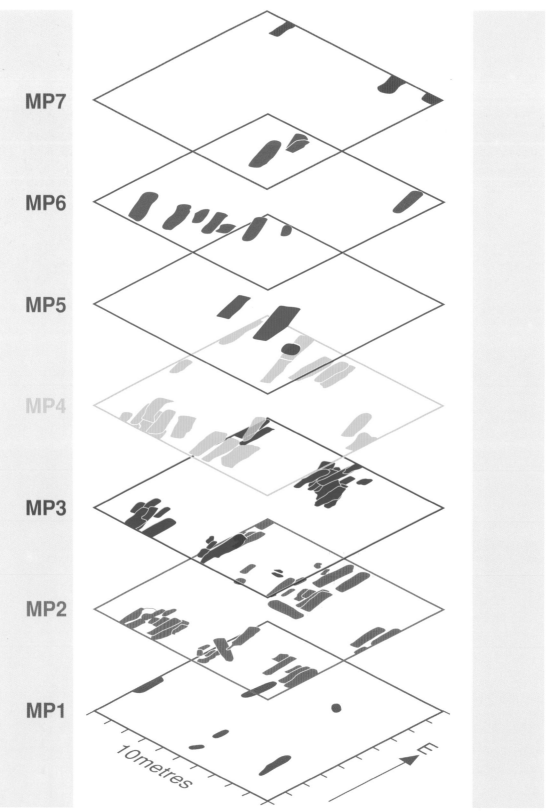

MP7

MP6

MP5

MP4

MP3

MP2

MP1

10metres

E

There are six graves in the earliest of seven mortuary phases. A newly-born infant came first, followed by two men, a woman, a second infant and a two-year old. The robust adult bones reflect a good diet, but there are also hints of illness. The two-year-old child suffered from a blood disorder which would have involved anaemia, and this also afflicted two of the adults, both of whom died when relatively young. Tayles (1998) has suggested that this disorder, probably a type of thalassaemia, would have provided for some resistance to malaria but with anaemia as a side effect.

If Khok Phanom Di had been abandoned, as was Nong Nor, after a brief period of occupation, we would have been left with two similar sites: both would have been dominated by accumulations of shellfish. These included layers of ash, and many potsherds, adzes, fishhooks and evidence for shaping and burnishing pots. We would have concluded that the inhabitants went out to sea to fish, and were involved in exchange relations with inland people who supplied high quality stone. Whereas the occupants of Nong Nor buried their dead in an upright seated position, at Khok Phanom Di we find extended inhumation burials with the corpse laid out on the back.

Neither community, it seems, knew of domestic dogs. No domestic animals were kept, though there was a little hunting. Only at Khok Phanom Di do we find fragments of rice, but was it grown locally? We think probably not, because the environment would have been unsuited. Rice does not thrive where the water is saline. Thompson (1996), in her analysis of the seeds, found a major concentration from the plant *Suaeda maritima* only in the early layers. This plant flourishes on salt flats often found behind the coastal mangrove fringe. The early rice could, given what we know of the estuary, have been obtained along with high quality stone, by exchange. The sort of site from which stone adzes could have been obtained, has been excavated at Don Noi, in Kanchanaburi. While there is little likelihood of a direct link between these two particular sites, Don Noi was clearly an inland site which specialised in the production of adzes from its rich local sources of stone. Raw materials found there include quartz, chalcedony, chert, jasper, slate, mudstone, conglomerate and petrified wood (Vongjaturapat 1991).

Khok Phanom Di, however, was not abandoned. The people lived on for over 400 years. And as we see the pattern of their lives unfolding, so we can trace a series of changes

65

64: *From bottom to top, we see the superimposed plans of graves in each of the seven mortuary phases at Khok Phanom Di.*

65: *During mortuary phase 2, the dead were laid out in clusters. Here we find from left to right, a man who died in his mid forties, a woman of similar age, and an infant who survived for about 9 months. Notice the two white burnishing stones beside the man's right ankle, and the lustrous black decorated pottery vessels.*

66: A hard loss for the parents to bear: a newly born infant buried on the knees of a five year old child.

which illuminate how hunter gatherers were able to adapt to a veritable kaleidoscope of influences over which they had little or no control.

We have divided the long burial sequence into successive mortuary phases (MP). With MP2, the dead were laid out in clusters which form a chequerboard pattern. A thick shell midden complements these clusters, and its linear edges and right-angled turns suggests that it accumulated against rigid structures, such as the wooden walls of collective tombs. This midden contained over 137,000 cockles, and was dominated by shellfish adapted to the mangrove and muddy intertidal zone. Apart from this midden, there was a change in the nature of the deposits associated with MP2. In place of ash spreads and hearths, we find many circular pits containing bivalve shellfish, many of which were unopened. Postholes indicate the presence of structures over the grave clusters. While the adzes, burnishing stones, anvils and awls continued as before, there were also two innovations. All the bone harpoons came from this part of the site, and a single shell knife, thought to have been used in harvesting a grass, such as rice, were found (Higham T.F.G. 1993). There was also an increase in the number of fishhooks and clay net weights.

Wild pig and macaque were still hunted, but we also find the first bones of the dog. This animal is exotic to Southeast Asia, and can only have been introduced in the company of human communities. The pattern of inhuming the dead with the head pointing to the east continued, but we find many more burials, with individuals set out in clusters. People were well fed and men had well muscled upper bodies, probably as a result of an activity like canoeing. We also find high infant mortality, much evidence for anaemia, and virtually universal female fertility. A notable amount of energy was also expended on mortuary rites. Bodies were wrapped in a fabric shroud, sprinkled with red ochre and laid on a wooden bier in individual graves. Pottery vessels were expertly made, brilliantly burnished and incised with complex designs (Hall 1993, Moore 1993). One man was found with about 39,000 shell disc beads, and shell beads in barrel and funnel forms were found with many burials. Cowrie shells included in one grave are almost certainly exotic, and bangles were fashioned from fish vertebrae (Pilditch 1993). Other grave offerings included the teeth of rhinoceros and deer, a stone adze, a fishhook and the stones used to burnish pottery vessels. The range of grave goods echoes some of the activities suggested by Tayles as possible reasons for stress on peoples' bones: making pots and paddling canoes. No clear differences have been detected in the mortuary rituals and grave goods found with men and women, although some individuals stand out on the basis of either their barrel beads, or association with shell beads and pottery vessels.

67: During the fourth mortuary phase, we find a row of burials in which the males were accompanied by turtle carapace ornaments. In the foreground is a male who died in his mid thirties and beyond him, first a younger man, then a child aged about 11 years in the same grave as a woman who had reached about 25 years of age.

During the third mortuary phase, which followed with no evident time lag from MP2, we find that the shell midden which ran round the grave clusters first tapered off in size, and then ceased. The stratigraphic sequence included many postholes, pits and lenses containing ash and charcoal. Artefacts included burnishing stones and clay anvils. Only one fishhook was recovered and net weights became rare. The first granite hoe was encountered, along with several more shell knives. Faeces from burial 67 included domesticated rice remains, while burial 56 provided food residue from the lower abdominal area which comprised fish bones, scales, and rice chaff. During this phase, there was a fall in the number of shellfish adapted to clean subtidal and intertidal marine sand, offset by a rise in those from the landward edge of the mangroves. It seems that the site was being distanced from the mouth of the estuary, and that siltation was affecting shellfish beds. The collection of shellfish from muddy marine conditions continued, however, for thousands of cockles were found, and there was no apparent rise in the number of shellfish adapted to freshwater. Only two dog bones were found in MP3 contexts, the macaque and pig dominating.

Just over half the graves contained infants or children. Males continued to develop strong upper bodies, indeed they were taller and more robust than at any other time. But anaemia still affected health. The grave goods included shell disc beads, pottery vessels some of which were burnished and incised with complex designs, burnishing stones and a fish vertebra bangle. One man was buried with four unique items: a nautilus shell, fish skeleton, shark fin spine and a small stone chisel. It was also during this stage that we find the first hint of different treatment of men and women: a man was interred with a turtle carapace ornament, and a woman with a clay anvil. This set a pattern to be followed regularly. It is also intriguing to note that, as shellfish of the clean intertidal conditions fell away in frequency, so the number of disc beads in burials declined. Three early MP3 graves had respectively 1,500, 859 and 1,260 such beads, but later MP3 graves had none. The decline continued into MP4.

Mortuary activity virtually ceased during the accumulation of layer 9 between MP3 and MP4. During this period, a series of midden, ash and charcoal lenses were deposited, and their distribution followed that of layer 10 lens 2. This suggests that existing mortuary structures belonging to MP3 remained in

68

69

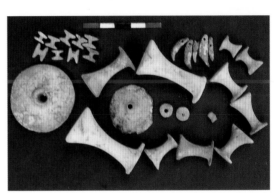

70

place and influenced the location of later deposits. During layer 9, shellfish from clean coralline subtidal and intertidal conditions were no longer present and estuarine species also declined, to be compensated for by a rise in freshwater shellfish. This change is matched by the distribution of fish and crab remains, freshwater species replacing those from sea or estuary. We also find the first remains of the water buffalo and small deer. But macaques and pigs continued to predominate. The first pygmy cormorants and pelicans were found, birds adapted to rivers and marshes. The last crocodile bone comes from layer 9. There appears too, to have been a change in fishing strategy, for fishhooks were no longer in evidence and net weights were rare. While adzes, burnishing stones and anvils were still found, shell knives surged in numbers.

Mortuary Phase 4 corresponds with the period identified by Mason (1991, 1996) as that most likely to have witnessed a major and possibly rapid environmental change. This could have involved a move in the channel of the adjacent river, or the cutting of an oxbow lake. At any event, we can pinpoint a

68: Uncovering mortuary phase 4 graves. Time flies, one is totally absorbed in the exercise.

69: Beside the right knee of the 'Princess' lay her clay potter's anvil and a shell containing her burnishing stones. We think that she was an outstanding potter and she may have made the lovely vessels which covered her ankles at death.

70: Some of the Princess's jewellery. There are shell discs, large and small shell beads, and the pierced canine teeth of a small carnivorous animal.

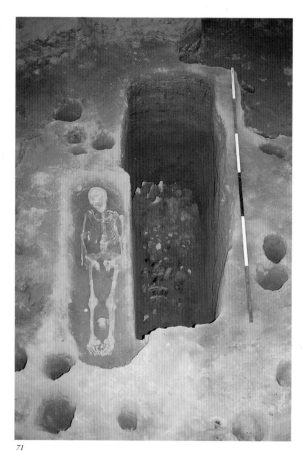

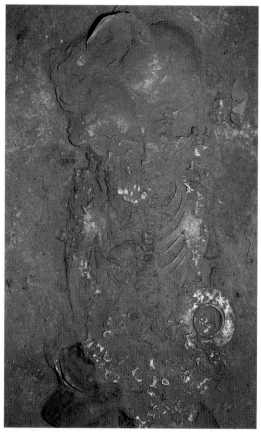

71

72

71: Revealing the Princess of Khok Phanom Di. On the right is the Princess still covered by a mound of clay cylinders and some pottery vessels. Note the large size of her grave compared with that next door, which contains the skeleton of a woman who, we think, was the Princess's grand daughter.

72: An infant no older than 15 months lay in a large grave beside the Princess. The burial was in many respects a mirror image of that containing the Princess, even down to a miniature clay anvil beside the infant's ankle.

73: The complete frame of the infant in burial 16 at Khok Phanom Di reveals a mirror image of the adjacent interment of the Princess.

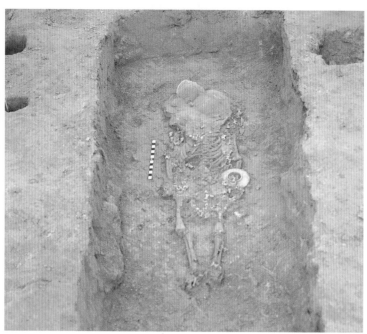

73

number of other changes which might relate to such an event. Shellfish remains show a further decline in the seaward mangrove habitat, and the rise in freshwater species seen in the preceding hiatus was followed by a decline. Only one fishhook was recovered, and a few net weights. Nevertheless, several granite hoes were found, and numerous shell knives. An ostracode from this context is from a freshwater habitat, such as rice fields. Freshwater fish and crabs again rose in frequency compared with marine or mangrove species.

74: The Princess of Khok Phanom Di wore over 120,000 shell beads, shell discs, a bracelet, and headdress. Her bones were red with ochre.

It is possible that burning, resulting in a series of ash lenses, preceded the renewal of the tradition of interring the dead in clusters during MP4, and within the mortuary area, we find a number of postholes, but markedly fewer pits. The burials, while still in their traditional clusters, were now less crowded, and were provided with individual graves. The trend towards distinguishing between males and females by the provision of turtle carapaces for the former, and anvils for the latter, was strengthened. Other grave goods included pottery vessels, now bearing less ornamentation, burnishing stones, and a single fishhook. Again, shell disc beads were rare compared with MP2 and early MP3.

The human remains reveal a number of profound changes. Infant mortality fell, but child mortality rose. Four of the five dead children had suffered from severe anaemia. The rise in infants surviving to childhood would have involved a greater investment in child rearing, and probably, a reduction in the number of births through greater spacing between pregnancies. Men were now smaller, lived shorter lives and lacked the powerful upper bodies of their forbears. Tooth wear declined in both sexes (Tayles 1998). Whereas tooth wear had caused most abscess formation in MP2-3 in males, caries was responsible in MP4. It seems highly likely that the diet involved less abrasive food. Stratigraphically, this mortuary phase includes burial 33, the grave cut for which was recognised at a depth of 3 m. It is possible that the cut was higher, and that this interment belongs to MP5. The nature of the child interment is much closer culturally to MP5 than to MP4, because it is so rich: there are 7,845 disc beads, 108 of the I-shaped beads so distinctive of MP5 burials, four pottery vessels and a small clay anvil.

Only 15 cm of cultural deposit accumulated between the last burial of MP4 and the interment of burial 15, which belongs to MP5. But the mortuary ritual changed dramatically.

75

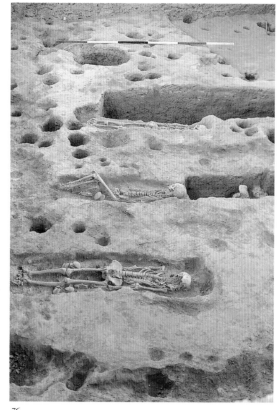

76

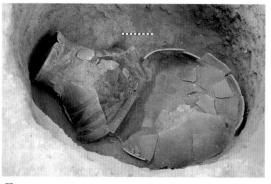

77

78

75: The structure seen in figure 79 contained the remains of a woman, seen on the right. She was buried next to two earlier females and died when she was in her mid twenties. Notice her whole pots and clay anvil.

76: In front of the raised structure, there lay a row of burials which were probably housed within their own wooden building. They were much poorer, in terms of grave goods, than those associated with the rectangular structure.

77: Exposing two pots in a circular pit.

78: They contained the skeleton of an infant, and more pots.

Clustering of graves ceased, and three people were buried in an area not hitherto used for this purpose. These graves were large and the dead were richly endowed with grave goods. Ornaments included thousands of shell disc beads and new forms of jewellery made from tridacna shell, such as discs, bangles and I-shaped beads. Burial 15 was interred with ten complete pots, some of novel form. It is also likely that the woman, who died in her mid thirties, was involved in pottery making. She had strong wrist muscles, was interred with an anvil and two burnishing stones, and her body was covered by clay cylinders destined, we think, for shaping into pottery vessels. The infant buried in an adjacent grave was also accompanied by novel shell jewellery, fine pots and a miniature clay potter's anvil. A second infant was found within two large, impressively decorated pots. The narrow stratigraphic band associated with MP5 burials saw the advent of land snails, indicating that the site was now linked to dry land.

Mason has suggested that this reflects the delayed impact of an environmental change which occurred earlier in the sequence. This period also lacked any shellfish from the clean coralline habitat to which tridacna is adapted, suggesting that the new range of shell jewellery was exotic. Ivory bangles were found for the first time, although not with burials. The last shell knife was found just before the start of MP5.

The earliest MP6 burials followed with little interval from MP5. There is much evidence for environmental instability, seen in an increase in shellfish from estuarine and seaward mangrove habitats. At the same time, sickles fashioned from freshwater shellfish ceased to be found. After a long interval, a few seeds of a plant adapted to salt flats reappeared, and fresh water remains became rare. It is possible that rice cultivation became marginal through the invasion of salt water. The mortuary ritual involved investment in substantial structures, one containing rich interments, the other a row of burials with far fewer grave goods. A more marine or at least brackish water habitat seems to have continued into the currency of MP7, the final phase which is represented only by a handful of graves.

Khok Phanom Di: A Rich Hunter-Gatherer Society

During the analysis of all this material, we were struck by the way in which the dead were superimposed over such a long time

79

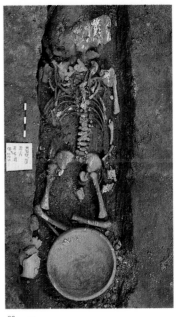

80

79: With mortuary phase 6, we encountered a rectangular building. We wondered what lay within.

80: Asbestos fabric used in ancient Rome was more valuable by weight than gold. The white streaks on this infant skeleton from Khok Phanom Di are asbestos, the earliest use of this material in the world.

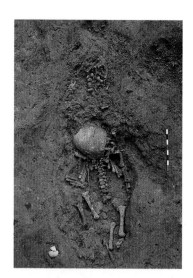

81: Two infant skeletons emerge at Khok Phanom Di. Infant mortality was very high.

span. Our detective work continued in the laboratory, and we puzzled over the possibility that people within each cluster were related to each other. If a man and woman were buried in adjacent graves, were they husband and wife, brother and sister, father and daughter? If a woman and infant shared the same grave, were they mother and child? So we began to sketch out a sequence of graves, and their possible relationships. Two clusters proved particularly long lasting, others petered out. We ended up with a series of possible descent groups two of which encompassed about 17 generations covering MP 2 to 6. This number, when you include MP1 and MP7, probably adds up to somewhere in the vicinity of 20 generations. At 20 years each, we end up with 400 years, a number which fits well with our radiocarbon dating results.

We then tested this idea in several ways, such as the recurrence in the skulls and teeth of inherited characteristics and found a good measure of support. We think that there are grounds then, for the validity of these genealogies, which are unique in the prehistoric world. What can we learn from them? Most burials were associated with grave offerings, including pottery vessels and shell ornaments. Some people were also interred with carved turtle carapace ornaments, others with clay anvils, or burnishing stones. The complexity of the mortuary ritual and quantity of grave goods inform us on the extent to which the living spent energy on the funeral of a particular person. What we have found is that, despite basic continuity in the ritual of death over the generations, there were also significant changes. Until MP3, for example, we can find no differences in the treatment of men and women, but thereafter, only men had turtle carapaces, and only women and some infants were buried with clay anvils. We also note an extraordinary increase in wealth with MP5, when a woman was buried in a large grave with over 120,000 shell beads, beautiful pots and a clay anvil with two burnishing stones. Next to her lay an infant with thousands of beads, and a miniature clay anvil. Both had exotic, heavy shell ornaments as well. During MP6, three rich people were found buried in a raised chamber while others, poorer in terms of grave goods, were laid out in front of it within a wooden building.

We have suggested that during MP1-3, the hunter gatherers made pottery vessels of great beauty and probably exchanged some of them for necessary items, particularly high quality stone and rice. Some individuals probably achieved prestige through their particular ability or ambition. There was then a change in the environment, and the people of Khok Phanom Di began to cultivate some rice in the newly formed freshwater swamps. They also used granite hoes to turn the soil, and fashioned harvesting knives from freshwater shellfish. But the fickle environment was soon to change again, as the sea level rose slightly, bringing a return to saline mangrove conditions. At this point, rice cultivation ceased, but there was a surge in exchange relationships. We envisage that women, skilled in pottery making, now turned out their wares for exchange, and many new and exotic materials were obtained, not least tridacna shell, ivory and slate for turning into jewellery. Rice may once again have come into the site through trade. Ban Tha Kae is just the sort of inland site with which coastal communities such as Khok Phanom Di might have traded. So the women of Khok Phanom Di grew in status, but when a daughter died young, it was a serious loss and young girls were sometimes given lavish funerals. Some men also prospered and were buried with rich sets of grave goods, including heavy, exotic shell discs. But at this point, we are reaching the sunset of this long and vibrant community. Perhaps the habitat changed again, the inhabitants may have decided on a new location. By about 1600 years BC, Khok Phanom Di was abandoned. But the way of life we have reconstructed ensures that our perception of hunter gatherers in Thailand has changed beyond recognition.

82

83

82: The people of Khok Phanom Di made, and were buried with beautiful pottery vessels.

83: The great depth of Khok Phanom Di is clearly to be seen, and there was more to come.

Hunter-Gatherers: Summary

Most people, when asked how they imagine life must have been as a hunter-gatherer, reply that it meant being constantly on the move in small groups, in order to find sufficient food. This is a myth. Particularly when occupying rich environments, hunter gatherers rarely if ever need to move, have little if any concern for their food supply, can develop large communities and are known to have sharp distinctions in rank and wealth. In Thailand, we have identified hunter gatherer sites in upland caves, beside rivers and along former shorelines.

The upland groups, known generally as Hoabinhian, took advantage of the shelter offered by the front of caves. But this does not mean that they were not equally if not more at home out in the open, near rivers, or within the forest to exploit seasonal harvests. It is simply that caves provide greater

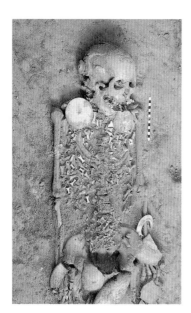

84: "She would have dazzled in reflected sunlight". The Princess of Khok Phanom Di.

protection for habitation remains, and are more easily located. These inland groups consumed a wide range of food resources, and are sometimes labelled 'broad spectrum' gatherers as a result. Anything that moved seems to have attracted their attention: crabs, fish, shellfish, tiny squirrels, deer and even rhinoceros. They must have been adept at fashioning traps and projectiles which, to this day, call on the supreme qualities of bamboo. But most of the surviving implements were roughly chipped from stone and only the traces of wear betray their likely use in shaping wood. This hunting tradition lasted with few changes for thousands of years, and its ancestry stretched back much further still, as has been seen in 40,000-year-old occupation remains at Lang Rongrien. Provided population levels were stable and people were not troubled by other human groups, or did not grow beyond the capacity of the environment, there is no reason why such a tradition should not continue indefinitely.

We must, however, set this possibility against the many gaps in our understanding of this inland Hoabinhian, as has been emphasised by Shoocondej (1996a). She has pointed out that much remains for investigation. We must pinpoint the nature of the subsistence, the duration of occupation of the rock shelters and not least, the way of life of these hunter gatherers beyond the confines of cave shelters. Perhaps Hoabinhian people who may have lived near lakes or rivers, developed agriculture independently. This is only an idea, and needs to be tested through fieldwork designed to find riverine sites. Yet, while we know virtually nothing of settlement in such areas, we are beginning to find out what life was like on the coast.

The warm shallow sea and broad estuaries and embayments of the Gulf of Siam provide one of the richest habitats on earth. We can only focus on the hunter gatherer adaptation to this shore after about 4000 BC, when the sea reached a high point, and then began to recede. There must have been a long tradition of maritime hunting and gathering before then, but the rising sea has drowned the relevant settlements. The abundance of food encouraged permanence, and moving away from the security of an estuary would have only opened the way for other groups to move in. We think that the rich coastal fringe would have encouraged a strong sense of territory. Certainly at Khok Phanom Di, we encounter a stable community which prospered over a period of at least 400 years from 2000 BC. Some changes in the environment would have been imperceptible as the generations came and went: sedimentation of the estuary took a century or more to have an impact. Other changes were swift, as when a nearby river, swollen with monsoon rains, burst its bank and found a new channel miles distant. Yet the people adapted to both. They continued in their traditional ways to make and exchange pots, and projected status through the ownership of shell ornaments, and probably the provision of mortuary feasts. A woman whose clothing, embellished with over 100,000 shell beads, dazzled in the sunlight does not provide us with the widespread conception that hunter gatherers were beset by concern over the next meal. During one brief period at this site, we think that the inhabitants began to cultivate rice. Throughout its occupation, they were able to obtain rice. Who was responsible for the first rice farming in Thailand? When and why did this transition take place? This is one of the most important questions in Thailand's past and to it we will now turn.

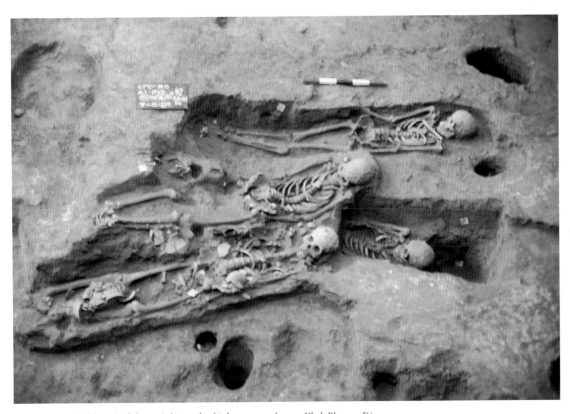

85: *Densely packed burials of cluster C during the third mortuary phase at Khok Phanom Di.*

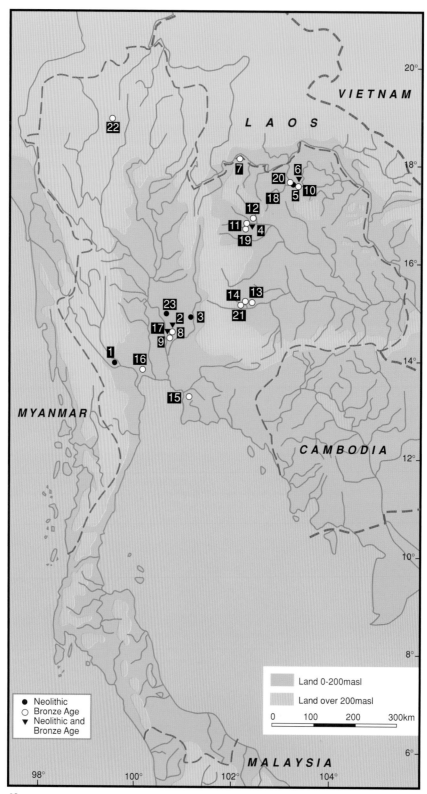

Chapter Three
The First Farmers

"The transition to agriculture is perhaps the most remarkable event in the entire course of human prehistory." Price and Gebauer 1995:3

The transition to agriculture is one of the key behavioural changes in the history of the human species. Why is this so? For over 99% of the human span on earth, our ancestors were hunters and gatherers. It is true that some of these groups, as we have seen at Khok Phanom Di, were able to live permanently in one place and develop a degree of social complexity. We have found that some individuals achieved high status and were buried with rich grave furnishings. But there are limits to the size and complexity of hunter gatherer societies. We never find, for example, literate civilizations that relied solely on the natural wealth of nature. The intentional cultivation of fields, human intervention in the breeding of plants and animals, and the adoption of agriculture permit the production not only of sufficient food for survival, but also a disposable surplus, a form of wealth. An agricultural community has the potential for growing far larger and more complex than one reliant on hunting and gathering.

Agriculture requires more labour than most hunting and gathering systems of food procurement. It often involves clearing trees, and tilling the soil. Altering the environment in this way also changes the relationships between human and other animal communities. Imagine forest being converted into a field of ripening wheat, or maize, or rice. This is an opportunity for birds, insects or mammals ranging in size from

87   (height 21.5 cm)

86: The location of Neolithic and Bronze Age sites mentioned in chapters III and IV. 1. Ban Kao, 2. Non Pa Wai and Non Mak La, 3. Khok Charoen, 4. Non Nok Tha, 5. Non Kao Noi, 6. Ban Chiang, 7. Phu Lon, 8. Nil Kham Haeng, 9. Lopburi Artillery Site, 10. Ban Na Di, 11. Non Pa Kluay, 12. Non Praw, 13. Ban Prasat, 14. Ban Lum Khao, 15. Nong Nor, 16. Khok Phlap, 17 Tha Kae, 18. Lake Kumphawapi. 19. Non Nong Chik, 20. Ban Phak Top, 21. Ban San Thia, 22. Ob Luang, 23. Ban Mai Champongkhon.

87: The earliest pottery found with agricultural settlements like Non Kao Noi and Ban Chiang, date to about 2100-2300 BC. (Photo: Fine Arts Department of Thailand)

(diam. 30 cm)

88: This ceramic stove from Tha Kae shows a mature tradition of ceramic firing. (Courtesy Surapol Natapintu)

a mouse to an elephant, to plunder. So farmers must protect their fields or their labour will be wasted. In Thailand, a traditional and doubly useful means of protection was to ring the clearance with bamboo traps, using the crop to attract animals to their death. So agriculture encourages people to live permanently in one place. Groups became sedentary, beyond the few rich places, like estuaries, where hunter-gatherers had lived permanently for many generations. Sedentism, occupying the same locality and investing in food production, has a number of implications. It opens the way to increasing the population. Hunter gatherers who move their base regularly have to carry their belongings, unless they have access to boats or, in the case of later American Indians, the horse. This includes young children. Consequently, they usually space births so that a woman does not have to carry more than one infant. Sedentism removes this limitation, and more frequent births means population growth, provided health problems do not intervene.

When the number of people living in one community reaches certain population thresholds, we often find that social stresses develop. Whereas 100 people in a village could take decisions communally and through agreement, consensus is more difficult where five times that number is involved. Resolution of disagreement and friction within a group approaching this size can be achieved by vesting authority in a dominant elite. Alternatively, a splinter group may move elsewhere and establish a new community. One phenomenon often, but not always found with the transition to agriculture, therefore, is that as populations grew, new settlements were founded and there was, over the centuries and millennia, an expansion of the area sustaining farming groups.

Another series of changes often associated with sedentary agriculturalists, is the development of new forms of artefact and the accumulation of possessions. We have seen that hunter gatherers at Khok Phanom Di and Nong Nor made and used pottery vessels, but that itself is a reflection of more permanent settlement. With intensified production and the storage of surpluses, people could construct large, permanent dwellings, increase the ownership of goods irrespective of weight and through exchange relationships, acquire quantities of rare or exotic valuables.

The Origins of Agriculture

Was there a transition to agriculture in Thailand, or did the first farming communities arrive from elsewhere? Thailand was and remains a country where wild rice flourishes, and of the native wild mammals, there are at least two species of cattle, the pig, water buffalo, elephant and jungle fowl that are now domesticated. There are no barriers in the path of local domestication, but is it possible to trace origins? This is achieved in other parts of the world by finding an archaeological sequence in which there were a series of changes in the size and shape of the domesticates. Some animals, for example the water buffalo and cattle, become smaller when domesticated. Domestic rice also undergoes a series of changes. When remains of these species change in tandem with cultural developments, like a different diet, larger settlements, the development of agricultural implements and the clearance of forests, then we can think in terms of a local transition.

Several archaeologists have suggested how such a transition may have happened in Thailand, and then looked for the evidence. Chester Gorman, for example, proposed that the Hoabinhian hunter gatherers brought certain plants into cultivation. He identified the marshes lying at the piedmont between plains and uplands as a likely habitat. Perhaps hunters and gatherers in such habitats tended taro, and then experimented with cultivating rice (Gorman 1977). He had no evidence to support this model, which saw root crop horticulture beginning about 14,000 years ago, followed about 9,000 years ago by rice cultivation. But at the stage when models are formulated for testing, there is no need for such evidence, only the will to go out and seek the necessary sites to excavate. This was undertaken, and no evidence was found. At this point, the model foundered.

In 1984, when we were planning the excavation of Khok Phanom Di, we substituted a model of our own. We suggested that the coastal habitat, while unsuited to rice cultivation due to the saline soil, was nevertheless subject to changes. If, for example, the sea level were to fall and the habitat came to include freshwater swamps, then the inhabitants might have begun to expand their food base by favouring the growth of rice. Once recognised for its potential, settlement by early rice farmers could have introduced this practice by expansion up the river valleys into the interior plains (Higham and Bannanurag

(diam. 8 cm)

89: *Two shell ear ornaments from Ban Mai Champongkhon, Nakhon Sawan. (Courtesy Surapol Natapintu)*

90: Shell disc and H-beads from a burial at Huai Yai are virtually identical to those from late Khok Phanom Di. (Courtesy Surapol Natapintu)

1990). In 1984, we knew that rice had been found during earlier investigations at the site, but were not to know until our radiocarbon dates were complete that the site was only occupied from 2000 BC, too late for its serious consideration as a place where rice cultivation actually began and then spread. So this model too, fell by the wayside.

Sørensen proposed a third alternative following his excavations at Ban Kao in Kanchanaburi (Sørensen and Hatting 1967). He suggested that its inhabitants were part of an expansionary movement of farmers from southern China. When published, the notion of such migratory movements was unfashionable among archaeologists, and few regarded his suggestion with enthusiasm. However, some recent developments have required us to return to his proposal.

Language, Archaeology and Human Biology

When a community divides and one group moves elsewhere, members take with them not only their tradition of tool making and subsistence, but also their language and genes. In theory, therefore, the distribution of languages today will inform us on past events, just as a person's genes will reflect ancestry. It is not quite so easy as this, because languages can be learnt and genes mutate. The descendants of a Chinese immigrant to Thailand may speak Thai rather than Cantonese. Perhaps the clearest example of the relationship between language and the spread of a particular people is the present distribution of Austronesian languages from Malagasy to Easter Island, and New Zealand to Taiwan. When people move into unoccupied islands, as in Polynesia, they will retain their own language with no borrowing from other groups. But languages change with time. New words are coined, others die out. Historic linguists can, nevertheless, identify linkages which suggest that the greatest time depth in Austronesian languages is found on the island of Taiwan. Bellwood (1989, 1992, 1993) has suggested that the speakers of Austronesian languages gradually colonised the Pacific Islands over the past 5,000 years, from an original homeland probably located in the valley of the Yangzi River.

Renfrew (1987), in a controversial hypothesis, has linked the spread of agriculturalists from their original homeland in Turkey and the Levant westward into Europe and north and eastward to continental Asia and so to India. This, he has suggested, is the most economical hypothesis to account for the remarkably widespread distribution of Indo-European languages. The idea has an attractive simplicity. How else did Indo-European languages, including Spanish, Portuguese and English reach their present distribution other than through human expansion? They even reached Thailand, for Sanskrit and Pali are Indo-European languages.

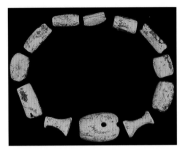

91: Shell barrel and I-shaped beads from Ban Mai Champongkhon look exactly like examples from Khok Phanom Di. (Courtesy Surapol Natapintu)

Do the languages of Thailand shed light on the remote origins of agriculture? We think they might, but the picture is blurred and the pattern, complex. Even early European visitors to the court of Ayutthaya noted this. The French diplomat, De la Loubère, wrote in 1693:

"As for what concerns the origine of the Siameses, it would be difficult to judge whether they are a single people, directly descended from the first men that inhabited the contrey of Siam, or whether in the process of time some other nation has not also settled there, notwithstanding the first inhabitants. The principal reason for this doubt proceeds from the Siameses understanding of two languages, viz. the vulgar, which is a simple tongue consisting almost wholly of monosyllables, without conjugation or declension, and another language, which I have already spoken of, which to them is a dead tongue known only to the learned, which is called the Balie tongue, and which is enrich with the inflections of words, like the languages we have in Europe". (De la Loubère 1693:14).

De la Loubère correctly identified the use of Pali words in the court of King Narai alongside the native Thai. Pali is, like Sanskrit, an Indo-European language, and its presence in Thailand will be considered later. But he missed the fact that at least two other languages were, and still are, spoken in remoter parts of Thailand: Khmer and Mon. These two closely related languages belong to a family known as Austroasiatic. Khmer is the national language of Cambodia and if you travel along the border country in Buriram, Sisaket and Surin provinces, you will find villagers speaking Khmer. They have friends and relatives in Cambodia, and move freely across the border on visits. Mon is now spoken only in isolated villages, but it was once the dominant language in the Chao Phraya Valley. Now, the interesting fact is that related languages in the Austroasiatic family stretch from eastern India to Vietnam and on into

92

92-93: Neolithic pottery vessels from Huai Yai and Phu Noi. (Courtesy Surapol Natapintu)

southern China. Moreover, some of these languages share the same word for rice and aspects of its cultivation (Zide and Zide 1976). The relationships between Munda, Mon and Vietnamese are slight, but most linguists think that they diverged from a common ancestor. Diffloth (1991) has suggested that divergence began over 4,000 years ago.

Until recently, linguists have paid little attention to a proposal advanced by the Austrian Schmidt (1906). He suggested that these Austroasiatic languages shared a common ancestor with Austronesian, and he called this super group, Austric. There are so few similar words between these two, that most specialists have been sceptical. But Reid (1993) has given particular consideration to the languages spoken on the remote Nicobar Islands. These fall within the Austroasiatic family, but he noted that some structural features were more akin to Austronesian languages. On this basis, he gave his support to a remote common origin. When this piece of the jigsaw fell into place, a pattern began to clarify. Robert Blust was prominent in suggesting a bold new hypothesis which linked the distribution of Austroasiatic languages with the origin and spread of rice agriculture (Blust 1996). He suggested that rice was first cultivated in the upper reaches of the Yangzi River valley. From this area, communities spread by degrees to the coast. Some may have crossed over the straits to Taiwan and set in train the expansion of the Austronesian speakers. Others, sharing at first a common language, infiltrated gradually down the rivers of the mainland. So agriculture and early Vietnamese speakers moved into the lower Red River valley. The Mekong was a conduit south for those speaking early Khmer and Mon, while the Brahmaputra could have provided passage for the Munda speakers of India. Like Renfrew's ideas on Indo-European, this pattern has an attractive elegance in its simplicity. But it has likewise attracted criticism and disagreement.

Such new proposals only gather weight when they are tested against the available information, and this takes us briefly to the Yangzi Valley itself. To many, this would seem deep in China. But it must be remembered that it was only from about 200 BC that Chinese speakers hailing from the Yellow River valley began to establish an empire which came to incorporate what is now China south of the Yangzi. It is more correct to think of this extensive area as a part of Southeast Asia. It shares the same monsoon climate, the same critical importance of rice cultivation and we can still find traces of Austroasiatic languages there. This even includes the very name of the Yangzi River. For many years, the prehistory of southern China has been neglected in favour of the Chinese nuclear area to the north, but this situation has now been reversed and we can identify a number of critical changes in the Yangzi Valley which help us to understand the prehistory of Thailand.

Foremost among these is the discovery of a series of mounded settlement sites in the swampy, low-lying land which surrounds Lake Dongting, just to the south of the Yangzi River. One of these, Pengtoushan, is a 4 metre high mound covering an area of about one hectare, located on the Liyang Plain where it meets the northern shore of Lake Dongting. Radiocarbon dates indicate settlement between 6500-5800 BC, a period which experienced a reduction in the temperature following a 1,500 year span of progressive warming (Huai-Jen and Zhiren 1984). Excavations have revealed the remains of four houses and 19 burials, some of which contained up to four pottery vessels. Each house covered about 30m². The material culture includes much pottery and flaked stone implements, but polished stone axes and adzes were rare. Pierced stone pendants of soapstone and siltstone were present, as in many other sites in the vicinity of Lake Dongting (Jiejun 1986). None of the large grinding stones and mortars typical of later sites in the area were found, but there were some small stone implements which might have been used for rice husking.

Screening and flotation lead to the recovery of rice, and pottery was tempered with rice chaff which Yan describes as being 'without a doubt cultivated'. Other sites of the Pengtoushan culture are known, especially in Hunan and Hubei provinces. They were small and have a shallow stratigraphy. Rice husks and straw were used as a pottery temper though again, no firm conclusions on its status have been published (Ahn 1990). It has, however, been suggested that the remains of deer, pig and buffalo from these sites come from wild animals.

The important point about these discoveries, is that rice was a part of the diet even by 6000 BC. This provides a possible home for the transition to rice cultivation by people who may have spoken a remote ancestral language to Mon, Khmer and possibly Thai. If so, then here lies a possible ultimate origin for the first farmers to move south and settle in Thailand.

93

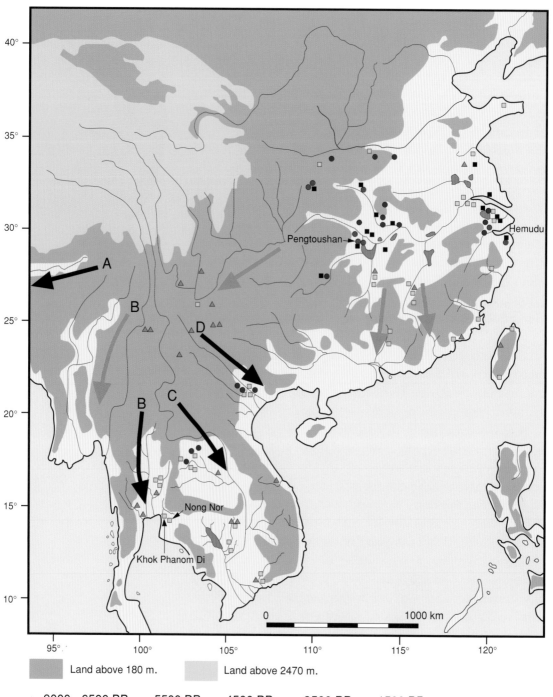

Pengtoushan

Hemudu

A

B

D

B

C

Nong Nor

Khok Phanom Di

0   1000 km

95°   100°   105°   110°   115°   120°

40°

35°

30°

25°

20°

15°

10°

Land above 180 m.   Land above 2470 m.

● -9000 - 6500 BP   ■ -5500 BP   ● -4500 BP   □ -3500 BP   ▲ -1500 BP

A. Proto Munda, B. Proto Mon, C. Proto Khmer, D. Proto Viet

94: Map showing the sites which reveal early rice agriculture, in the region of Pengtoushan, with arrows which point in the suggested direction of the expansion of early rice farmers.

The Archaeological Evidence
for the Neolithic in Thailand

By Neolithic, we mean a way of life which incorporated agriculture and the raising of domestic animals. It virtually always involves permanent communities, the making of pottery vessels and polished stone axes or adzes. There are two ways of tracking down the earliest farmers. We can identify agriculture and stock raising on the basis of the size and shape of the plants and animals recovered from excavations in settlement sites. There is a more subtle and elusive method which requires caution, and this involves the analysis of naturally deposited plant remains which have accumulated in lake beds or swamps. The care which needs to be taken with the latter approach is well illustrated by the conclusions of Bernard Maloney at Khok Phanom Di (Maloney 1991).

As part of his environmental research, he took deep cores from the natural deposits in the vicinity of the site, and then extracted the remains of pollen and charcoal. He found that there were phases in the past when intense burning cleared the local vegetation, and encouraged the growth of plants which prefer open, sunny conditions. These burning episodes were dated to 5500, 5300-5000 and 4000 BC, and one of the pollen types which increased in quantity following the fires was from grass. It would be convenient were it possible to identify pollen from cultivated rice, for its presence would strongly suggest that farmers burnt the vegetation when creating rice fields. Unfortunately, this is not possible. So we are left with several possible explanations for ancient fires. One is that they began when lightning struck the tinder dry forest at the start of the rainy season. This often occurs today. The second is that hunters and gatherers deliberately torched the forest to encourage grass growth. This attracts deer and other game, and makes it easier to hunt. A third possibility is, indeed, that agriculture was involved.

Five years after Maloney's research was complete, and still unable to determine which of these three alternatives was most likely, we returned to the vicinity of Khok Phanom Di, and excavated at Nong Nor. There, we found the remains of a hunter gatherer site dating to 2500 BC. It contained much evidence for burning: there were thick deposits of ash resulting from firing pottery vessels, but no evidence for rice. This is just the sort of activity which could have caused those increases in charcoal in Maloney's cores.

95   (length 15 cm.)

96

*95: An effigy vessel of a cow from Phu Noi.
(Courtesy Surapol Natapintu)*

*96: Turtle carapace was transformed into a
disc, and buried with a child, at Phu Noi.
(Courtesy Surapol Natapintu)*

More recently, similar investigations have been undertaken on cores taken from Lake Kumphawapi, located in Udon Thani Province, about 30 km southwest of Ban Chiang. One metre from the top of the lake sediments, there is a sharp rise in charcoal concentrations, dated to the 5th millennium BC (Penny *et al.* 1996). Burning phases have been noted on the basis of plant phytoliths taken in separate cores by Kealhofer (1996). White (1997) has suggested that these relate to the first rice farmers in the vicinity, and proposed that the Ban Chiang cultural tradition could be a thousand years earlier than 3600 BC. As was the case for Khok Phanom Di, however, such fires might have more than one cause. What we need, and currently lack, is any evidence from the land round Lake Kumphawapi for human settlement at the time of early burning episodes. It might be that the conversion of the lowland area to rice fields, involving much levelling, has destroyed the evidence. On the other hand, no excavated site in the area has any evidence for agricultural settlement before about 2300 BC, nor have concentrations of pottery which might be earlier than this date ever been found during site surveys. It is, therefore, considered wiser to stress only that the earliest acceptable evidence for the settlement of Thailand by rice farmers is in the region of 2300 BC, rather than push back the arrival of agriculture on the basis of insufficient evidence. Nor do we know of an archaeological sequence suggesting a local transition from hunting and gathering to the Neolithic in Thailand.

Ban Kao

During the course of the Thai-Danish expedition to Kanchanaburi Province, particular attention was paid to a prehistoric settlement known as the Bang Site, near the village of Ban Kao. Many potsherds and fragments of stone adzes were found on the surface of this mound, and in 1961-2, Per Sørensen opened an area of almost 400 m². This was a pioneering excavation, no one had previously worked in such a mounded site in Thailand (Sørensen and Hatting 1967). His team found what has subsequently become one of the most important sources of information for prehistoric Thailand: an inhumation cemetery. By degrees, they uncovered 44 graves, in which the dead were inhumed in a supine, extended position, associated with grave offerings which included pottery vessels, adzes and shell jewellery. Radiocarbon dates suggest occupation between 2300-1500 BC. Sørensen noted some parallels in the form of pottery vessels with examples from China, and suggested that the settlement involved an expansionary movement from that quarter (Sørensen 1963).

The lack of clear stratigraphy and of superimposed burials made it difficult to order the graves chronologically. Sørensen set them out in order of depth below a fixed datum point, on the assumption that earlier graves were the lower. He then divided the pottery vessels into different forms and sought a correspondence between the forms and the depth of the graves. He concluded that there were two phases of graves which belong to either an early or a late Neolithic. There are, however, intermediate graves, indicating that the two groups were not separated by a long interval.

Does the location of burials and treatment of the dead reveal social information? During the early phase, bodies were placed on their back, and there was no preference for an easterly orientation. Only one infant was reported. Perhaps they were interred separately, but it is hard to envisage a community without higher infant mortality, particularly given the skeletal evidence at Ban Kao for thalassaemia. The graves were not clustered in the manner of Khok Phanom Di, but there was an orderly pattern in which the dead were interred in pairs and on the same alignment. Burials 31 and 33, for example, were found alongside each other. One was probably a male aged about 30 at death. He was accompanied by a pottery vessel. The other was a 35-year-old adult with two pottery vessels. At the eastern edge of the excavated area, there are five early phase burials. The three intact graves are oriented in a southwesterly direction. From west to east, burial 18 was an adult, lying on the broken remains of three pottery vessels with the sherds from a further five being found over the lower limbs. Burial 29, which lay alongside, was also an adult. A stone adze head was found under the skull, and six broken pots were present in the region of the head and shoulders and below the knees. Burial 28 was associated with at least three pots, while with burial 27, we have another adult on a southwesterly orientation with an adze under the skull and twelve broken pots.

Such grouping continued into the late phase. Burials 9-11 lie parallel with each other on a northeast to southwest orientation, the two females have the head to the southwest, the male in the opposite direction. In each case, however, grave goods were richer and more varied then hitherto. Burial 9, a 35-

0   20cm

97: These pottery vessels from Ban Kao come from Neolithic burials. The tripod form is widespread, even as far south as Lang Rongrien and into Malaysia.

98: An early grave at Non Mak La, and showing bracelets of green stone, marble shell, and small disc beads. (Courtesy Dr. V. Pigott, Thailand Archaeometallurgy Project)

year-old woman, was accompanied by 11 pottery vessels, eight of which were disposed in a line beyond the feet, such that the grave would have been at least five metres long. Burial 10 lay almost two metres to the east. The male was over 50 years at death, and his grave goods included four pottery vessels and a large stone ring with a hole in the centre, traces of polish hinting that it was unfinished. There were also two stone adzes and a remarkable deer antler, the tines of which were cut at right angles to the shaft and shaped into tubular ends. The remains of two young pigs were also found beyond the head. Burial 11, a woman who died when about 30 years old, was particularly rich. There were nine complete pottery vessels, six adzes and a necklace made up of two strands of 642 shell disc beads and two tubular stone beads.

The majority of burial offerings are pottery vessels. Sørensen has divided these into twelve principal forms. The two major divisions involve vessels with or without supports. The former include so-called tripods and among the latter, we find beakers and bowls. Surfaces were burnished or cord marked and two vessels bear incised and impressed ornamentation, the designs including a series of six arcs and a snake. Shell beads are absent from early graves and present in only three late phase graves. There is much evidence for continuity between early and late phases at Ban Kao. When superimposed, burials from the latter do not disturb the former. Presumably the location of graves was known. The mortuary ritual, despite some modifications, remained similar. Graves in close proximity were found on a similar orientation, with males and females being placed in opposite directions. People were still interred with pottery vessels and stone adzes, although offerings were more varied and abundant. New items include shell disc and stone beads, worked shell, bone harpoons, a carved sandstone phallus, a modified antler and pigs' foot bones. A perforated stone disc was found in the same grave as the worked antler.

Ban Kao was a small inland settlement, located on a river flood plain where aquatic resources, and presumably marshland suited to rice cultivation, were available. Many sites with similar pottery forms are known which portray a widespread occupation from western Thailand south to Jenderam Hilir in Malaysia. Two burials with Ban Kao style pottery vessels and shell ornaments have been found at Han Songchram and a further similar burial comes from Rai Arnon (Shoocondej 1996b). The upper layers at Lang Rongrien have produced burials containing pedestalled pottery vessels which recall the Ban Kao repertoire (Anderson 1990). The same people pushed south across the border into Malaysia as well, where Leong (1991) has suggested that they represent the introduction of agriculture to the coastal plains of peninsular Thailand and Malaysia.

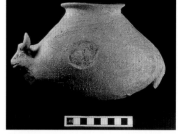

99

The Lopburi Area and the Khao Wong Prachan Valley

We will be hearing a lot about this valley, which lies about 15 km north of Lopburi. Here, the flat plain of the Chao Phraya River and its tributaries gives way to hilly outcrops some of which are rich in veins of copper ore. Recent research at the site of Non Pa Wai, where there is much evidence for copper mining and smelting, has also identified a Neolithic cemetery which partially underlies and extends beyond the Bronze Age layers. The published results of this excavation, which was directed by Vincent Pigott, are keenly awaited and at present, we have available two radiocarbon dates which suggest that settled agriculture was being established in this part of the Central Plain by about 2300 BC.

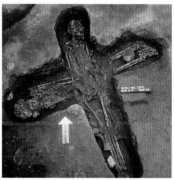

100

99: A superb pot from Non Mak La in the form of a cow, which was decorated with incised lines. (Courtesy Dr. V. Pigott, Thailand Archaeometallurgy Project)

100: These two Neolithic burials from Non Mak La were interred in the form of a cross. (Courtesy Dr. V. Pigott, Thailand Archaeometallurgy Project)

One of the most important excavations on a Neolithic site in this valley took place at Non Mak La in 1994. Under the direction of Vincent Pigott and Andrew Weiss, burials were uncovered which reveal the material richness of the early rice farmers in Central Thailand. They made and decorated superb pottery vessels including one in the form of a cow. Through exchange or local endeavour, they obtained personal ornaments of green stone, marble and shell. Infants were often buried in pottery vessels, adults in an extended position, in one case superimposed in the form of a cross.

Reports of the excavation at nearby Tha Kae also evidence settlement during the Neolithic. In 1979, officials from the Fine Arts Department found that this large, moated mound was being systematically destroyed for fill. Excavations followed in 1980, under the direction of Surapol Natapintu, and in 1983 by Rachanie Thosarat. Subsequent excavations were undertaken by Ciarla (1992). The cultural sequence has been divided into three distinct phases of which the earliest is Neolithic. Twenty one inhumation burials were found. They have in common a north-south orientation, and the placement of pottery vessels beyond

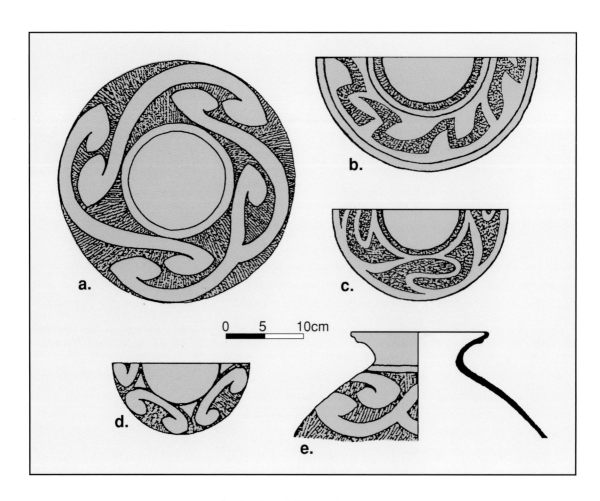

101: Designs found on Neolithic vessels from Ban Tha Kae.

the head and feet and in one case, under the knee. Other offerings include shell beads, bangles and earrings, a bone point and polished stone adze head. It is the pottery vessels which attract most attention, for we encounter not only a profusion of forms, but also of motifs. The latter were incised on the surface of the vessel, and highlighted by being surrounded by cord marking, or receiving impressions within the confines of the incised lines (Siripanish 1985). So we can appreciate the C and S shaped patterns, the line of stylised snakes and the assured way in which motifs were opposed in harmonious groups round the vessel necks. This particular method of pottery decoration is widespread, and characteristic in Yunnan and Vietnam as well as Thailand, of expansive farming communities. Hanwong (1985) has also described the artefacts from Tha Kae, and noted the presence of marlstone and turtle carapace bangles, and the central cores removed from tridacna shell to create bangles. The site was thus a centre for the manufacture of shell ornaments. Tha Kae is just the sort of community with which the inhabitants of Khok Phanom Di would have traded, and obtained their dogs and the notion of cultivating rice. Unfortunately, we do not have any radiocarbon dates for this site, but these earliest layers probably belong within the period 2500-1500 BC.

Natapintu (1988a) has exposed an area of 3 by 5 m at Phu Noi, 40 km to the north, and found a concentration of 32 burials. Grave goods include marine shell ornaments as well as items made from turtle carapace, ivory and exotic stone. Two animal figurines serving also as pottery vessels were found, forms virtually identical with an example from Non Nok Tha. Again, no radiocarbon dates are available, and the principal relevance of this site is the proof for exchange between inland and coastal communities during the second millennium BC.

Khok Charoen

Khok Charoen, located in the valley of the Pasak River, was excavated in four seasons between 1966-70, and only the material from the first two is available for consideration (Loofs-Wissowa 1997). Ho has suggested that the inhabitants had "some knowledge of rice cultivation". The date of occupation is not known with assurance, but there are two TL dates which suggest that it falls within the period 1400-800 BC and Ho (1984) ascribes them to the early Metal Age. No bronze grave goods were recovered, however, and only with a full set of radiocarbon dates will the issue be settled. At Ban Lum Khao on the Khorat Plateau, for example, we have uncovered 110 undoubtedly Bronze Age graves again with no metal grave goods. At present, all we can say with confidence is that Khok Charoen may be earlier than the Bronze Age.

The graves contained poorly preserved human remains, in

102: This person buried at Non Mak La wore a ceramic ear spool. Identical ornaments of bronze were found 2,000 years later at Noen U-Loke. (Courtesy Dr. V. Pigott, Thailand Archaeometallurgy Project)

103: As at Bronze and Iron Age sites, infants at Non Mak La were buried in large jars. (Courtesy Dr. V. Pigott, Thailand Archaeometallurgy Project)

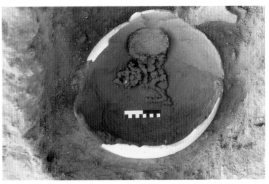

102

103

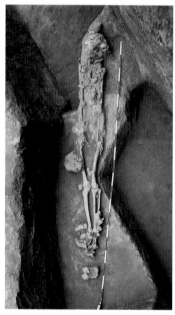

104: The excavations at Non Nok Tha in 1968 were a major contribution to our understanding of early agricultural settlement in Northeast Thailand. (Courtesy Dr. D.T. Bayard)

105: One of the earliest Neolithic burials uncovered at Non Nok Tha in 1968. (Courtesy Dr. D.T. Bayard)

association with pottery vessels. Decoration involves overall burnishing, as well as zones of red slip and cord marking. Some rare forms see patterns demarcated by incised lines infilled with stamped or impressed surfaces. Shell jewellery includes disc beads, but never in the quantities attained at Khok Phanom Di, the maximum number in any grave being 843. The shell head ornament from burial 15 at Khok Phanom Di is paralleled at Khok Charoen in form and size, each having a diameter of about 4 cm. This cemetery has also yielded a moderate quantity of trochus bangles and rings, and there are also two conus shell rings, and marble and green stone ornaments.

The Khorat Plateau

This region, lying in the great bend of the Mekong River to the north and east, is divided into two major drainage basins. In the northern part, we find the Sakon Nakhon Basin, where small streams thread across a gently undulating landscape which is favoured by relatively high rainfall. As we proceed south to the Mun and Chi river systems, it becomes increasingly dry, and monsoon rains are reduced. We know of no Neolithic sites in this latter basin, the earliest sites fall into the Bronze Age. In the Sakon Nakhon Basin, there have been a series of site surveys undertaken with the aim of identifying early settlements, and we have some evidence that rice farming communities were infiltrating into the area by about 2300 BC.

Non Nok Tha

Non Nok Tha is located in the upper catchment of the Chi River system, and nestles on the eastern side of an upland known as Phu Wiang, an outlier of the Phetchabun Range. Excavations by Parker, Bayard and Solheim in 1966 and 1968 were a landmark in our appreciation of prehistory in Thailand, because for the first time, an extensive area of a Bronze Age cemetery was revealed.

The prehistoric stratigraphy, which at just over a metre is not deep, incorporates many graves which intercut or overlie earlier interments. This has allowed Bayard to subdivide the sequence into Early and Middle Periods (EP and MP). The former is divided into three phases of which the first two lacked bronze, and probably date between 2000-1500 BC.

There are 17 secure burials from EP 1-2, two adult females, two adult males and 11 children aged between one and six years. Little can be said of the social organization on the basis of so small a sample, particularly when, as Bayard (1984) suggests, it may come in part from an area reserved for child burials. However, the mortuary ritual followed a widespread pattern. The dead were inhumed in a supine position, accompanied by grave goods. Pottery vessels predominated, other items included three individuals with strings of shell disc beads, and others with stone adze heads, grinding stones, offerings of domestic cattle or pig bones and bivalve shells. One person was found with some red pigment. There is no evidence to suggest that any of these goods were of remote and exotic origin, and insufficient information to draw any conclusions on the presence of different status groups.

Of one issue there can be no doubt. The early inhabitants of Non Nok Tha consumed rice, and used chaff to temper their potting clay. They also maintained herds of domestic cattle and pigs, and kept domestic dogs. The presence of the dog is particularly interesting, because it is descended from the wolf. Wolves do not inhabit Thailand, but they live in the wild in China. Did these dogs find their own way to Thailand, or did they come as part of the baggage brought by early rice farmers? The first settlers of Non Nok Tha also hunted the local game,

106   (height 16 cm)

107   (height 13 cm)

108

106-108: The severely looted site of Ban Phak Top yielded arguably the most impressive assemblage of early Neolithic incised pottery in the Sakon Nakhon Basin.

Dating Ban Chiang

Ban Chiang in Udon Thani Province is probably the most talked about prehistoric site in Thailand. It came to the public attention because of the beautiful red painted pottery found there, linked with claims that its bronze and iron artefacts were the earliest in the world. There have been many excavation programmes at this site, the 1974-5 seasons being the best known, because they produced the radiocarbon dates upon which the claims for the early chronology were made. We were part of the team which worked there in 1975, and remain indebted to the co-directors, Chester Gorman and Pisit Charoenwongsa, for allowing us to join them.

The series of dates from the excavations at Ban Chiang in 1974-5 were difficult to interpret, because they tended to contradict each other, and claims for very early bronze and iron were controversial. Fortunately, however, it is now possible to solve this problem by dating provenanced material by the AMS technique. Such dates from Ban Chiang show that the site is much later than was first proposed. The earliest grave is dated to about 2100 BC. There are two Neolithic skeletons associated with pottery vessels from the second phase of burials at the site. The AMS radiocarbon dates are 2050-1500 and 2190-1880 BC. There are two Bronze Age burials with dates of 1740-1450 and 1320-1000 BC. There is another burial with a date of 1950-1600 BC, which contains a nodule of bronze in the grave fill.

These Bronze Age graves should also be considered in relationship to two conventional dates obtained from firm contexts which suggest that the people were interred about 1000-1300 BC.

Many more dates have been obtained from Neolithic and Bronze Age sites in Southeast Asia since 1975. From Non Nok Tha, for example, we now have a set of AMS dates which suggest that the Bronze Age graves there belong within the period 1500-1000 BC. We also have a set of AMS dates from rice chaff found within burial pots at Nong Nor. It is on the basis of all this accumulating evidence, that we suggest that Ban Chiang was first occupied about 2100 BC, and that the earliest bronzes there were cast after 1500 BC, but before 1000 BC. In suggesting so, we realise that this framework may well change with the results of further research, just as our interpretations have changed in the past. But this is the nature of archaeological research, and no blame must be given to anyone for attempting, over the years, to clarify this vexing and difficult problem of dating Ban Chiang.

See Gorman and Charoenwongsa (1976), Vallibhotama (1996), Higham (1996) and White (1997).

109

110

111

collected freshwater shellfish and caught fish from the local streams and lakes.

Non Kao Noi

During Higham and Kijngam's 1980 fieldwork on the area east of Lake Kumphawapi, the site of Non Kao Noi (small old mound) was discovered. Although it was hard to estimate its size, it is thought not to exceed 75 by 50 m. A test square encountered five inhumation burials. The first, which was not complete, was accompanied by three pottery vessels. A group of green stone beads were found near the feet of one burial, and three pots were found with burial 4. One is black, and

109: The 1974 excavation of Ban Chiang took place in a private garden.

110: Barely perceptable, the small, low mound of Non Kao Noi yielded Neolithic graves.

111: The Non Kao Noi people were interred with typical early Neolithic pottery vessels.

112: The early graves at Ban Chiang, which belong to the Neolithic, date to about 2100 BC. The pottery vessels are similar in decoration to those of Non Kao Noi and Ban Phak Top.

decorated with incised motifs, and there is a small bowl with red painted patterns. The burials were oriented with the head to the northwest or the southwest. No radiocarbon dates have been obtained, but the pottery relates to that from early contexts at Ban Chiang. Nor was any bronze present, and the site is interpreted as an early settlement by rice farmers (Higham and Kijngam 1984). The distinctive black incised pottery found at this site is also found in abundance at the nearby site of Ban Phak Top (Schauffler 1976).

The site of Ban Chiang in Nong Han District, Udon Thani Province, has attracted an enormous amount of publicity since first discovered in 1957 (Rattanakun1991, Chaimongkol 1991). This began because of the attractive red painted pottery discovered there during excavations initiated by the Fine Arts Department, and directed by Nikhom Suthiragsa (1979), Pote Kueakoon and Vithya Intakosai. The first scientific excavation took place in 1967, when Vithya uncovered skeletons associated with this red painted pottery, glass beads and bracelets made of iron and bronze. In 1972, Pote opened excavations in the grounds of the temple Wat Pho Sri Nai, and uncovered further graves in which the dead had been covered with painted vessels. Encouraged by this wealth of prehistoric finds, the Fine Arts Department organised still further excavations, this time in the southeastern quarter of the present village, under the direction of Nikhom. He found five cultural layers, in which the red painted pottery was present in later levels, but absent from the lower ones. A skeleton, associated with cord-marked pottery vessels, was found cut into the natural substrate under the site. Suthiragsa returned in 1973, and this time opened an area in the middle of the ancient mound. He found a cultural sequence over a depth of 3.5 metres. The lowest level, which again had no painted vessels, included burials which were associated with a black burnished style of pottery often incorporating incised designs. Rice fragments were also recovered, and one person, buried right at the bottom of the excavation square, was found wearing bronze bracelets. Only in the upper layers did he find any painted pottery vessels.

There the situation rested. No satisfactory dating evidence was available, although the thermoluminescence technique, which has proved unreliable in Thailand, had been applied to some excavated potsherds from the 1972 excavation and furnished a date of 4420-3400 BC for a sherd found at a depth

of two metres. More needed to be done, and an excavation programme was planned by the Fine Arts Department and the University Museum, University of Pennsylvania. Under the direction of Pisit Charoenwongsa and Chester Gorman, excavations took place in 1974 and 1975 (Gorman and Charoenwongsa 1976). This programme called on specialists in many fields, and was designed to provide a full picture of the prehistoric occupation of the site. The first season revealed a sequence with some black pottery vessels at the base incised in a similar manner to those from Non Kao Noi. None of the early burials had bronze grave goods, and they probably belong to the Neolithic. The 1975 season saw excavations next door to Nikhom's 1973 square and again, the earliest burials belong to the Bronze Age. This occupation phase was followed by Iron Age graves, some associated with the red painted pottery vessels.

The Neolithic burials, like those of Non Nok Tha, reveal again the inclusion of fine pottery vessels and items of personal jewellery in the mortuary ritual. Clay for the former was tempered with rice chaff, and there is much evidence for domestic cattle, pigs and the dog. Fish and shellfish formed an important component of the diet, and deer and a variety of small mammals were hunted or trapped. The people, too, appear from their robust bone development to have enjoyed a good diet. Indeed, with such an abundance of fish to eat with their rice, it would be hard to imagine there being a problem with the food supply.

114 (height 15.8 cm)

114-115: The earliest pottery found with agricultural settlements like Non Kao Noi and Ban Chiang, date to about 2100 BC. They bear many complex incised designs. (Photos: Fine Art Department Thailand)

Where did the first farmers come from?

Tracing the origins of people in prehistory is notoriously difficult, particularly for the first farmers in Thailand, due to the rarity of sites. One approach is to examine the artefacts people made, particularly one as potentially variable as pottery. In Europe, for example, prehistorians have tracked a particular style of vessel decoration from Hungary west into Holland, and use it as, in effect, the footprints of pioneer farmers. Yet even this is difficult, because pots can be traded, or copied. Of one issue, however, we can be confident: there is no evidence for a local transition to agriculture and stock rearing within Thailand.

Pottery vessels from the earliest layers of Non Pa Wai, Ban Tha Kae, Non Nok Tha and Ban Chiang are, again, different in form from those found on the coast at Khok Phanom Di and Nong Nor. Yet the radiocarbon dates indicate that the inland and coastal sites were roughly contemporary. It seems, however, that coastal shell of high quality was converted into jewellery to be used in exchange transactions. The flow of valued commodities, like shell, stone and ceramics also implies the exchange of ideas and knowledge. By this means, perhaps the idea of rice cultivation reached the hunter gatherers of Khok Phanom Di.

To follow this line of enquiry involves a brief excursion beyond Thailand. We have already seen that pottery like that from Ban Kao recurs in Malaysia. By tracking sites with a similar economy and style of incised and polished pottery in adjacent regions, we encounter an intriguing pattern. In the lower valley of the Red River in Vietnam, agricultural villages were founded at about the same time as the settlement of Ban Kao, that is somewhere between 2500-2000 BC. These sites, called collectively the Phung Nguyen culture, had a similar economy and made elaborately decorated and incised pots similar to those from Ban Chiang and Tha Kae (Khemnak 1991, Rispoli 1992). There are also two sites in Yunnan, up the valley of the Mekong River, which have the same characteristic pots and a similar tradition of burying the dead. In Vietnam, there is no evidence for a local transition to agriculture witnessed at Phung Nguyen. Shixia is the earliest Neolithic site in southern China, and is dated to about 2800 BC. It is also in direct line of expansion by river from the middle Yangzi Valley. The question, and that is all it is at present, is, could all these sites, including those in Thailand, represent the gradual expansion of farming groups, people who spoke early

Austroasiatic languages and incised their pots with similar designs, from an original home in the Yangzi Valley?

Some archaeologists find this an elegant and likely proposal. Others disagree. Among the former is Peter Bellwood, and he has advanced an intriguing idea. There is a group of hunter-gatherers adapted to the rainforest habitat of southern Thailand known as the Semang. Related groups live across the border in northern Malaysia. They are negrito, with dark skins, short stature and curly hair. They speak an Austroasiatic language. There is a second group known as the Senoi, who are agriculturalists, speak Austroasiatic languages but lack the negrito racial features of their Semang neighbours. Both groups differ from the Malays, who are racially southern Mongoloid and speak Austronesian languages. The question posed by Bellwood (1993) is, where do the Semang originate? His proposal is, in short, that they are ultimately descended from the Hoabinhian hunter gatherers, whose cave sites are to be found in the forested interior. The Senoi might also have some Hoabinhian ancestry, but have also intermixed with intrusive Southern Mongoloids who brought with them agriculture and Austroasiatic languages. These proposed ancestors would have been responsible for the introduction of agriculture, and we see them represented at sites like Ban Kao. It would be most intriguing if only the original languages of the Semang survived, but they have been lost with the arrival of the speakers of languages in the Austroasiatic group.

This bold proposal, when applied to Thailand, would see a population of negrito hunter-gatherers being responsible for the coastal and inland Hoabinhian sites. They were exposed to intrusive Southern Mongoloid agriculturalists. Doubtless there was much intermixing with time, a process that would naturally make it difficult to identify the racial affiliations of the prehistoric groups in question. At present, this hypothesis stands ready for further research and testing. One possible avenue lies in extracting DNA from prehistoric bone. It would be interesting, for example, if the Hoabinhian people differed significantly in their genetic inheritance from Southern Mongoloid agriculturalists.

115   (height 18 cm)

116

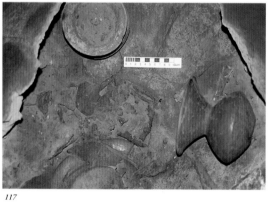

117

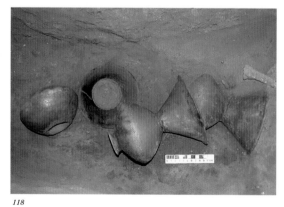

118

Chapter Four
The Bronze Age

Bronze is an alloy of copper and various other metals, particularly tin, lead and arsenic. By varying the proportions, the metalworker can alter the properties of the alloy. Tin and arsenic impart hardness, lead makes for easier casting. If the ratio of tin to copper exceeds 20 per cent, the alloy becomes brittle and hard to work, but it also takes on a golden colour. Thailand has some of the richest deposits of tin in the world, and good quality sources of copper and lead ore. Prehistorians are interested in the Bronze Age for a number of reasons.

Metallurgy opens to human societies, a new range of opportunities. We can appreciate this best by examining what prehistoric people cast from bronze. There are many socketed axes that could have been used in clearing forests to create rice fields, or to work wood for houses, boats and a range of other requirements. We also encounter socketed bronze spearheads and arrowheads, so bronze may have been used in conflict, or possibly in hunting. Bracelets and anklets are most abundant, probably because they were preferred grave goods. The potential of bronze ornaments to project a person's status is one of the most significant aspects of this period. Another attraction is that the ores of tin and copper are often located at considerable distances from the prehistoric settlements where the finished artefacts are found. This enables us to trace exchange routes between suppliers and communities they serviced and consider whether a nodal location was advantageous. Commanding the source of ore, or critical part of an exchange network, might have allowed certain individuals or groups high social prestige.

119

116-118: During the Bronze Age, we encounter at Ban Lum Khao many burials containing beautiful pottery vessels and other offerings.

119: The pottery vessels from Ban Lum Khao included numerous examples of the potter's skill. This mortuary jar contained the remains of a newly born infant and is 43 cm in height.

Bronze and Iron

The transformation of a metal ore into a finished metal artefact was one of the most significant technological advances in the history of the human species. It requires a mastery of pyrotechnics, of applying heat, for the regular use of copper, tin, lead or iron entails smelting. This technique permits the production of efficient tools that allow communities to modify their environment more readily. We often find that weapons were cast in bronze or forged from iron. A third and more subtle result was the demand for objects that could be used to advertise personal prestige. In China for example, overlords used elaborate decorated bronze vessels in ostentatious feasting. Bronze is an alloy involving copper mixed with tin, lead, arsenic or antimony. Tin makes the alloy stronger, lead makes it easier to cast. Molten bronze can also be cast in many different ways: in an open mould, a bivalve mould with two matching opposites of clay or stone, by the lost wax technique or by means of a number of clay piece moulds. Iron ore is much more widespread in nature than copper or tin, and was usually converted into artefacts by smithing, that is heating the iron until it glows red and then hammering it into shape. One of the great advantages of working in rural Thailand, is that one can still see such iron forging being undertaken. In China, however, smiths cast iron into moulds by 500 BC, a process entailing control over considerable heat.

Until 1966, standard texts described three major centres where metal working was discovered: the Near East, Middle America and China. Two other possible centres were

120: The smelting and forging of iron was a crucial development in Thai prehistory. Iron is still forged into useful tools in Thai villages in the northeast. Here, the red hot iron is being forged, while in the background, the forge and bellows are clearly visible.

the Balkans and Iberia (Spain and Portugal). Imagine then, the impact of an article published by Professor W.G. Solheim, based on radiocarbon dates from Non Nok Tha, which claimed that there was another such centre of bronze technology, in Thailand, which was even earlier than China (Solheim 1968). Pending a full excavation report, many scholars put the proposal in a suspense account, or were frank in their disbelief (Loofs-Wissowa 1983). Apparent confirmation of a fourth millennium BC date came with an article by Chester Gorman and Pisit Charoenwongsa that described the results of their excavations at Ban Chiang. In addition, they also suggested that iron at Ban Chiang was being smelted and forged earlier than anywhere else in the world (Gorman and Charoenwongsa 1976). These claims soon found their way into the world's media, but still, many scholars remained sceptical.

All concerned have agreed that time, the excavation of further sites and the development of new dating techniques, would resolve the controversy. We feel that this has now taken place. Bronze casting became established in Thailand soon after about 1500 BC, and iron a thousand years later. We can now focus on the implications of bronze and iron technology in Thailand, rather than debate the dates. We find that artefacts were cast in copper and tin as well as being combined to make bronze. Tin is not often found unalloyed, and thus far, only a few graves at Nong Nor include tin ornaments. Most metal artefacts between 1500-500 BC were bangles, often cast using the lost wax method. Axes, spearheads and arrowheads were cast in bivalve moulds made of clay or sandstone. With the Iron Age, bronzes became more abundant and the bowls, belts, torcs and bangles called upon greater expertise. Iron was used for ornaments as well as spears, knives, sickles and hoes.

121: These sandstone moulds reveal how Bronze Age metal workers cast their axes and spearheads.

0 _____ 5cm

125: Excavations under way at the Pottery Flat ore processing area, Phu Lon. (Photo courtesy of the Thailand Archaeometallurgy Project)

The archaeological record in Thailand provides us with a rare opportunity to explore every stage of bronze metallurgy, from mining through processing the ore, casting, exchange and final use of the desired objects. Investigating the copper sources was seen as a critical area of research by Vincent Pigott and Surapol Natapintu, and the first stage of their Thailand Archaeometallurgy Project saw them at Phu Lon in Nong Khai Province (Natapintu 1988a). This is an outcrop containing copper ore located close to the bank of the Mekong River. They were attracted to the area by the presence of green staining on the rock surface, and initial test excavations at an area called the Pottery Flat proved promising. The excavators found an accumulation of copper ore, stone tools for ore crushing and processing, fragments of crucibles, a stone and a ceramic mould for casting, much charcoal and prehistoric pottery. A radiocarbon date showed that this activity took place about 400 BC. Later excavations produced three more radiocarbon dates. That from the lowest context suggested that occupation of the site began within the period 1750-1425 BC, and that ore processing took place between 1000-275 BC.

The excavators then opened the shafts of copper mines, to reveal mining debris mixed with prehistoric stone mauls. Charcoal from a mine shaft was dated to 830-590 BC. On the Lower Flat site, they found mining and ore-crushing tools, together with cord-marked pottery interspersed with clean lenses of sand. These suggest that mining was seasonal, or at least intermittent, but it continued over a long time span, because soundings have revealed that the mining debris accumulated to a depth of over 10 metres. The so-called Bunker Hill mining and processing area has been dated to 390-5 BC, while at Ban Noi, excavations have revealed yet another ore processing facility incorporating fragments of crucibles, copper slag, and a socketed axe, dated to 1100-615 BC.

The excavators have noted that ore-crushing implements concentrate in clusters, as if small task-orientated groups worked together. This, linked with evidence for intermittent rather than continuous activity, indicates that the copper mining and processing were undertaken on a seasonal basis. The proximity to the Mekong River, a great conduit for exchange, might also help in appreciating how copper ingots or cast objects could have been distributed rapidly within its catchment.

The Khao Wong Prachan Valley

After completing fieldwork at Phu Lon, the staff of the Thailand Archaeometallurgy Project transferred their attention to the Khao Wong Prachan Valley in Lopburi Province. Archaeologists have discovered several sources of copper ore in this area, including Khao Phra Bat Noi, Khao Phu Kha, Khao Tap Khwai and Khao Si On (Bennett 1988, 1989, Natapintu 1988a, Ciarla 1992, Cremaschi *et al.* 1992). Ores include malachite, azurite and chrysocolla with up to 10% copper. Prehistoric sites which evidence the exploitation of copper ring these hills. One of these, the Lopburi Artillery site, has been well known for 25 years as a rich later prehistoric cemetery in which about fifty burials have been recovered, associated with bronze and iron artefacts (You-di 1976). According to the excavator, some individuals even had a bronze ring in place on each toe. Two TL dates suggest occupation from the second well into the first millennium BC. In 1984, Natapintu (1988a) collected fragments of copper ore and smelting slag there, indicating that it was also a processing site.

126: This mine shaft was excavated at the Phu Lon copper mining complex. (Photo courtesy of the Thailand Archaeometallurgy Project)

Huai Yai has furnished burials associated with discs of marine shell and H-shaped beads paralleled at late Khok Phanom Di. This site has also provided evidence for the manufacture of polished stone adze heads, and bracelets of shell and stone. It was a centre for copper extraction and casting, for excavations have produced crucible fragments and casting slag, but the chronological relationship between the H beads and the copper slag is not known. Natapintu excavated Non Mak La in 1985, and found that copper and iron working had been undertaken there during the first millennium BC. Non Khok Wa, the object of limited excavations, is another ore-crushing site, while at Nil Kham Haeng, the remains of crushed ore and slag fragments have accumulated to a depth of five or six metres. The successive layers have yielded ceramic moulds, including some for the casting of circular ingots, and a burial interred with a bracelet that combines bronze and iron segments. Of all these sites, however, Non Pa Wai stands out as being the largest and most significant.

127: Nil Kham Haeng is a vital site in understanding how copper was smelted. Here is a scene of the excavation. Note burial 4 in the foreground, and many pits and postholes. (Photo courtesy of the Thailand Archaeometallurgy Project)

Non Pa Wai

The remains of copper smelting and casting at Non Pa Wai cover about 5 ha (Pigott and Natapintu 1988, White and Pigott 1996). The Neolithic occupation was followed by a five century hiatus. When the site was reoccupied, graves were cut into it. One contained the remains of a 25-year-old man with two halves of a clay mould for casting a socketed copper axe while a second grave contained such an axe. The layer from which the grave was cut included copper slag and crucible fragments, heralding a phase of copper processing which was to last for eight centuries and accumulate to a depth of 2-3 m. There are three radiocarbon dates from the lower part of this phase, which come from the earliest context we have for copper smelting in Central Thailand. They are 1690-1225, 1450-1136 and 1270-800 BC. A fourth date from later in the sequence is 834-530 BC (Natapintu 1991). It would seem that copper smelting began at this site within the period 1500-1000 BC.

This dense concentration of metal-working debris, taken in conjunction with the other sites that cluster round the copper deposits, is one of the largest prehistoric extracting complexes in Southeast Asia. Ore was smelted in crucibles or shallow bowls set in the ground, over which a circular, clay furnace chimney was positioned. These contained three holes, probably to provide access for the tuyères (White and Pigott 1996). The furnace would have been charged with ore and wood or charcoal. With the aid of the bellows, a temperature of 1200°C would have been sufficient to obtain a sulphur-rich copper. This would then have been cast. Perhaps the most important aspect of this material is the quantity of clay moulds shaped to produce circular metal ingots. Few artefacts were encountered, but these included barbed points and socketed axes. The moulds were made from clay, and bear incised markings which might well indicate ownership. No alloying with tin took place.

In a series of experiments, successful smelting following the techniques documented at Non Pa Wai has been achieved (Rostoker and Dvorak 1989). It took 90 minutes to reach smelting temperature in bowl furnaces set in the ground. The problem faced by the discharge of poisonous arsenic vapour was solved by sealing the crucible with clay.

(length 8 cm)

128: These two socketed copper artefacts from Nil Kham Haeng are of unknown function. Could they be small axes, or chisels for wood working? (Photo courtesy of the Thailand Archaeometallurgy Project)

Nil Kham Haeng

Nil Kham Haeng is a second copper-working site. It has been partially destroyed, but covers at least 3 ha, and has a cultural stratigraphy over 6 metres deep. There are two principal phases. The earlier already contains evidence for copper production and pottery similar to that for period 2 at Non Pa Wai. It has been dated by a single radiocarbon determination to 1301-900 BC. The second phase comprises many thin horizontal lenses which Weiss (1992) has interpreted as the remains of dry season metal working redeposited by monsoon rainstorms. The deposits included crushed slag, while there were also many ash lenses rich in charcoal. Enough material has survived, however, to reveal the presence of activity areas that involved ore preparation, smelting and casting. There was, it seems, no permanent work force repeatedly using fixed copper-working facilities. Rather, metal working continued as a small-scale, probably seasonal, occupation in which the principal activities began with mining, then ore preparation and sorting, smelting and casting. The

129

130   *(width 7 cm)*

129: Non Pa Wai is the mound in the foreground with Khao Wong Prachan in the distance. (Courtesy Surapol Natapintu)

130: Clay moulds from Non Pa Wai were used to cast an axe. (Courtesy Surapol Natapintu)

physical remains comprise mauls, clay-lined bowl furnaces or smelting crucibles, clay chimney furnaces for concentrating heat, crucibles and ceramic moulds. Weiss has suggested that the workers at Nil Kham Haeng used lower grade ores than at Non Pa Wai, perhaps due to the early exhaustion of the highest quality sources, and therefore had to break them down more finely to concentrate the copper-rich material. The radiocarbon dates from this phase are 900-400 and 800-380 BC.

From about 700 BC, there are signs of change at Nil Kham Haeng. Fourteen inhumation burials have been excavated, the north-south orientation being preferred. The head of one burial lay on a cache of copper ore, and there were three pots beyond the head. A series of copper and iron bracelets were present, the first use of iron being for decorative purposes. Another burial in the same area included a sea turtle over the head, a copper bracelet, copper ring, three pots beyond the head and a mass of copper ore. The presence of copper ore recalls the placement of clay cylinders, the raw material for pottery working, in graves at Khok Phanom Di. A further grave contained five pots, iron bracelets, a complete furnace and five carnelian beads.

At this juncture, during the period from 700-300 BC, there appears to have been a surge in production at Nil Kham Haeng, with particular emphasis on casting small socketed implements which Weiss has described as projectile points. They continued to be made from the high arsenic copper, but one or two items, in particular a socketed spear, included 10% tin. These are alien to the local metal tradition, and are best interpreted as imports.

The site of Wat Tung Sing-to has not been excavated, but surface finds include ingots, ingot moulds, stone crushers, traces of copper ore and crushed slag. Natapintu (1988a) has suggested that the material dates to the first millennium BC. Two mounds at Huai Yai have also revealed much relevant material. One has furnished burials with a series of shell ornaments, including marine shell discs and H-shaped beads. There is also evidence for the local production of stone adzes and bracelets, shell bracelets and the casting of copper-based artefacts. A later phase at the site has also produced iron slag. The latter context probably equates with occupation at Huai Yai Reservoir site, where iron, bronze, carnelian and agate items have been recovered (Natapintu 1988a).

Copper Technology in Central Thailand

Bennett (1989) has cast much light on the techniques of prehistoric metal workers by her analysis of the slags. She has described at Khao Phu Kha, one of what may have been many mines, the ore being malachite and chrysocolla with up to 10% copper. Non Pa Wai, Non Mak La and Nil Kham Haeng are located nearby. She has suggested that most ore crushing and sorting occurred near the mines, where some final processing took place at the slag sites, for large ore-dressing stones have been found. Slag accumulated in the archaeological build-up, but was also found adhering to the walls of what Bennett has termed clay reaction vessels. There are numerous fragments of these and possible reconstructions reveal a vessel about 12 cm in height and up to 20 cm in external diameter. The organic temper would have increased thermal resistance. Analysis of the associated slag shows that smelting was facilitated by employing a haematite (iron ore) flux. Little metal remains in the slags, which shows that smelting successfully liquefied most of the copper, at temperatures of between 1150-1250°C. The recovery of complete cakes of slag suggest that the metal was poured from one smelt in the reaction vessel into the waiting ingot moulds. Some of the moulds had a long base, which may have helped secure them before pouring molten metal. Nil Kham Haeng has also produced a copper axe head and ingots. This industry is significant because it provides the evidence for casting and exchanging unalloyed copper, a procedure often cited as a necessary condition for the presence of an independent centre of metallurgy.

Circular copper ingots were the most numerous casting. These, it is assumed, were used in exchange relationships, and so ended up far from the copper mines. During the past 30 years, several settlement sites have been excavated, and it is in these that we can trace the further use of copper and tin once ingots reached their final destination. The most complete evidence for casting bronze artefacts away from the actual mines, comes from Ban Na Di, located in Udon Thani Province (Higham and Kijngam 1984).

131: Excavations under way at Nil Kham Haeng. (Courtesy Surapol Natapintu)

132

(length 12.5 cm)

133

132: Two crucibles from Ban Na Di were used for pouring bronze into the waiting mould.

133: Prehistoric clay moulds from Non Pa Wai were used to cast ingots of copper. The ingots seen here are modern, experimental ones. (Photo courtesy of the Thailand Archaeometallurgy Project)

Ban Na Di

Ban Na Di was recognised as a potentially important prehistoric settlement during a site survey in 1980, and excavations were undertaken a year later in two areas 30 metres apart at the centre of the mound. The eight archaeological layers accumulated to a depth of nearly 4 metres, and the three lowest belong to the Bronze Age. Even in the lowest layer, along with the remains of freshwater shellfish, domestic animal bones and numerous fish bones, the excavators recovered fragments of bronze and the crucibles used to pour molten metal into the mould. There are two radiocarbon dates from the charcoal found in early hearths and they suggest that initial settlement probably fell within the period 1400-1000 BC. In layer 7, which probably dates between 700-400 BC, the excavators came across a cemetery in which the skeletons were laid out in rows and with time, over earlier graves in a manner reminiscent of Khok Phanom Di. It was within this layer that an interesting bronze casting complex was uncovered. It comprised a clay-lined bowl furnace still filled with charcoal, round which there was a scattering of more charcoal mixed with crucible fragments and a piece of sandstone bivalve mould. An analysis of the metal scoria adhering to the inside of the crucibles indicated that they had been used for melting an alloy as part of the casting process. Two complete crucibles were found. They are bowl shaped with a pouring spout and many still have the remains of bronze adhering to the inner surface. One is 125 mm long, the other slightly larger and each would have held between 75-80 ml of metal, sufficient to cast a socketed axe.

134

135

It is evident, then, that the inhabitants of Ban Na Di
participated in an exchange network which linked villages on
the Khorat Plateau with copper mines like those of Phu Lon
and Khao Wong Prachan. Moreover, the dating evidence
suggests that this activity was established at least by 1000 BC.
Ban Na Di also provided a sample of 60 prehistoric graves and
it is in this mortuary evidence that we can approach the society
and way of life of the Bronze Age in Thailand.

Both excavated areas included burials. Area B contained a
row of inhumation graves in which men had the head to the
south, women to the north. Burial 47 was the earliest, the grave
being excavated 20 cm into the natural substrate. It contained
the remains of a man who died when aged between 30 and 35
years. His grave offerings are most interesting and in the context
of the Thai Bronze Age, unusual. They included a single pottery
vessel which contained fragments of fish bone and a small piece
of bronze. A marble bracelet was present on the right wrist. It
had been broken twice, and repaired by casting bronze in the
form of wire through two holes, one on each side of the break.
Since marble and bronze were exotic to this part of Thailand,
it seems that the bracelet was treasured and care attended its
repair. To judge from its smooth interior, it had been worn
frequently while this man was alive. Apart from the necklace of
shell beads, which may again have been of marine origin and
therefore exotic, the twelve clay figurines are the most
interesting feature of this burial. These represent eight cattle,
an elephant, deer and two human beings. The excavators have
suggested that they represent wealth.

*134: The excavations of Ban Na Di in
1980-1 uncovered a fascinating Bronze Age
cemetery.*

*135: This man was interred with a
necklace of dog canine teeth.*

136

137   (height c. 10 cm)

*136: This marble bracelet on a man's wrist
had been broken in antiquity, and repaired
with cast bronze ties.*

137: A figurine of a deer from Ban Na Di.

Burials alongside this man also included clay figurines. A fifty-year-old woman had been buried with three representing cattle that even bear the fingerprints of the maker. An infant who died aged about 6 months was found with six cattle figurines and another bracelet repaired with bronze. This was the only bronze found in the earliest phase of graves. Other early graves in this area were found with shell disc beads, the most in any burial being 7,850 with a young man, large shell beads and pottery vessels. Although the samples are small, eight burials from area A and nine from area B, it is intriguing to note that there are no clay figurines nor exotic stone bangles with the former group. Moreover, one grave from Area A includes 242 shell disc beads while seven of the Area B graves have just over 10,000. Did this disparity in wealth between the two groups persist?

Burials of the second phase overlay earlier interments. There are ten in area A and eleven in area B, with men, women and infants in each. Pottery vessels were evenly distributed between both groups, and the vast majority were locally made. When we turn to exotic goods, however, the division persisted. All 23 bronze, both the stone and all three shell bracelets were found in area B. Four area B burials included almost 800 disc beads against 29 from just two area A interments. Both clay figurines of cattle came from area B and we also find that the

138

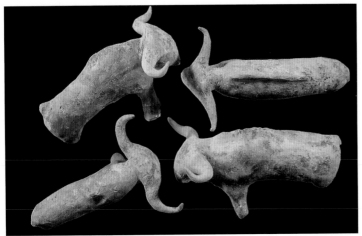

139

(width c. 15 cm)

140

(height c. 7 cm)

141

(height c. 15 cm)

138: An infant at Ban Na Di was buried with clay figurines of cattle.

139-141: Clay figurines are a unique feature of the Bronze Age cemetery at Ban Na Di. They include cattle and humans.

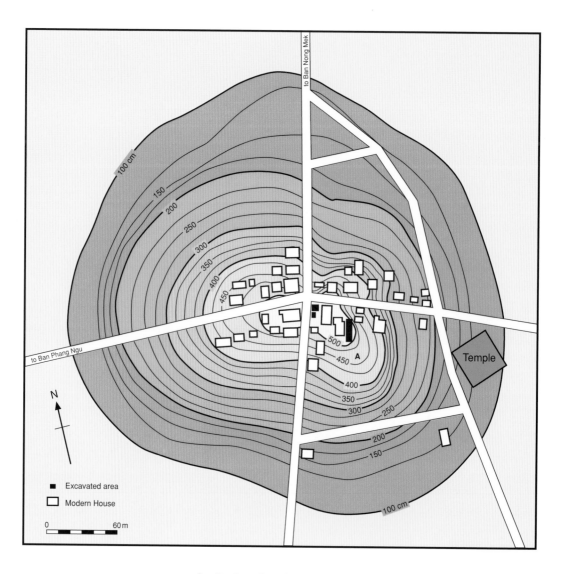

142: The village of Ban Na Di, showing the areas excavated.

forelimbs of cattle were placed with some individuals. Of the five instances of this practice, all but one came from area B. This is interesting, because the bones lay in perfect articulation, and probably involved sacrificing an animal as part of mortuary feasting. So the concentration of both the cattle figurines and the remains of cattle with area B graves reinforces the idea that wealth display was involved. Finally, we find a further intriguing set of grave goods. A five-year-old child in area B was buried under a crocodile skin shroud – rows of articulating bony scutes covered the human remains. Nearby, a woman had been interred with a large bone pendant on her chest, fashioned from the skull of a crocodile. These animals survived in the nearby Lake Kumphawapi within living memory. Could it be that the area B people were in some totemic way, associated with the crocodile?

In the third and final phase, seventeen of the burials were found in area B and only seven from Area A. Again, men women, children and infants were present. Bronze artefacts were rare, three bracelets and two anklets coming from Area A, and a single bracelet from Area B. Area B burials again had a monopoly on the stone and shell bracelets, the single cattle figurine and at the very end of the life of the cemetery, the first few items of iron. Pottery vessels and cattle forelimbs were evenly distributed between the two areas.

We can draw several inferences from this cemetery. The mortuary ritual continued over several generations, for people were interred in rows and in time, over the presumed ancestors. By degrees, the range of grave goods and the variety of pottery vessels grew, but always within the same tradition. The rites involved the slaughter of animals and inclusion of part of the carcase with the dead: in one case, the forelimb of a pig had been placed within a pottery vessel. Exotic goods included shell, marble, slate and bronze ornaments and two pottery vessels. Most of these were consistently found within one group of graves. Archaeologists always seek larger and more reliable samples, and Ban Na Di is no exception. If this concentration is not the result of chance, however, it would seem that one social group at Ban Na Di had easier access to these precious valuables, and conspicuously placed them with their dead. This is quite possibly the result of their having higher social status in their community than a contemporary group. Perhaps they were the senior line of descent from the founding ancestors. The distinctions are not great, both groups were interred on the same principles and were not far apart from each other in the ground. We do not argue for a major social division into rulers and ruled, rather a recognised higher affiliative status.

143

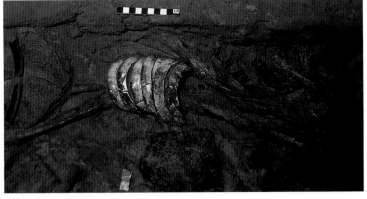

144

143: The woman next to the shroud burial wore a crocodile skull pendant on her chest. height 30 cm.

144: This man wore a row of exotic shell bangles on each arm.

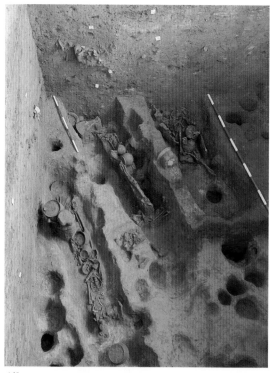

145

146

147

148

145: *Burials at Ban Na Di included many grave offerings of locally made pottery vessels. Some contained food for the after life: rice, fish and pork.*

146: *This five-year-old child was interred under a crocodile skin shroud.*

147: *Pottery vessels in Thailand are still made with the paddle and anvil technique.*

148: *The people of Ban Na Di made ladles of clay. Length 13 cm.*

149: *Pottery vessels were fashioned at Ban Na Di with the age-old technique of using a clay anvil in conjunction with a wooden paddle. Height of smallest, 8 cm.*

149

The People of Ban Na Di

One of the most important aspects of prehistory is the health
of the people. Human remains are the source of all our
information, and Ban Na Di is no exception. Houghton and
Wiriyaromp (1984) have studied the remains of 63 people from
this Bronze Age cemetery, and found that the people enjoyed a
good diet. The values of Nordin's Score, a measure of bone
development, reveal equality with modern Finns and
Norwegians. We have seen that the people of Khok Phanom
Di suffered from anaemia, but there is no evidence for this at
Ban Na Di. The inhabitants of this site were also relatively tall,
the average height for males being 1.73 m and for females,
1.61 m. All seven available female pelves showed evidence for
pregnancy, even in a woman who died when about 17 years of
age. This indicates the onset of menarche when she was about
two years younger, again a reflection of a good diet.
Nevertheless, life expectancy was short: 22.8 years at birth, and
men over 15 years could expect to live on average to the age of
29.5. Women in the same situation could anticipate living to
nearly 38 years. In the event, two women but no men lived
beyond 50. Rather, women died with particular frequency when
aged between 15 and 19, perhaps due to the risks of pregnancy,
and again when over 40. Men died with greater frequency when
20-34 years old. One of the most intriguing elements of this
mortality pattern, from a modern perspective, is the youth of
the leaders of this prehistoric community.

At Khok Phanom Di, we found evidence in the skeleton
that men in Mortuary Phases 2 and 3 had strong upper bodies
which might have resulted from an activity such as canoeing.
This was not found at Ban Na Di. What evidence is there,
however, for the diet?

*150: A man and a woman at Ban Na Di
were interred in the same grave, but in
opposite directions.*

The Diet at Ban Na Di

At best the dietary pattern will only be partially reconstructed
from archaeological evidence, for many possible food items,
such as taro or yams, do not survive. There are, however, ways
of maximising the recovery of information. One is to put a
sample of cultural material through a fine screen, and another is
to use the technique of flotation to recover tiny organic remains.
Both were employed at Ban Na Di, and we therefore have at
least some good information on the diet. The remains of milled
rice kernels suggest to Chang and Loresto (1984) a cultivated

151

152

151-152: Bronzes were cast at Ban Na Di from imported copper and tin ingots, probably mixed on the site in crucibles. Above, we see a cross section through a crucible showing the scoria left behind after a pour, still containing pieces of copper (width 6 cm). Below, there is a piece of a bivalve sandstone mould for the casting of bronze arrowheads (width 5.5 cm).

variety. The animal bones also include a significant proportion of bones which come from domesticated cattle, pigs and dogs. But the people also undertook a lot of trapping or hunting, for several varieties of deer were represented among the animal bones, as well as some small mammals. If measured in terms of the number of individuals, however, we find that fish were totally dominant, along with the remains of frogs, turtles and shellfish. This predominance of aquatic species should be considered in conjunction with the evidence in the Bronze Age layers for the deposition of thin sand lenses which are thought to result from the passage of floodwater over the site. During the wet season, Lake Kumphawapi would have expanded, and rivers probably backed up and spread well beyond their dry season channels. This, as is the case with modern rice fields, would have encouraged aquatic species.

The Bronze Industry at Ban Na Di

We have seen that the inhabitants of this settlement obtained copper and tin, but are unsure whether it arrived as an alloy, or in ingot form for local mixing. According to the analysis of their artefacts, the preferred alloy was a combination of copper and tin in the proportions of 9:1. Bracelets were the most numerous artefact, but the repertoire included arrowheads, axes, fishhooks, anklets and beads. They used two methods of casting. For axes and arrowheads, they used bivalve sandstone moulds. In the case of bracelets, some of which were decorated with rows of bosses or transverse grooves, they followed the lost wax technique. This involved making a model of the desired form in wax, often over an inner clay core, then coating the wax in further layers of clay before melting out the wax and pouring in bronze. Pilditch (1984) has found the actual remains of insect wax on one of the Ban Na Di bracelets. In order to repair stone bracelets, clay moulds were built up over the holes pierced on either side of the break and bronze was poured. For this process, a ternary alloy of copper, tin and arsenic was used. Once cast, the bronze bracelets received no obvious further treatment. But the arrowheads were annealed. This involved heating and hammering in order to increase hardness.

Ban Na Di: Summary

Ban Na Di was settled by a community conversant with rice cultivation and the raising of domestic stock which, over several centuries, maintained a cemetery for the ancestors. The inhabitants had a good diet, were tall and had robust bone development. Local industries included the manufacture of pottery vessels and the casting of bronzes. In the latter case, the raw materials were obtained by exchange, a mechanism which also brought exotic stone, ceramics and shell to the site. One social group seems to have had preferential access to these exotic goods, probably due to higher status. Towards the end of this cemetery, knowledge of iron forging reached Ban Na Di which, taken in conjunction with the radiocarbon dates, suggests that later burials date to 400-500 BC.

Ban Chiang

The excavation of Ban Na Di was originally designed to expand our knowledge of the prehistoric culture revealed during the excavations at Ban Chiang. We had worked there together in 1975, and one of us (R.T.) returned to excavate further in 1991. During the 1975 excavations, we helped uncover a Bronze Age cemetery similar in many respects to that from Ban Na Di. Again, burials were laid out in rows with men, women, infants and children in close proximity and interred with a range of grave goods. While most of the associated pottery vessels were different in form and decoration between the two sites, one was virtually identical, and suggests that the later graves at Ban Chiang and Ban Na Di were contemporary. This is supported by the presence of iron artefacts in the latest burials. At Ban Chiang, however, the Bronze Age cemetery contains a series of graves earlier than those of Ban Na Di, including one young male associated with a socketed bronze spearhead, and a second grave containing the remains of a child with bronze bangles (Gorman and Charoenwongsa 1976). A man nicknamed "Vulcan" was buried with an axe and several bangles. Burial 40, which came late in the sequence, included a T-shaped bronze bangle similar in form to one from the Central Thai cemetery of Nong Nor, and to the marble and slate examples from Ban Na Di, while other bangles match closely in form, examples cast using the lost wax technique from Ban Na Di. Burial 23, which was slightly later than Burial 40, included a spear with a bronze haft cast onto a forged iron blade. This technique was

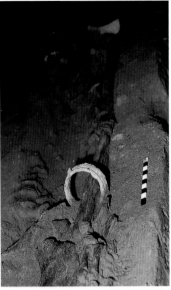

153

154

153-154: This man, nicknamed Vulcan by the excavators when he was uncovered in 1974, was found with several bronze bangles and a socketed axe at the left shoulder.

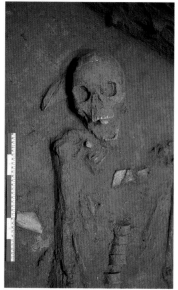

155

156

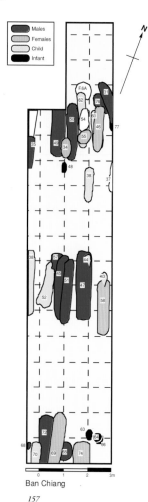

Ban Chiang

157

widespread in southern China towards the end of the first millennium BC, and examples have also been found in Vietnam.

While the pottery forms may have differed between Ban Na Di and Ban Chiang during the Bronze Age, we can also identify some similarities. A bronze casting area with similar small clay crucibles and sandstone bivalve moulds recurs at Ban Chiang, as do small cattle figurines, and the practice of interring the remains of animals with the dead. At Ban Chiang, the preference was for the jaws of domestic pigs. The people of Ban Chiang during the Bronze Age cultivated rice, chaff of which was used as a ceramic temper, and maintained herds of domestic cattle and pigs. The remains of dogs have been found and one complete cranium has a form which indicates descent from the wolf. But numerous animals were also trapped or hunted, reminding us of one grave which contained the skeleton of a man associated with pierced tiger canines, deer antler and a bone spear. Fishing was clearly important, and the remains of shellfish and turtles reflect an environment incorporating rivers and low wetlands during the monsoon. The way of life of the people at Ban Chiang, according to a study of their bones, saw rather more fractures than at Ban Na Di, Ban Kao or Khok Phanom Di, but there is no evidence for conflict or strife (Douglas 1997). Most men lived until between 45-50 years, while most deaths among women occurred when they were 35-

40 years of age. There was a peak of mortality among infants meaning that the average age of death for the available sample was just over 24 years.

Non Nok Tha

The 1975 excavation at Ban Chiang was only 3.5 metres wide, as it was constrained by houses on each side. But at Non Nok Tha, there were no such problems, and Donn Bayard has excavated more extensively. This is an important point, because the greater the area of a cemetery exposed, the clearer is the spatial pattern observed. Non Nok Tha is a small mound lying on the eastern edge of an outlier of the Phetchabun Mountains in Khon Kaen Province. It was discovered in 1964, and excavations took place in 1966 and 1968. The shallow stratigraphy – barely over a metre in depth – and maze of intercutting graves made dating difficult, but a series of AMS dates on rice chaff used as a ceramic temper suggest that the Bronze Age cemetery belongs within the period 1500-1000 BC. The layout of the graves in the latter season suggests a series of rows, and the size of the sample has permitted Bayard to provide a comprehensive relationship between graves, the sex and age of the person buried, and the range of grave goods.

No group defined by age, sex or location stands out as being particularly rich in terms of grave goods. Pottery vessels are the most common mortuary offering, and these come in a wide range of forms. There are also stone adzes, shell disc beads, large bivalve shellfish and in nine cases out of 217 mortuary contexts, bronzes. Again, bracelets dominate with a total of 28 from five graves. We also find five socketed axes. One man was interred with a crucible and a sandstone mould for casting such an axe, perhaps with copper obtained from the Phu Lon mines 140 km to the north. It is self evident that bronze casting took place at this site, the alloy including up to 15% of tin. Some individuals were also interred with the remains of domestic cattle, pigs and dogs.

Since the excavation of Non Nok Tha, several nearby sites have been examined in an exploratory way, and all contain burials associated with bronze grave goods. One of these is Non Pa Kluay, 25 km to the west (Wilen 1989). Although the area excavated was not large, sufficient was found to indicate a similar mortuary ritual to that documented at Non Nok Tha. Even the pottery vessels had similar forms, and we find the same

158

159

155-156: The Bronze Age burials at Ban Chiang were laid out in rows. One male was buried with tigers' teeth at the neck and a bone point directed towards the antler of a muntjak. Was he a hunter? The excavators nicknamed him Nimrod.

157: The layout of early Bronze Age graves at Ban Chiang shows clear clustering.

158: The Bronze Age burials at Nong Nok Tha included socketed axes among the grave goods. Here, an axe can be seen on the man's chest. (Courtesy Dr. D. T. Bayard)

159: The same axe in close up. At first thought to be made of copper, it is now known to have comprised an alloy of copper and tin. (Courtesy Dr. D. T. Bayard)

160

161

160: Three vessels placed in graves at Non Nok Tha. The tallest is 15cm high.

161: The prehistoric mound of Non Nong Chik is seen here, in the shadow of the Phu Wiang upland.

interest in placing the limbs of cattle and pigs with the dead. No bronze grave goods were found, but local villagers have described finding a socketed bronze spearhead and bracelets with some skeletons when digging in the area. A fragment of charcoal found within a mortuary vessel suggests that the cemetery dates towards the end of the 2nd millennium BC, and the average date for all four determinations is 1311-977 BC.

Higham and Parker excavated Non Nong Chik in 1970, and revealed in the small area exposed, burials matching those from later Bronze Age contexts at nearby Non Nok Tha (Buchan 1973). Non Praw is a two hectare mound located 30 km northeast of Non Nok Tha, and excavations by Metha Wichakana in 1993 have revealed an inhumation cemetery (Buranrak 1994a). As at Ban Na Di, males and females in the earlier of two phases were interred on opposing orientations, and grave goods included shell disc beads, bangles and pottery vessels, but no bronze offerings were found. Bronze, however, was found with later burials, including axes and bracelets. One of these axes is particularly interesting, having a crescentic shape identical to one from Non Nok Tha. Marble bracelets are also found, with precise parallels at Ban Na Di. No radiocarbon dates are available, though these burials probably belong to the same time span as Non Nok Tha.

As we proceed south to the relatively broad flood plains of the Chi and Mun rivers and their many tributaries, so we find several more Bronze Age sites. Amphan Kijngam excavated Ban Chiang Hian, located just south of the Chi River in Mahasarakham Province, in 1981. He found Bronze Age graves five metres deep, associated with radiocarbon dates of 950-800 BC. Two pieces of crucible point to local casting activity (Chantaratiyakarn 1984). One interesting aspect of this fieldwork was the recognition of a pattern in where people chose to settle. Bronze Age sites were found at or near the confluence of small tributary streams, or along the margins of the Chi flood plain. These are areas that would probably have seen regular but not severe flooding, and the soils near the sites would have been suited to the cultivation of rice.

163: Excavations at Non Nong Chik in 1970 revealed a Bronze Age cemetery similar to that of Non Nok Tha.

The Mun Valley

David Welch and Judith McNeill have undertaken similar fieldwork in the Phimai area of Nakhon Ratchasima Province. This region has also seen two major excavations, at Ban Lum Khao and Ban Prasat. Again, the Bronze Age sites were located on slightly elevated terrain within easy reach of a river or stream and soils suited to the cultivation of rice (Welch and McNeill 1991). Ban Prasat is located on the southern bank of the Prasat Stream, and was excavated by Suphot Phommanodch in 1991 (Phommanodch 1991a, Monkhonkamnuanket 1992). This is a large site, ringed by old river channels, but the lowest levels included a Bronze Age cemetery of great interest. The burials, which probably date from about 800 BC, included rows of interments of men, women, children and infants. Bronze offerings were rare, one man being found with a socketed bronze axe on the chest and a child had some bronze bangles. The range of grave goods found in the sites to the north is repeated: shell disc beads, marine shell and exotic marble bracelets and the remains of cattle and pigs. The profusion of pottery vessels is a singular feature of this cemetery. Many were red slipped and polished, the most popular form having a broad, trumpet-shaped upper body. One male was interred with at least 50 of these vessels, and was surely a significant member of his community. As the excavators continued uncovering the graves, they also encountered a crucible and a clay mould for casting an axe.

163

163: Ban Prasat has been left as an open museum following excavations there. Burial 5 in the centre of this picture is the richest known interment from Bronze Age Thailand. Burial 3 at the lower right hand side of this picture belongs to the Iron Age.

164: Before excavating at Ban Lum Khao, the owners made offerings to the spirits of the dead.

Ban Lum Khao

One of the larger excavations of a Bronze Age site on the Khorat Plateau took place in 1995-6 at Ban Lum Khao, only five km west of Ban Prasat. We opened an area of 14.5 by 10 metres, and over a period of three months, uncovered 111 burials. These overlay a thin layer of occupation that, we think, represents the initial occupation in the area. It includes several pits filled with animal and plant remains and much charcoal. According to the radiocarbon dates, this initial settlement took place between 1400-1000 BC. The first inhabitants found themselves in a habitat of forest and river, where low-lying wetlands supported herds of wild water buffalo and a wide range of fish and shellfish that, hitherto untouched by human collection, were huge compared with their modern counterparts. The people introduced domestic pigs, cattle and the dog, but quickly turned their attention to the large water buffalo and the deer of the forest and forest fringe. Soon after initial occupation, we find no more of the water buffalo, but the deer proved resilient and were hunted well into the Bronze Age occupation period. It was during this period, probably dated between 1000-500 BC, that the rows of graves were laid down. As at Ban Prasat, the trumpet-rimmed vessels dominated among the sample of over

164

165   *(height 18 cm)*

166   *(width 13 cm)*

167   *(width 14 cm)*

165-167: The pottery vessels buried with the dead at Ban Lum Khao were red slipped, sometimes with painted designs, and of elegant shapes.

500 vessels recovered, but other forms were many and varied. Some incorporated attractive painted designs. Although the occupation layers furnished undoubted evidence for bronze casting in the form of moulds and crucible fragments, none of the graves incorporated a bronze mortuary offering. But, again, exotic ornaments were often found, particularly marine shell, stone adzes and marble bangles. As at Non Nok Tha, many burials were also accompanied by a large, iridescent bivalve shellfish, while pigs' foot bones and dog bones were often found in later graves. We also found some large, lidded pots, some up to 60 cm across. Taking off the lid revealed the remains of new born or young infants, associated in death with small versions of the pots found with adults. These infant burials were often found placed beyond the heads of women.

In 1986-7, Preecha Kanchanagama undertook several excavations in Nakhon Ratchasima, and at Ban San Thia, he found a complete inhumation burial that follows in the same tradition as the interments from Ban Lum Khao and Ban Prasat. The adult was buried with the head pointing to the east, with a set of Prasat style red slipped vessels beyond the head and feet. There was also a stone and a bronze bangle on the right wrist (Kanchanagama 1996).

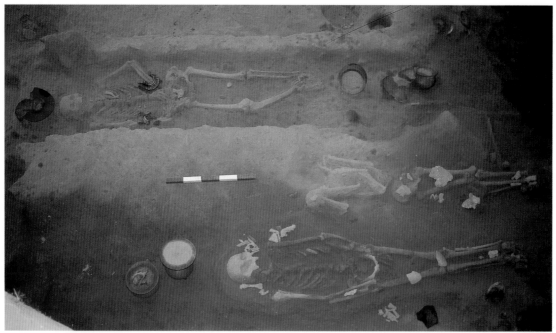

168

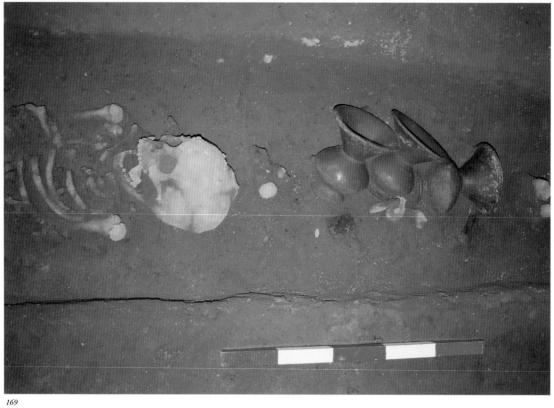

169

168-169: The dead at Ban Lum Khao were laid out in rows, with pottery vessels placed beyond the head and feet.

170

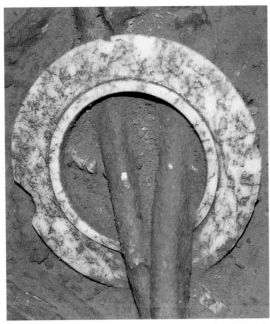

171

(width 10 cm)

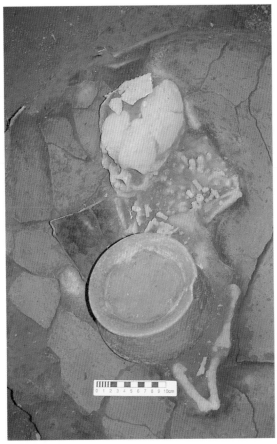

172

173

170-171: *The people of Ban Lum Khao wore exotic shell and marble bracelets.*

172-173: *Infants at Ban Lum Khao were buried in lidded jars. When opened up, this jar contained a tiny skeleton and a miniature pottery vessel.*

174

175

174: *At Nong Nor, Bronze Age graves were cut into a much earlier settlement site.*

175: *Aerial view of the Khao Wong Prachan Valley. Non Pa Wai is the large, dark area in the left foreground. Non Mak La lies along the right side of the creek bed which winds from the reservoir across the valley floor. (Photo courtesy of the Thailand Archaeometallurgy Project)*

Central Thailand

The network of settlements seen on the Khorat Plateau, which incorporated the copper mines of Phu Lon, is matched on the plains of Central Thailand. In the Khao Wong Prachan Valley we find a concentration of copper processing and casting sites, some of the products from which reached agricultural settlements by exchange. At Non Pa Wai, the second mortuary phase falls within the Bronze Age, and includes a 25-year-old male interred with a set of bivalve clay moulds for casting an axe. Another grave contains such an axe. A second ore processing and casting site at Nil Kham Haeng has furnished a radiocarbon date which suggests that copper extraction was under way by 1300-900 BC. This site comprises many lenses of ash and metal processing debris that probably represent material picked up and redeposited by monsoon rains. Weiss (1992) has suggested that this indicates dry season metal extraction. Fourteen inhumation graves have been uncovered, dating it is thought from about 700 BC. Burial 5 included as grave goods, a sea turtle skeleton over the head, a copper bracelet, copper ring, three pottery vessels and a mass of copper ore. One of the singular features of this and other Khao Wong Prachan sites is this presence of copper without the addition of tin. Among the artefacts so cast at Nil Kham Haeng, there is a range of small, thin socketed implements with chisel like working surfaces. We will meet with similar artefacts at Nong Nor.

Nong Nor

We excavated Nong Nor over three seasons in 1991-3. In addition to the 4500 year old coastal habitation site, we found a Bronze Age cemetery, in which the graves were cut into the earlier settlement layers, or on occasion right through them and into the natural substrate. After three seasons, we had uncovered 400m², one of the largest areas of any prehistoric excavation in Thailand, and uncovered a total of 166 graves. Not all were complete, for prehistoric and more recent disturbance has taken place, but it remains a fascinating collection, because we can recognise spatial patterning in the distribution of graves, and apply a statistical analysis to the variation in mortuary offerings to see if any people were given special attention. This is a method for identifying social organisation. If a small group of graves in a particular place was distinguished by opulent or rare offerings, they might represent a group with high social status.

The method of burying the dead followed the same basic procedures as have been described for the cemeteries on the Khorat Plateau. A grave was excavated, in this site through the dense shell midden, and the body was placed on its back with the head facing towards the rising sun. Pottery vessels were located beyond the head, beside the body or beyond the ankles. Many of these were red slipped, open bowls on a pedestal. They

176

176-177: Nong Nor graves were, as is always the case in Bronze Age cemeteries in Thailand, laid out in rows. This cemetery dates within the period 1100-600 BC.

177

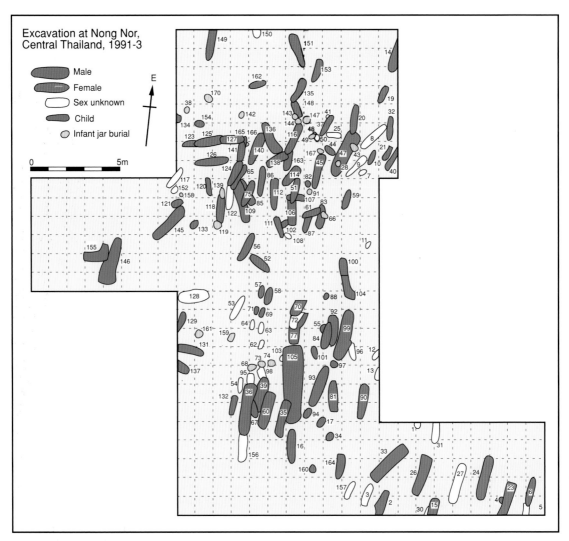

Excavation at Nong Nor,
Central Thailand, 1991-3

Male
Female
Sex unknown
Child
Infant jar burial

E

0   5m

178: The layout of the Bronze Age
cemetery of Nong Nor.

may have been used to display food: on one occasion, we found
a chicken bone lying in one. We have seen how animal bones
were often placed with the dead. Nong Nor was no exception,
but was also unusual, for the most common offering was a dog
skull placed beyond the head. Sometimes, we found pigs' foot
bones, just like those from Ban Lum Khao and Non Nok Tha.
Personal jewellery was worn by some of the dead, and again we
find the same marble and shell bangles as have been seen in the
northeastern sites. We also, however, found a range of jewellery
made from stone sources not hitherto seen in such cemeteries,
including talc, serpentine, carnelian and jade.

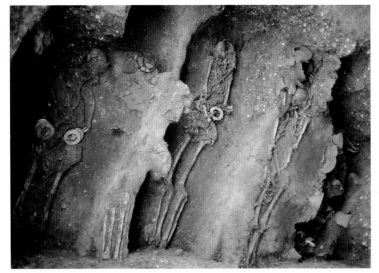

179

189: This group of graves at Nong Nor stands out for the wealth of the dead. We can see the many marble, shell and bronze bangles and whole pots. Most individuals also had a dog's skull beyond the head.

180-183: The people of Nong Nor wore these bangles of bronze, serpentine and shell. The two serpentine bangles have been repaired with bronze tie wires. Each is about 11 cm wide.

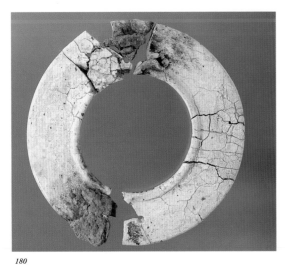

180

181

182

183

184

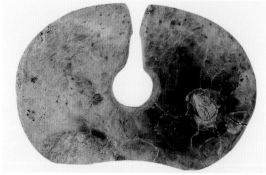

185

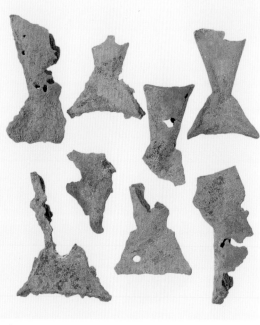

186

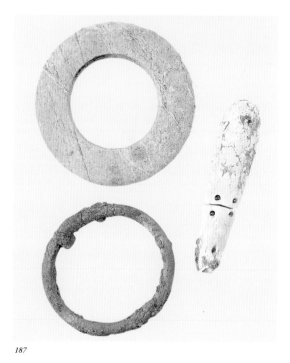

187

188

184: *This jade ear pendant has been refashioned from a broken bangle. Width 4.6 cm.*

185: *Ear pendants like this one in serpentine were found as grave offerings at Nong Nor. Width 3.3 cm.*

186: *These socketed chisel-like implements were cast in copper. Virtually identical moulds have been found at Nil Kham Haeng in Lopburi province. They are about 5 cm. in length.*

187: *These grave goods from Nong Nor are bangles of marble and bronze, and a shell neck pendant repaired with bronze tie wires. Length of shell pendant, 10.8 cm.*

188: *Carnelian beads were found with a man buried at Nong Nor. The largest is 6.6 mm wide.*

Burial 105 is a good example of a complete grave from Nong Nor. It is one of the longest known for Bronze Age Thailand, measuring almost four metres. It contained the remains of an old adult male, centrally placed with a series of pottery vessels placed beside and beyond the head. A large bronze bangle was found on the right wrist, and a marble bangle on the left. The bronze example is particularly large, and matches almost perfectly one described for Ban Chiang. The shin bone of a pig had been placed beside the head, and a large shellfish valve on the opposite side. When we removed one of the pots, we found the skull of a young dog beneath. We also found one of the several shell ornaments which are, to our knowledge, unique in Thailand, a long shell pendant worn round the neck. The last and most unusual offering was reserved for much later, long after the bones had been removed from the ground. When preparing the skull, Nancy Tayles found a dark circle in the area of the ear, which turned out to be the decayed remains of a tin earring.

This was not the only tin artefact found. One woman was found interred with two spiraliform tin bangles, one on each wrist. She lay near a second large and opulent male interment, burial 109. In this instance, the adult man was buried in a long and deep grave cut right through the earlier shell midden and into the natural substrate. Some care had been given to the placement of grave goods beyond the head, for there lay four conus shells in a row. A series of five pottery vessels had also been arranged round the skull. The mourners had also selected three sandstone whetstones and placed them beside the head and under the left hand. A shark's vertebra was found by the other hand, and between the hands, there was a serpentine bangle which had been subjected to heat and broken in antiquity. As at Ban Na Di, it was repaired with cast bronze tiewires. A shell neck pendant completed the offerings with this man. Another man was interred with many grave offerings, but what stood out was a set of bull's horns placed round his skull.

We have noted the presence of a large bronze bangle with burial 105. Some other individuals were also interred with bronze bangles, but if we consider the 50 complete graves, only seven were found with bronzes. Of these, simple bracelets in the form of a band dominated, and these were cast from tin bronze. But two graves also contained small, socketed implements with chisel-like working edges already noted as coming from Nil

189

190

189: Burial 105 at Nong Nor was found in a grave 4 metres in length. The man wore a large and heavy bronze bangle.

190: In the case of burial 145 at Nong Nor, the man's skull lay between the horns of a large bull. We called it the bull burial.

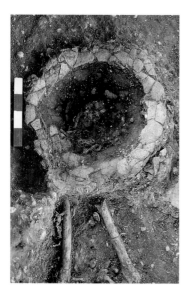

191: At Nong Nor, infants were buried in complete pots placed beyond the head or feet of an adult.

Kham Haeng. When analysed in the laboratory, it was found that these were cast from copper with no evidence of alloying. This parallels examples from the copper casting sites of the Khao Wong Prachan Valley, and surely provides strong evidence for the existence of an exchange relationship.

It is always intriguing to discover how people treated infants and children in death. The people of Nong Nor interred the latter exactly as they did adults. For infants, they made large jars and placed the tiny corpse inside, often with its own grave offerings, like a tiny shell bangle. We found groups of such jar burials, often placed beyond the head of a dead woman.

What can we say about the distribution of graves from Nong Nor? The plan reveals two major groups. The western incorporates three rows of graves. Infants were found in clusters, children were given the same treatment as adults, and on some occasions, earlier graves were disturbed by later interments, and the bones were relocated with some care. In the eastern group, there is a less clear pattern of rows, and more superpositions. We also find that graves cluster in the centre and thin out at the edges, suggesting that the edge of the cemetery was reached. There is one cluster of four infant jar burials and a sub group of four adult inhumations that follow a north-south rather than the more typical east-west axis. Where graves were found on top of earlier ones, there is no evidence for a time lag, for the pottery vessels belong to the same forms. In some cases, males and females were buried alongside each other. Burial 148, a female, was found associated with three infants and a child. We have suggested on this basis that the groups have some biological coherence, and probably reflect a relatively brief period of time.

The actual dating of the cemetery has proved difficult due to the lack of large charcoal samples. One concentration of charcoal, however, was found within an infant jar burial, and other radiocarbon dates, using the AMS technique, have been obtained on the basis of rice chaff used as a ceramic temper. The results indicate that the cemetery dates within the period 1100-600 BC.

Although we identified 166 burials, only 50 were intact and therefore available to analysis by multivariate statistics. Essentially, this involves the search for patterns that incorporate the age and sex of the individual, and the nature and association of the grave goods. Is it, for example, the case that graves in one corner of the cemetery were unusually rich? Were older individuals relatively wealthy? Are there distinctions between men and women? Such issues contribute to identifying social organisation, or where there is a tangible sequence, changes with time. Two statistical tests reveal that there was no major disparity in the nature or the quantity of grave goods, although some individuals were interred with more than others. Males and females were not differentiated by mortuary wealth, nor did age at death determine relative richness. Children were accorded the same burial rite and range of grave goods as were adults. There is, however, consistent evidence that a group of women and the male burial 105 represent a particularly rich lobe or group in the cemetery, measured in terms of bronze, marble and shell bangles, pottery vessels and dogs' crania.

192: This ornate bronze bracelet was recovered from a burial a Khok Phlap. (Courtesy Sod Daeng-iet)

One of the most interesting results is that bronze artefacts are not associated only with richer burials. Certain items of jewellery were manufactured from exotic serpentine, jade, talc and carnelian. These are found so rarely, that they have no obvious impact on the results of the statistical analysis. The burials with ornaments of carnelian, jade and talc are, with one exception, located in the eastern sector. In terms of the assemblage of pottery forms, this seems most likely to reflect the passage of time. Eastern graves were probably later, by which juncture exchange relationships saw the availability of these new sources of stone.

The people of Nong Nor cultivated rice, and used some of the chaff to temper their pottery vessels. They also maintained herds of cattle and pigs, and sacrificed their dogs as part of the ritual of death. They must have lived near the sea, even today it is little more than 20 km distant, and participated in an exchange network that brought in copper, tin, sandstone and an unusually wide range of exotic stone. There was thus much interaction between the Bronze Age communities of Central Thailand, and many sites surely remain to be identified and investigated. One such site, also located near the shore, is Khok Phlap.

Khok Phlap

Located between the Chao Phraya and Mae Klong rivers, this low mound with an area of 1.5 hectares was excavated by Sod Daeng-iet (1978). He encountered several human burials, accompanied by whole pottery vessels, bracelets of bronze, turtle carapace, stone, shell and bone. Some pots were filled with

193: This individual at Khok Phlap was buried with a pottery vessel and exotic stone ear pendants. (Courtesy Sod Daeng-iet)

194: Note how this burial from Khok Phlap was accompanied by a pottery vessel containing cockle shells. (Courtesy Sod Daeng-iet)

marine shellfish. One grave hearkens back to Khok Phanom Di, in that three potters' anvils were found. A socketed bronze spearhead and arrowheads recall items found at Ban Chiang and Ban Na Di. No radiocarbon dates have been obtained, but it would be surprising, given the material culture, if it was not contemporary with Nong Nor.

Northern Thailand

Compared with the wealth of Bronze Age sites in Central and Northeast Thailand, little is known of this period in the North. The first recognition of the presence of Bronze Age communities came from Ob Luang, where a grave was excavated in 1986. Grave goods included bronze and shell bangles, shell and carnelian beads and pottery vessels. To judge from the presence of carnelian, this grave is likely to be late in the Thai Bronze Age, for this material, while common in Iron Age graves, is otherwise known only from Nong Nor in a Bronze Age context (Prishanchit *et al.* 1988).

The Bronze Age: Summary

The existence of a Bronze Age in Southeast Asia has been known for over a century. Early French archaeologists found bronze axes, spearheads and arrowheads well back in the 19th century at sites in Vietnam, Laos and Cambodia. These belong to the same bronze casting tradition as those from Thailand, and the consensus of all available radiocarbon determinations indicates that the Bronze Age was underway some time between 1500-1000 BC.

If this dating framework is confirmed with further research, then we can relate it to an intriguing pattern which will, again, temporarily take us beyond the borders of the Kingdom. Excavations in Bronze Age settlements situated in Vietnam and along the coast of southern China to Hong Kong have uncovered the same range of bronzes, and the same casting techniques, as have been found in Thai sites. Some of these sites have been dated, and we find again, a consensus that they belong within the period 1500-500 BC. Now, southern China, particularly the provinces of Guangdong and Guangxi, are linked by river routes to the Yangzi Valley. During the second millennium BC, rich and powerful states were developing in this valley. Sanxingdui in Sichuan is a city, from which large and impressive bronzes have been recovered. These communities traded with the equally powerful states of the Huanghe Valley, where some of the world's largest and most impressive bronzes were routinely cast.

The important point to stress is that some of these bronzes, and also jade artefacts, found their way down the exchange routes into southern China and Vietnam. Indeed there are Neolithic cemeteries in these areas which contain the occasional Chinese jade. Is it possible that it was through such exchange contacts that knowledge of the properties of bronze reached Southeast Asia, including Thailand? We cannot yet answer this question one way or the other. It is certainly a possibility, and will remain so until we find undoubted evidence that there were Bronze Age sites in Southeast Asia which date back as early as 2000 BC. So far, they have not been found, but one day, they might be.

195

Life in the Bronze Age

Bronze Age sites, when we can ascertain their size, were not large, and perhaps never exceeded 5 hectares. Nothing is known of the nature of houses, where people lived, nor how many occupied a given community. To judge from the many postholes found in some sites, people may have lived above ground level in stilt houses similar to those we see in Thailand today. In modern villages, it would be highly unusual to find more than 100 people living in one hectare, and 50 would be a more typical figure. We are, therefore, probably dealing with communities of no more than 250 people, and some villages might have been smaller still. They were occupied over quite long periods, measured in centuries rather than decades. In favourable terrain, including good potential rice land laced with suitable streams, they might have become quite densely distributed. Where a group commanded a favoured stream confluence, it would be sensible to stay. And rice is a most important plant in this context, because it can be grown over successive years on the same plot without periods of fallow, due to its capacity to absorb energy from the water which percolates

196

195: Life and death were never far apart in the Bronze Age. This lidded jar from Ban Lum Khao contained the remains of a newly born infant. Note the holes in the lid and pot. Were they to release the spirit?. This huge vessel stood half a metre in height.

196: Life in the Bronze Age involved much trade in exotic jewellery. Here are two bangles, one of slate and the other of marble, from Ban Na Di graves. (width 11 cm)

197: This burial informs us on life in the Bronze Age. There is a bronze bangle, cast by the lost wax technique, figurines and the bones of cattle and a locally-made pottery vessel.

past its stems. Today, rice will grow to maturity even on what look like poor soils, provided there is sufficient rainwater to sustain it.

In addition to rice, there were domestic animals and an abundance of wild animals, fish, shellfish and plants. Biological activity in the wet season is so high, given the rain and heat, that it is hard to envisage a food shortage, a suggestion confirmed by the robust bone development of the prehistoric people themselves. The dry season might have been slightly more difficult to cope with, but we must remember that there was much more forest cover then, and the forest acts to retain water in the ground, and therefore provide for perennial streams. Where now you see a landscape with few trees and dried up stream beds in much of the Khorat Plateau, then there would have been a quite different habitat. Now one sees hardly any wild mammals outside the National Parks. Then, the forest teemed with game.

While daily activities in the Bronze Age doubtless centred on the routine of rice cultivation, caring for the domestic herds and fishing, there would also have been seasonal rhythms. There is some evidence that copper mining was a dry season activity, and making pottery almost certainly was, given the difficulty of properly drying and firing during the period of rains. Leaders in these communities were usually in their 20s or 30s. Death came long before what would now be called middle aged, and a widespread pattern of mortuary ritual has been recognized. No two villages are alike, but all follow the same theme: interment next to or over a relative or ancestor, and association with a range of grave offerings. There is a further consistent thread of evidence for the employment of items of jewellery made from exotic raw materials, such as marble, slate, marine shell, copper and tin. The care given to the repair of some of these, and the intrinsic value of an object obtained from afar, both serve to stress their symbolic role as indicators of achievement or status.

At two sites, Nong Nor and Ban Na Di, there are hints that groups of individuals buried in close proximity had an unusual concentration of mortuary wealth, but never to the extreme degree noted in later Iron Age sites. There appears rather to have been a moderate differential between wealthy and poor, consistent with a separation between a family group which for one reason or other was able to achieve and maintain higher status. This could reflect, perhaps, seniority in descent from the founding ancestor, or unusual ability in making desirable objects or communicating with the spirit world. This system of social organisation is embodied in what we term segmentary, that is autonomous, communities in which decisions affecting the community were taken from within, by its own membership without heed to any outside authority. But competition for the precious valuables, an increasing population within the confines of the village, a threat from a rival group, the life of a person of prowess and charisma, the availability of a new medium for making tools or weapons, all these taken singly or in combination could tip the balance and lead to pervasive social change. This is what we think happened from about 500 BC, a period known as the Iron Age.

(height 26 cm)

198: The pottery vessels from Ban Lum Khao have spectacular shapes.

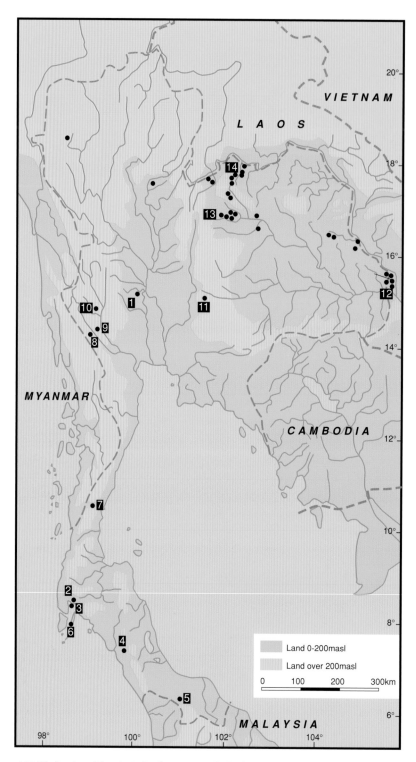

199: The location of the principal rock art sites in Thailand . 1. Khao Plara, 2. Tham Pee Hua To, 3. Khao Khiew, 4. Tham Traa, 5. Tham Silp, 6. Tham Wai King, 7. Khao Na Ma Phraaw, 8. Tham Rup Khao Khiew, 9. Tham Ta Duang, 10. Tham Pha Daeng, 11. Khao Chan Ngam, 12. Pha Taem, Pha Mon Noi, 13. Tham Lai Thaeng, 14. Phu Phrabat (Tham Khon and Tham Wua).

Rock Art

The existence of rock art in Thailand, paintings on the walls of caves or open rock faces, has been known for almost a century (Lunet de Lajonquiere 1912, Kerr 1924). This section describes some of the principal sites, styles and scenes, but it is unfortunate that we have no accurate information on chronology. At Pha Chang, red ochre which could have been used as a pigment, has been found in Hoabinhian layers under shadowy figures painted in the same colour on the walls above. What is needed, is the extraction of any organic material in the paint for AMS radiocarbon dating. Only such future research will determine the dates of the various sites, and how the corpus can inform us on the people who created the many vivid and fascinating scenes.

There is a wide range of sites and scenes from which to choose. Many include human beings, perhaps our first glimpse of the prehistoric peoples' activities as they portrayed themselves. We see many animals, both wild and domestic as part of fishing, agricultural and hunting scenes.

There are also abstract motifs and human hands placed at times on sheer rock faces, or hidden away in rock shelters (Charoenwongsa *et al.* 1985).

One of the most intriguing sites is Khao Chan Ngam, located in the Phetchabun Range just on the western edge of the Khorat Plateau. Set round a hidden circle of rock, there are numerous scenes painted in red. One reveals a group of people, with a dog, engaged in what was probably a hunting scene, for one man is firing an arrow. The people include men and at least one woman, and they seem thinly clad, the men wearing a sort of kilt, the woman an elaborate hat and what looks like a feathered tail. Two children sit on the ground next to the dog. The presence of the dog suggests a date

0   40cm

200: Cave art. from Khao Chan Ngam.

later than about 2000 BC, for dogs are not found in Hoabinhian sites prior to that date, and the first archaeological evidence is found in Neolithic contexts. Hunting with a bow and arrow is also seen at Pha Mon Noi in Ubon Ratchathani Province. Here, a large hind seems to be in danger and beyond, a stag and another hind are seen. Is it possible that the symbols behind the two deer represent a rice field? Pha Taem is nearby, and has a remarkable frieze of humans and animals. The former are depicted in a stylised manner, with triangular heads associated with solitary hands which appear as silhouettes outlined in paint. The people are linked with elephants and the huge catfish which are still to be found in the Mekong River. While the humans from this site are stylised, those from Tham Lai Thaeng in Loei Province are shown in virtually the same manner as those from Khao Chan Ngam. One man appears to wear a tail which reaches down to the ground behind him. A woman sits on the ground dandling a baby in her arms. Several bulls appear, recalling those modelled in clay from Ban Na Di.

One of the most important concentrations of sites is found Phu Phrabat in Udon Thani Province. At Tham Khon, for example, there is a frieze of red-painted human figures, and from Tham Wua, there is a row of cattle. The numerous superpositions over faded earlier motifs suggest that the rock faces of this region attracted artists over many years.

There are many rock art sites in Kanchanaburi, which suggest a widespread style of portraying human figures with animals. One of the most impressive sites, Tham Pha Daeng, is located in the remote Mae Lamun Stream a tributary of the Kwae Yai River. Here, the male dress is clearly to be seen: a kilt, tail, headdress and even what might be feathers at each shoulder. In the background, we see the outline of a leaping bull.

0   50cm

201: Cave art from Pha Thaem, Khong Jiam.

From Tham Ta Duang, downstream and on the right bank of the Kwae Yai River, we have a procession, in which men are carrying what might be a large circular drum.

One of the most fascinating and important rock art sites is found in Uthai Thani Province at Khao Plara. Here, on a spectacular wall of stone, visible for miles, are found the same human figures with kilts and headdresses, but this time with domestic animals. One man is accompanied by two dogs, and another has a bull attached to a line. He also wears a large bangle on each wrist. Both man and beast are portrayed in an X-ray style, the bones being seen in panels. There is also an outline drawing of three dancing human figures one of whom has an animal's tail.

The distribution of rock art extends right down to southern Thailand. At Pee Hua To cave in Krabi Province, there are human figures associated with fish and dolphins (Chaimongkol 1988). The presence of the dolphin recalls that from Khao Khiew in Phangnga Province, which is reputedly the first prehistoric painting to be identified in Thailand. Dolphin bones have also been found in the first phase layers at Nong Nor.

These many examples of a vibrant artistic tradition have the potential to add much to our appreciation of the prehistoric people of Thailand, but first and foremost, there needs to be a dating programme so that we can relate them to the cultural sequence.

202: Cave art from Khong Jiam.

0   2 m

203: Cave art from Tham Pha Daeng.

0   60 cm

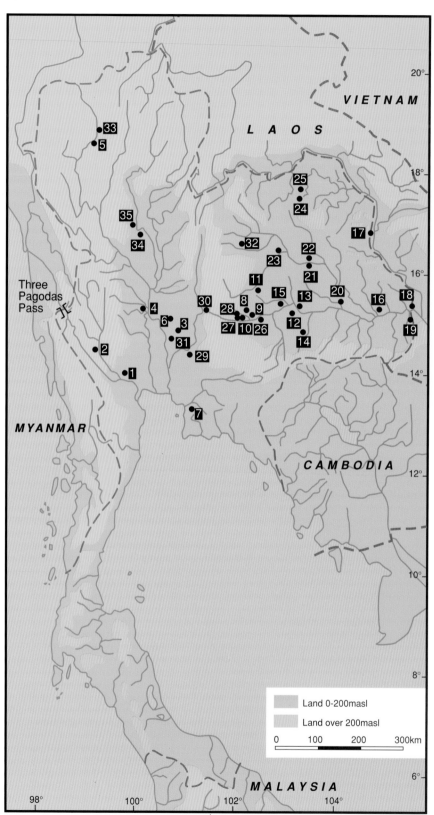

Chapter Five
The Iron Age

The period from 500 BC saw a series of deep and significant changes in the cultural and social fabric of Thailand. It is possible to recognise some on the basis of the artefacts recovered during excavations, while others are documented in Chinese or Indian historic sources. One of the most important in terms of its implications for society, was the development of iron working. Some sites also contain objects which originated in India, thus providing evidence for the establishment of distant trade relations, and the arrival of new ideas. We also know that the last few centuries of the first millennium BC saw a major expansion to the south by the Yin and Han dynasties of Central China, bringing the threat of foreign conquest. Finally, there is much evidence for an expansion of population in the lands bordering the major river valleys of Thailand.

Although the copper working areas in the Khao Wong Prachan Valley and at Phu Lon were extensive, it must be recalled that they were in use for many centuries, and the actual quantity of copper or bronze at the living sites beyond the mining complexes was not great. Metal, while a significant factor in the rituals of death, and doubtless too in signalling status among the living, was not a dominant material in daily activities. This changed with the coming of the age of iron. Iron ore is much more widespread than are sources of copper or tin. As laterite, it is readily available over much of Northeast and parts of Central Thailand. It requires a higher smelting temperature than does copper, and was not cast, but rather forged into the desired artefacts. The iron which came from early Thai smelting furnaces would have been brittle and riddled with unwanted impurities, but by heating and hammering, these

205 (length 6.7 cm)

204: The location of Iron Age sites mentioned in chapter V. 1. Ban Don Ta Phet, 2. Ongbah, 3. Noen Ma Kok, 4. Ban Lum Khao, 5. Ban Wang Hi, 6. Chansen, 7. Ban Bon Noen, 8. Noen U-Loke, 9. Ban Prasat, 10. Non Muang Kao, 11. Non Tung Pie None, 12. Ban Don Phlong, 13. Non Yang, 14. Ban Takhong, 15. Ban Krabuang Nok, 16. Ban Kan Luang, 17. Don Tan, 18. Ban Na Pho Tai, 19. Ban Chi Tuan, 20. Non Dua, 21. Ban Chiang Hian, 22. Muang Fa Daet, 23. Non Chai, 24. Ban Na Di, 25. Ban Chiang, 26. Ban Samrit, 27. Ban Dan Thong Lang, 28. Ban Ko Hong, 29. U Taphao, 30. Sri Thep, Ban Nong Daeng, 31. Tha Kae, 32. Non Muang, 33. Ban Yang Thong Tai, 34. Ban Bung Ya, 35. Ban Wang Hat

205: The carnelian lion from Ban Don Ta Phet. (Courtesy Dr I.C. Glover)

206: Iron was converted by forging into a wide range of new and vital artefacts. Here is a spade, or possibly a socketed ploughshare, from Noen U-Loke. It was found in a pottery vessel, covered in rice. Length, 18.5 cm.

could be removed and the very act of placing the iron into a forge of glowing charcoal and then hammering has the effect of carburising it, that is mixing carbon with the iron and thereby giving it more tensile strength.

It is hard to overemphasise the potential of iron. If you study a map of Northeast Thailand, you will find many villages named Ban Khi Lek, meaning Iron Slag Village. Visit them and you will almost invariably find a mound the surface of which is densely covered with iron slag and late prehistoric pottery. With iron tools, trees were more easily felled and the soil was turned with less effort. Iron smelting called on supplies of fuel wood to charge the furnace, so leading to deforestation. As the trees were cleared, so more land was opened to agriculture. And with iron digging implements, it became easier to consider hydraulic engineering works, to retain and control the flow of water. During the Bronze Age, there are hints of raiding or friction in the form of arrowheads and socketed spearheads. With the Iron Age, particularly in Central Thailand, heavy iron weapons proliferated.

Nobody can be sure how the knowledge of iron working began. It could have had a local origin, rooted in the accumulated metallurgical skill of the Thai copper smelters, who were using iron ore as a flux in their operations. Knowledge might have been gained from early contacts with the Chinese, or with Indian traders. This same period also saw the first known direct exposure of Thai communities to foreigners. India had by then developed various states within which merchant venturers undertook trade with Southeast Asia. They sought spices, bronzes and gold, and brought a new range of exotic goods: glass, agate and carnelian, as well as new ideas rooted in the Buddhist and Hindu religions. The communities which had early access to these novelties, or which themselves went to sea on trading ventures, reaped the reward of controlling the accumulation and flow of these goods. For their leaders, there came an unrivalled opportunity to gain in social standing. The corollary was that any demands for novel local goods on the part of Indian traders would have fostered production and the control of the distribution network.

During these same centuries, the Han Chinese began a southward move into Southeast Asia with an unashamed objective of imperial expansion. Most of what is now southern China, including Yunnan, Guangxi and Guangdong provinces, and the Red River Delta in Vietnam were absorbed into the empire, but the energy behind this push ebbed and finally ran out at the Truong Son Cordillera or, as the Chinese called this range, the "Fortress of the Sky". The impact on Thailand was therefore indirect. It involved the rapid establishment, in the decades leading to Han domination, of powerful chiefdoms, polities which vested authority in warrior leaders. In Yunnan, we can see these leaders, depicted on their bronze drums, or represented as gilded figures on the bronze cowrie containers which were interred in royal tombs. Naturally, the development of such chiefdoms opened a new and exciting range of novel bronzes, and established new markets for exotic goods from the south. This quickening of exchange could only have provided opportunities for the people of Thailand.

With the Iron Age, there is also evidence for a rapid growth in population. Settlement sites proliferated where formerly there was little evidence for occupation, and some sites grew to be up to ten times larger then their Bronze Age predecessors. Ban Chiang Hian in Mahasarakam, for example came to cover 38.5 hectares and if we assume a density of 50 people per hectare, then the population might have measured 2000. The area of these sites is readily defined, because many were demarcated by old river channels.

207

208

207: This iron knife from burial 85 at Noen U-Loke was found still within its bamboo sheath. Length 14 cm.

208: Another knife, this from burial 113 at Noen U-Loke, was covered in woven cloth. Length, 12.5 cm.

Ban Don Ta Phet

In September 1975, schoolchildren in the village of Ban Don Ta Phet in Kanchanaburi Province noticed curious potsherds and beads emerge from the ground when contractors were digging the foundations for a new fence. This attracted the attention of the local authorities, and the Fine Arts Department began excavations, under the direction of Chin You-di. It turned out to be the richest, most important Iron Age site yet excavated in Thailand. Many burials were uncovered, which included as grave goods iron tools and weapons, ornamental bronze jewellery and bowls, and beads of glass, agate and carnelian (You-di 1976). Some of the jewellery recalled examples from India, while the bronzes were at that time unparalleled in Thailand. A site of such potential called for further research, and in 1980, more excavations began under the direction of Ian Glover and Pisit Charoenwongsa. They uncovered a further 19 graves, and their research provided some new and interesting

209

210

211

209-210: *The excavations at Ban Don Ta Phet in 1985 produced an unparalleled assemblage of Iron Age grave offerings. (Courtesy Dr I.C. Glover)*

211: *This picture shows the carnelian lion of Ban Don Ta Phet as discovered, along with carnelian and etched agate beads. (Courtesy Dr I.C. Glover)*

212: *The excavation of Ban Don Ta Phet. (Courtesy Dr I.C. Glover)*

212

information. First, the range of grave goods showed little variation, suggesting a brief span of time for the cemetery. Acid soils meant that little human bone has survived, but the orientation of the grave offerings suggested that most graves had an east-west orientation, a pattern familiar at Nong Nor and Khok Phanom Di. They considered it possible that the burials were secondary, that is they had been relocated from elsewhere, and placed within a mortuary precinct defined by a ditch which enclosed an area 40 metres across. After digging a grave up to 40 cm deep, soil had been heaped over the grave to form a mound. Still more excavations were undertaken by the same team in 1984-5. Thirty more burial contexts were identified, and of no less significance, the margins of the cemetery were traced.

Compared with the preceding Bronze Age burials, the individual interments of Ban Don Ta Phet were considerably richer. Take, for example, burial 55. It contained 26 pottery vessels, 11 bronzes, four objects of iron, nine spindle whorls and 185 glass beads. Burial 46 also included many pots and among the bronzes, some bowls, bangles and a most remarkable bronze figurine of a fighting cock standing on top of its cage. Burial 56 incorporated two bronze vessels, one of which looks remarkably like those cast in northern Vietnam at this period for its style is quite alien to that of Ban Don Ta Phet. There are also 20 pottery vessels, more glass beads, examples in agate and carnelian and 13 iron objects, including digging tools and spearheads. One of the most important finds comes from burial 73 which, apart from a bronze bowl and anklet and 12 iron implements, included a carnelian statuette of a leaping lion which beyond any doubt indicates exchange contact linking the site with India.

It is in the bronze industry that we can identify major changes from the preceding centuries in Thailand. During the second and third seasons, 288 bronzes were recovered, but not one was connected with war or conflict. It is clear that bronzes were rather used as items of display and show. Bracelets became more complex, finger rings and bells appeared, but the most extraordinary aspect of this industry is the collection of bronze bowls. These were cast from an alloy of copper with about 23% tin, a mix which, while imparting a golden colour, is also brittle and hard to work. According to Rajpitak and Seeley (1979), these bowls were first cast using the lost wax method, then reduced on a lathe to their finished form. Some were reduced to a thickness of 0.3-0.5 mm. At this point, they were incised with

213   (width 11 cm)

214

215

213-214: Bronze bowls of high tin bronze were one of the most important categories of mortuary offerings at Ban Don Ta Phet. (Courtesy Dr. I.C. Glover)

215: This elegant woman is one of the first images we have of prehistoric people in Thailand. She was incised onto the outside of a bronze bowl from Ban Don Ta Phet. Her face and hair are 2.7 cm wide. (Courtesy Muang Boran)

216

(length 4.5 cm)

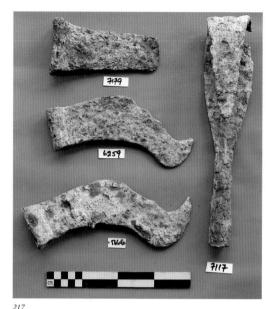

217

218

219

(length 20 cm)

216: Close up of the jade double-headed animal ornament. (Courtesy Dr I.C. Glover)

217: Iron was most important to the people of Ban Don Ta Phet. Here we see billhooks an axe and a bent spearhead. (Courtesy Dr I.C. Glover)

218: A view of the jade double-headed animal pendant, alongside two bronze bowls, from Ban Don Ta Phet. (Courtesy Dr I.C. Glover)

219: A deliberately "killed" or damaged iron spear from Ban Don Ta Phet. (Courtesy Dr I.C. Glover)

designs and scenes: we see women with elaborate coiffures and long ear ornaments, a range of animals including elephants and what look like sheep and horses, neither of which is native to Thailand. There are structures which may be houses, flowers and geometric designs. The inference to be drawn from these objects is that they required specialised, highly skilled craftspeople, who would quite probably have plied their craft full time. Moreover, their works were not confined to local consumption, for virtually identical bowls have been found in contemporary sites in India.

The iron objects, by contrast, were designed for agriculture, hunting or fishing and in conflict. The commonest implement was a socketed tip for a hoe or small spade, but we also find curved billhooks, spears and arrowheads. It was common practice to bend or destroy the spearheads as part of the mortuary ritual. Fabric, perhaps the remains of clothing, sometimes survives and interestingly, it seems that in addition to hemp, the people of Ban Don Ta Phet also knew of cotton. This plant probably came to Thailand from India (Glover 1996). The beads are one of the largest and most important assemblages of this period in Thailand. The majority, about 3,000, were made of glass, while 600 were made of carnelian, agate, rock crystal and jade (Glover 1996). A particular feature among the latter group is the technique of etching, whereby patterns were imparted to the surface of the stone by applying caustic soda and heating. This technique had reached a high pitch of perfection in India at the period of occupation at Ban Don Ta Phet which, according to the available radiocarbon dates, probably fell within the period 395-350 BC. A further ornament which informs us on the widespread exchange networking at the time is a curious double animal-headed pendant in jade. Virtually identical ornaments are found in Iron Age sites along the coast of Vietnam, and across to the Philippines (Reinecke 1996).

The location of Ban Don Ta Phet would have facilitated its participation in a trading network for, in a sense, it lies at the Thai gateway to India. The Three Pagodas Pass to the west connects the rich lowlands of Kanchanaburi with the Andaman Sea and so to India. Glover (1989, 1990) has emphasised the strong evidence in favour of exchange contacts between these two regions from at least the fourth century BC which brought not only a new range of exotic ornaments, but also ideas. We have noted the presence of a carnelian lion: the lion was an early means of representing the Buddha before it became acceptable to portray him in human form. So here, in this early Iron Age cemetery, we can detect the first seeds in the spread of Buddhism into Thailand which were to provide for such strong and vigorous growth over the ensuing millennia.

Tham Ongbah

Ban Don Ta Phet is not alone in documenting this major change to increased cultural complexity during the Iron Age. For further evidence, we return to the great cavern of Ongbah, in the upper reaches of the Khwae Yai River. This site is located near a source of lead ore, and lead was in demand for adding to copper to produce an alloy more easily cast. Sørensen (1973, 1988) has described with feeling the frustration of reaching the site in the wake of looters, who had ravaged the boat-shaped wooden coffins containing the remains of Iron Age aristocrats.

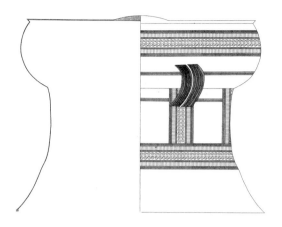

220: One of the bronze drums from Ongbah, showing the superb decorative scene to be found on the striking surface. This drum is 53.5 cm high and 67 cm wide. (Courtesy Per Sørensen)

221

221: Burials at Ban Wang Hi reveal groups of adults, children and infants laid out on the same orientation. (Courtesy MAFT J.-P. Pautreau and P. Mornais)

222: The minute care with which burials were uncovered at Ban Wang Hi is shown clearly in this picture from the 1998 season. (Courtesy MAFT J.-P. Pautreau and P. Mornais)

223: This person was interred at Ban Wang Hi with an extraordinary array of iron weaponry, including a sword in the left hand, and spearheads by the skull. Blue glass beads are seen round the neck. (Courtesy MAFT J.-P. Pautreau and P. Mornais)

The site had once housed over 90 of these coffins, and the few pieces recovered, along with three which survived the depradations, show that they were cut from a local hardwood, and embellished with birds' heads at each end. The lids were similarly constructed of hardwood and fitted to the coffin proper with mortice and tenon joints. Grave goods, to judge from a few surviving pieces and reports of the local villagers employed by the looting gang, included glass and stone beads, bronze ornaments and iron weapons and tools. Eye witnesses describe long strings of beads in the form of necklaces and belts. A radiocarbon date from a fragment of coffin wood (403 BC-25 AD) suggests contemporaneity with Ban Don Ta Phet.

By far the most interesting of the grave goods recovered by Sørensen was a group of six bronze drums which may well have been grave offerings, set as pairs within or beside the coffin. These drums, named after the site of Dong Son in Vietnam, were of impressive size, the largest being about 60 cm in height and 70 cm wide. One of the first surviving reports of Southeast Asia, contained in the History of the Chinese Sui Dynasty and describing the years 586-617 AD, noted that "The different Lao tribes make bronze drums . . . . before going to war, the chief summons the warriors of the tribe by beating the drum". During the period of the Iron Age in Thailand, many contemporary groups in southern China and Vietnam cast these drums and used them in their rituals. Two major concentrations of sites are known, one in Vietnam and the other in Yunnan, but few have been found in Thailand. In the northeast of the country, they have been found in sites near the junction of the Mun and Mekong rivers, suggesting riverine routes of exchange from the north (Nitta 1994). In Central Thailand the most important assemblage comes from Ongbah, which accentuates its wealth and strategic location. It is highly likely that these drums reached Ongbah by exchange. Their decoration is a rich source of information on their creators. First, to cast such a large bronze demands skill of a very high order. Most were cast by the lost wax method, whereby sheets of wax were first placed over a clay mould to take the chosen patterns of decoration, and then applied to a clay core in the form of the drum. More clay was then applied to the wax, and held in place with bronze chaplets. This meant that, when the wax was melted out, bronze could be poured in to fill the void and so create a decorated drum.

222

If this procedure took place in Vietnam or Yunnan, it is not informative on the skill of the Thai bronze caster, nor of Thai prehistoric society. We have already seen the languid scenes of houses, lotuses and sophisticated women on the Ban Don Ta Phet bronze bowls. But the drums rather portray an austere aristocracy, with plumed warriors, armed to the teeth, engaged in parades or manning war canoes. We see rituals, music making, rice processing and flights of crane egrets, birds of the marshlands of Vietnam. But the most telling point about these drums and their presence at Ongbah, is that there was a demand for them by the rising Thai Iron Age aristocracy. They sought such prestigious artefacts, had the means to acquire them, and then the wealth to immolate them at the time of their leaders' funerary rites.

Sørensen also found a small group of five graves which had escaped the looters' attention. None was interred within a boat coffin, but a group of five had the head orientated to the east, while three others were on a northeast orientation. Associated artefacts included iron hoes, knives, a spear blade, arrowheads and chisels. These graves, rather poorer but contemporary with the boat coffin burials, hint that the community of Ongbah included an elite group, and commoners.

As more sites belonging to this critical period in Central Thailand are excavated, so we find further strands which we can weave into a pattern. Among the earliest investigations took place at Tha Muang, part of the later Dvaravati centre of U-Thong (Loofs 1970, 1979). Excavations in 1969 revealed an

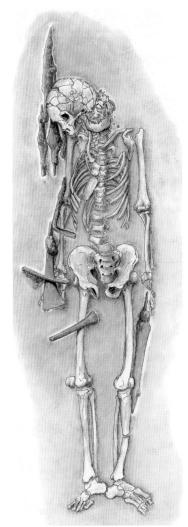

223

224

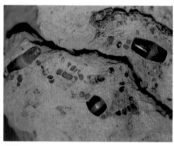

225

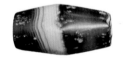

226

224: Excavations at Ban Wang Hi revealed Iron Age graves of considerable wealth. (Courtesy J.-P. Pautreau)

225-226: Agate and glass beads from Ban Wang Hi very similar to those from Northeast Thailand. (Courtesy J.-P. Pautreau)

Iron Age occupation which incorporated among the earliest evidence for the local manufacture of glass beads in Thailand, dated by Loofs in the 4th century AD, as well as abundant evidence for iron smelting and a material culture closely akin to that of at least one other emerging state, that of Funan in southern Vietnam.

At Noen Ma Kok, just north of the Khao Wong Prachan Valley, Mankong (1989) has found agate, carnelian and glass beads matching those from Ban Don Ta Phet, as well as similar forged iron tools. The middle phase at Tha Kae has yielded agate, carnelian, glass and nephrite ornaments belonging to this period (Hanwong 1985). Natapintu (1988b), in his excavations at Ban Lum Khao in Uthai Thani Province has uncovered three burials associated with glass beads, green stone earrings and an assemblage of pottery vessels. Elsewhere in the site, he found beads of carnelian and agate, and iron slag attesting the establishment of a local iron industry. Tankittikorn (1987) has opened the site of Ban Wang Hi just south of Lamphun, and encountered seven inhumation burials with the head orientated again, to the east. Glass and agate beads, large bronze bangles and socketed iron implements were found in association. A further season of excavations in 1996 added four further inhumation graves, one of which was that of an infant, but the poor preservation of the bone ruled out sexing or ageing the adult skeletons (Pautreau *et al.* 1997). The excavators have suggested that the dead were interred in a shroud of organic material, associated with a range of grave goods which include glass beads and earrings, agate beads, complete pottery vessels and tools made of iron. One finely decorated bronze bracelet was also recovered. The suggested date of this cemetery lies in the last century or two BC or AD.

The same date probably applies to the single inhumation grave uncovered at Ban Yang Thong Tai, just east of Chiang Mai. There, Prishanchit found the inhumation grave of a woman in her thirties, together with two spindle whorls, several pots, an iron spearhead and three bronze bangles, the latter decorated with curvilinear designs (Prishanchit 1986).

Saraya (1997) has emphasised the importance of recent excavations in the Yom River basin in identifying a vigorous series of Iron Age communities which precede the establishment of states. At Ban Wang Hat, for example, excavations have revealed much evidence for iron smelting, while the presence of glass, agate and carnelian jewellery points to inter-regional exchange (Songsiri 1997). Burials unearthed in early 1997 at Ban Bung Ya and in Khamphaeng Phet tell a similar story (Pisnupong 1997, Wilaikaeo 1997).

In the second occupation phase at Chansen, a site later to be enlarged and ringed by a moat, Bronson (1979) found a most interesting object, an ivory comb decorated with geese and horses, as well as Buddhist symbols, which has been dated in the vicinity of 100 AD. Part of a similar comb was found at nearby Tha Kae. Many exotic glass beads have also been recovered from the upper layers of Ban Bon Noen, a site in Chonburi Province which we excavated in 1990 (Pilditch 1992).

Sri Thep is a large moated site in the Pasak Valley best known for its historic monuments. However, excavations in 1988 within the moats have revealed a late prehistoric Iron Age occupation represented by five burials at a depth of four metres. A complete female inhumation, oriented with the head to the north, was accompanied by a bronze bangle and a pointed iron tool 50 cm long. A carnelian bead was found in the neck area (Tankittikorn 1991).

An iron tool was also found near the hand of a second burial, and the adjacent grave of a child included a large pottery vessel and some glass beads. Twelve kilometres to the southwest lies Ban Nong Daeng. Excavations in 1990 encountered six burials and grave goods include pottery vessels, polished stone axes and iron tools and ornaments. The pottery vessels are similar to those from Noen Ma Kok (Tankittikorn 1991).

Excavations in the huge moated site of U-Taphao, undertaken in 1989, encountered Iron Age graves at a depth of 3 metres. Burial 2 overlay burial 1, only the lower part of the body of burial 3 was found. The grave goods included slate bangles and polished stone adzes. Iron ore, and three clay moulds for casting ingots are also reported (Wilaikaeo 1991a,b).

227

228

227: A late grave from Nil Kham Haeng included many bronze bangles as grave goods. (Courtesy Surapol Natapintu)

228: An adult with a sword is seen here interred with children. There is much structural evidence for elaborate mortuary ritual at Ban Wang Hi during the Iron Age. (Courtesy MAFT J.-P. Pautreau and P. Mornais)

Northeast Thailand

There is a point on the highway linking Saraburi with Nakhon Ratchasima, where you suddenly see unfolded the flat expanse of the Khorat Plateau. Here, the streams flowing east from the Phetchabun Range gradually come together to feed the Mun River which joins the Chi at Ubon Ratchathani before itself losing its identity in the Mekong. To a prehistoric person standing in this same position, the plain in front must have

229: Aerial view of the Iron Age settlement of Ban Non Wat, Non Sung, Nakhon Ratchasima Province.

appeared as an unbroken pattern of treetops vying for a place in the sun. We know that there were a few Bronze Age communities dotted across the plain, but it was only with the coming of iron that the first serious inroads were made into the virgin forest of the Mun Valley.

Today, the Khorat Plateau has lost most of the natural forest cover, and lying in the rain shadow of the Phetchabun Range to the west and the Truong Son Cordillera to the east, it now suffers a long, arid dry season. We do not know if it also presented difficulties during the Iron Age, but certainly, it was the season when rice did not absorb the energy demanded at other times of the year. So, there was time for other activities, and we can, on the basis of archaeological evidence, track some of these down.

Archaeological fieldwork on the plateau began just on a century ago with explorations by Aymonier (1901) and Lunet de Lajonquière (1907). Just after the second world war, further impetus was given to this interest in the prehistoric sites by an officer in the Royal Air Force of Britain. Peter Williams-Hunt took a series of aerial photographs of the plateau, and recognized many large settlements demarcated by what he called banks and moats. These he ascribed to the prehistoric past, and further research on the ground has confirmed that they were occupied during the Iron Age (Williams-Hunt 1950).

Virtually all subsequent workers have accepted that these sites were ringed by moats (Moore 1989, Parry 1992, Higham 1996). McNeill (1997) has reported a date in the first few centuries AD for the construction of the moats at Muang Phet. But for years, these moats and their intervening banks have presented an enigma and a challenge to archaeologists, particularly given the importance of water control during the subsequent development of early states (Groslier 1979). Imagine the problems of investigating the site of Noen U-Loke, which is located in the upper Mun Valley. Air photos reveal what look like at least five concentric moats, which stretch over a distance of about 200 metres. At one corner, they link with what looks like a canal which proceeds, straight as a dye, to the stream 2 km distant. Are these in fact moats, and if so, were they dug for defence? For water conservation to ensure a supply to the occupants of the settlement within? Were they intended to aid in drainage during times of excessive flooding, for a source of food or indeed, for any of these singly or in combination?

Resolution of these important issues can only be achieved by excavation, to examine the nature of the moat profiles, and determine the circumstances under which any sediment was deposited. In association with our colleague William Boyd, we initiated a programme to investigate the Noen U-Loke moats by excavating sections across them with a powerful mechanical digger. Boyd found, to our surprise, that at Noen U-Loke and Non Muang Kao, there is no evidence for moat construction at all. Rather, the 'moats' cover a series of old river channels and swamp deposits, indicating that the sites were situated in low-lying flood-prone terrain. The moats, and their banks, he suggests, were formed recently as the local rice farmers levelled the rich clay soils round the sites to expand the agricultural area. The alleged canals can hardly relate to these sites either, since the rivers they lead to did not exist during the Iron Age.

We were very surprised by this finding, and have since opened similar cuts through the channels surrounding four further sites near Noen U-Loke. Boyd found exactly the same situation: old river or stream beds, but no signs of prehistoric activity. This does not rule out the possibility that moats were formed round some Iron Age sites in Northeast Thailand, but does stress the importance of excavation and analysis by a geomorphologist before concluding so.

A second problem also involves scale. There are hundreds of Iron Age sites, some virtually within hailing distance. Were they all occupied simultaneously? If so, there must have been a population explosion with the Iron Age. Some are very large, covering over ten times the area of the largest preceding Bronze Age sites. What was their internal organisation we wonder. Perhaps they were densely packed with houses. Alternatively, there could have been industrial, residential and mortuary areas interspersed with open spaces. What was their date of occupation, and why are so many now abandoned, miles from the nearest settlement. As there are so many, was there perhaps a settlement hierarchy. That is, a particularly large, central site which housed a paramount leader, with subsidiary settlements occupied by members of his chieftaincy.

We share these problems with other prehistorians. By no means all have been resolved, but slowly and painstakingly, we are inching forward in our understanding of this Iron Age of the Khorat Plateau.

230: Opening the 'moats' at Non Muang Kao revealed a series of old river channels. The excavations can be seen on the mound in the far distance.

231

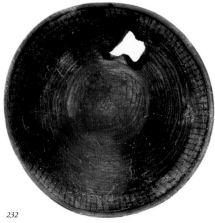

232

233

231: This view of the excavation of Non Muang Kao shows an Iron Age floor, with wall partitions and postholes, some still containing the form of the wooden posts. A number of later disturbances are also visible. (Photo: Dougald O'Reilly)

232-233: A Phimai Black pottery vessel from Noen U-Loke, the interior of which has been decorated with burnishing strokes. (16 cm in diam.)

The Upper Mun Valley

Our assumed prehistoric observer of the Khorat Plateau would have seen the panorama of the upper valley of the Mun River. This region has been examined by David Welch and Judith McNeill, and they have combined the study of aerial photographs with ground surveys to trace the pattern of Iron Age occupation, a period they describe as the Phimai Phase. This phase, which they have dated to 200 BC-300 AD, is recognised on the basis of a style of pottery which involved burnishing in clear lines and firing in an enclosed environment to produce a black finish. Named Phimai Black, its presence made it possible to trace Iron Age settlements from the alluvial plain to the surrounding old terraces and so to relatively elevated terrain (Welch and McNeill 1991). It is evident, when viewed through their detailed surveys in each of these environmental zones, that there was a considerable growth in the number and the size of settlements which commanded the alluvial plain when compared with the preceding Bronze Age. Moreover, about half of these low-lying sites were ringed by old channels. They have also found that people were beginning to found settlements in areas less favourable to rice cultivation, for on the terraces above the alluvial plain, they traced a number of smaller (1-5 ha) sites,

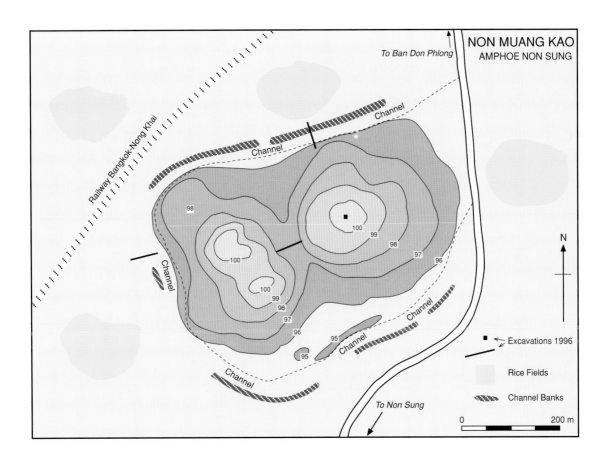

To Ban Don Phlong

Railway Bangkok-Nong Khai

Channel

Channel

Channel

Channel

Channel

Channel

Channel

98

100

100

100

99

98

97

96

95

95

100

99

98

97

96

N

Excavations 1996

Rice Fields

Channel Banks

0   200 m

To Non Sung

234: The twin peaks of Nong Muang Kao, a huge settlement dated to the Iron Age.

some again being surrounded by channels. Even the uplands were settled, all six sites being located in small enclaves where some rice cultivation was probably possible.

At Ban Prasat, the Bronze Age cemetery underlay a series of graves belonging to this Iron Age period. The thin-walled Phimai Black pots were accompanied by bronze grave goods, including a remarkable bronze headdress.

Non Muang Kao, Mound of the Ancient City, lies 20 km east of Ban Prasat, and was first recorded by Lunet de Lajonquière (1907). In 1906, it was visited by H.R.H. Prince Damrong: on the morning of 19th December in that year, the Prince, while en route for Bua Yai, heard from villagers at Ban Don Phlong of a site nearby called Non Muang Kao (H.R.H. Prince Damrong 1995). Ninety years later, we were finishing a day seeking sites when we drove south from Ban Don Phlong and encountered the contour of this huge mound. At first, we could hardly believe what we saw, but ascended to the top of the mound and there, we picked up numerous prehistoric potsherds. It covers about 55 hectares, and comprises two

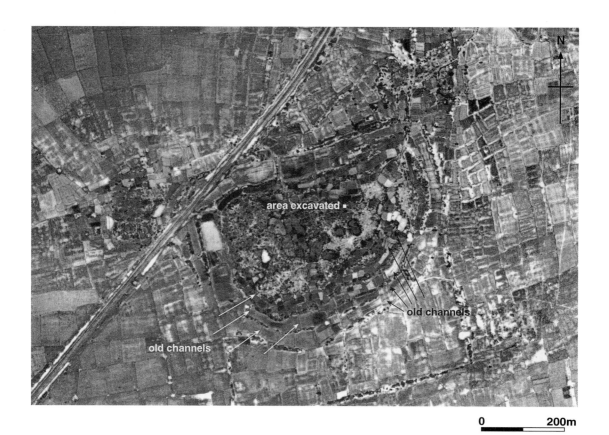

N

0   200m

235: Air view of the site of Non Muang Kao, showing the old channels which run round the site and the area excavated.

mounds ringed by multiple channels. We felt then that it must be excavated on account of its size and commanding position. In due course, we set our graduate student Dougald O'Reilly the exciting task of opening a square where we had stood on the mound's summit.

O'Reilly encountered a complex series of superimposed plastered floors containing what look like house foundations. Some postholes even retained the pattern of the wooden supports for possible houses. There were also graves, which were lined and covered with a thin layer of plaster, and filled with rice. The dead, who lay in these rice beds, wore bronze earrings and were accompanied by glass and agate beads and beautiful, eggshell-thin Phimai Black pottery vessels. The radiocarbon dates from these contexts date the excavated layers to 0-400 AD, but settlement seems have have commenced by about 50 BC.

Noen U-Loke

Excavations at this mound, which viewed from the air appears to be ringed by a series of channels, were undertaken in an area of 15 by 14 metres in 1997-8. The natural substrate was reached at a depth of 4.85 metres. The occupation in this area began with the Bronze Age, but virtually the entire sequence belongs to the Iron Age. Wichakana (1991) also found Bronze Age graves in a different part of the mound. The sequence began with evidence for a small stream running across the excavated area, in the channel of which were many small, redeposited potsherds. There followed four major cultural layers which contained evidence for industrial, occupation and mortuary activity.

The industrial activity involved the construction of a series of clay-lined furnaces equipped with tuyeres. Their precise function is uncertain, but they were clearly used on several successive occasions, for we have found that the clay was relined with intervening layers of asbestos. Possibly they were used in iron forging, but McDonnell doubts this in the absence of hammer scale, the chips of iron which accumulate round the working blacksmith. Alternatives include glass making, for we found pieces of glass rod, iron smelting: some contained iron slag, and bronze casting. We found part of a clay bivalve mould for casting an axe.

The occupation remains included rows of deep postholes. Both hearths and pits have provided large samples of carbonised rice. Many of the pottery vessels and potsherds of a white residue on the interior which Heron has identified as a resin of probably dipterocarp origin, which would have assisted in waterproofing.

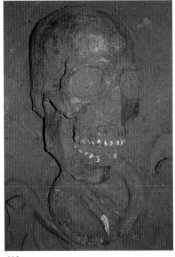

236

236: Noen U-Loke burial 27: The bronze torcs and tiger's canines are part of a rich assemblage of early Iron Age grave goods.

237-238: The earliest burials recovered from Noen U-Loke in 1997 involved two males interred next to each other. The richer, burial 27, had been buried with an iron and two bronze spears, an iron socketed hoe, several pots containing fish skeletons, two bronze bangles, shell discs, two bronze torcs at the neck and four tiger's canine teeth.

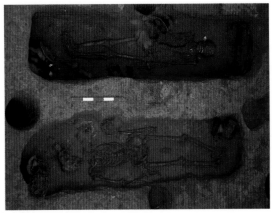

237

238

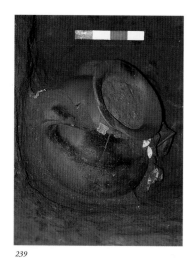

239

239: The pot at the feet of burial 27
contained a fish skeleton, and was
associated with two bronze spearheads and
several shell discs.

240: Burial 108 from Noen U-Loke,
Nakhon Ratchasima. Such bones as these,
in excellent condition even after 2,000
years, provide clues for peoples' health and
way of life.

241: Burial 69 wore four bronze belts.

Most interest, in terms of assessing aspects of social organisation
at this site, derives from the burials. The sample of 126
inhumation graves include five phases, ranging in depth from
5.0 to 0.65 metres below the present surface of the mound All
but the lowest belong to the Iron Age. The sequence is now
dated by 17 radiocarbon determinations from the laboratory at
the University of Waikato in New Zealand. The earliest Iron
Age phase is represented by six interments which date to
between 100-200 BC. Burial 27 was found associated with a set
of two bronze torcs, a broad bronze bangle on each wrist, and
two socketed spearheads of bronze beyond the feet. A large
socketed iron implement, probably a spear, was placed beside
the head, and a socketed iron hoe was found beside the left
ankle. At least two of the four associated pottery vessels
contained the complete skeletons of fish. Several shell discs were
also found, two beside the head and four beyond the feet, while
four tiger's teeth in the neck area were probably strung as a
necklace. The adjacent interment had fewer grave goods, the
pottery vessels containing fish skeletons while a pig's foot had
been placed between the thighs. Burial 108 was particularly
intriguing: it was interred with an iron torc and three iron

240

241

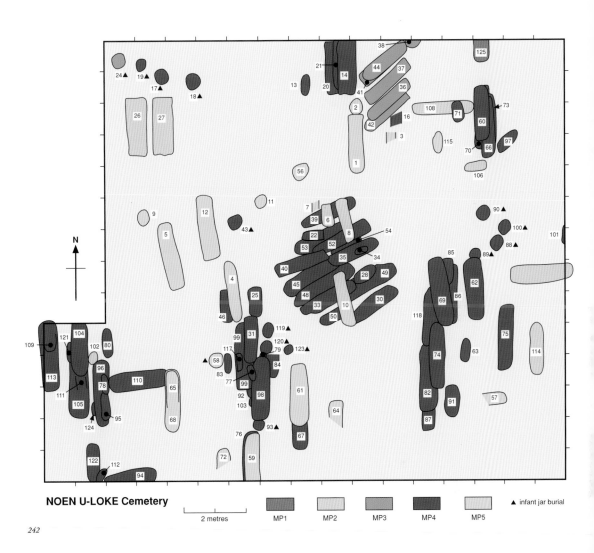

NOEN U-LOKE Cemetery

2 metres

MP1　MP2　MP3　MP4　MP5　▲ infant jar burial

242

243

242: *The distribution of graves in the Noen U-Loke Iron Age cemetery, 1997-8 seasons.*

243: *The gold beads of Noen U-Loke burial 113. Each is about 4mm across.*

244

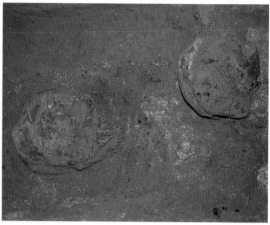

245

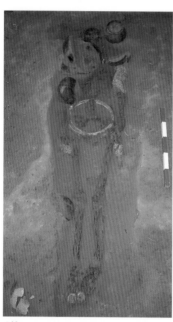

246

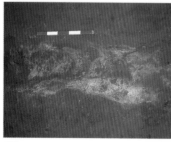

247

bangles. It is likely that this represents a very early phase of the Iron Age, when iron was used only for ornamental purposes.

The third mortuary phase is dated in the first or early second century AD. It incorporates a cluster of inhumation graves with the head pointing to the northeast. These were interred at a depth of 2.95-3.35 metres below the present surface of the mound, and show a number of differences from those ascribed to phase 2. Apart from the tight clustering and different orientation, two were associated with complete young pigs, and we find the first evidence for glass beads. One person had been buried prone, all others were supine. Burial 37 was found with an agate neck pendant, which was to recur in all later phases, while some of the individuals wore bronze finger rings. The latest burial in this group was a lidded jar containing the remains of an infant.

The fourth mortuary phase dates not long after 250 AD, and incorporates clusters of graves between two and three metres below datum. The dead were now buried in what we have termed rice beds. This involved filling the base of the grave with a layer of burnt rice before interring the body. A further layer of rice then covered the human remains to a present depth of about 10 cm, although subsequent compaction makes it difficult to estimate the depth of the rice at the time of burial. This same practice was applied to adults and infants. Although there was a common ritual element to the clusters, each also has some particular characteristics. One had no pottery vessels, but all the carnelian beads. Another had many pottery vessels and much wealth besides in the form of agate beads and pendants, gold beads and bronzes. A third had little if any agate but a lot of

248

249

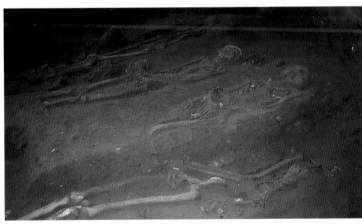

250

bronze. One burial in this group, number 69, wore four bronze belts. The richest burial in another cluster was associated with the most remarkable assemblage of bronzes known to the excavators for this period in Northeast Thailand. The adult male was found in association with silver earcoils covered in gold foil. A bimetallic bronze and iron ring was found in the neck area. On each arm, there were approximately 75 bronze bangles covering the body from the elbow to the shoulder while the finger bones were covered with rings. Three bronze belts were found round the waist, and the toes bore large, bronze rings. In addition to these finds, the body was associated with pottery vessels, glass beads in the area of the neck, chest and ankles, and an iron knife. An infant buried nearby was also richly endowed with bronze and glass ornaments.

Burials of the final phase were found between 0.65 and 1.35 metres below the surface of the mound, and date to not

244-245: The jewellery from phase 4 graves at Noen U-Loke included a glass bead necklace, and agate pendants worn at the neck.

246: Burial 14 is the richest Iron Age grave at Noen U-Loke, and included about 400 bronze ornaments including finger, toe and earrings, three bronze belts, about 150 bronze bangles in addition to glass beads, pottery vessels and an iron knife.

247: During mortuary phase 4 at Noen U-Loke, we encountered a fascinating innovation. The dead were buried in what we called 'rice beds'. First, a layer of burnt rice was laid in the grave, and when the body was in place, it was covered in rice. The burnt rice is white in these pictures of burials 33 and 34 as the skulls of an adult and a child appear through their covering of rice.

248-249: Bronzes were abundant in mortuary phase 4 graves, including bells and a unique spiraliform ornament on the side of a skull.

250: The burials of phase 3 at Noen U-Loke were tightly clustered and relatively poor in terms of grave goods. There were no pots and few bronze rings and bangles. Two adults were accompanied by complete young pig skeletons. Is this a prehistoric extended family?

251

252

251: Uncovering burial 14 at Noen U-Loke. The weight of all the bronzes surpasses the combined weight of all the bronzes from over 300 burials from Ban Na Di, Nong Nor and Ban Lum Khao.

252: There were about 75 bracelets on each arm of burial 14 .

long after 300 AD. The orientation remained with the head to the north, but rice beds were no longer in evidence. Continuity was seen in the use of jar burials for infants, the presence of agate pendants and beads in the neck area, and the bronze jewellery. Burial 1, for example, included bronze finger rings, bracelets, earrings and bimetallic bronze and iron rings. A feature of these later burials, however, is the marked increase in iron implements, which include knives, sickles and in one case, a socketed spearhead. One person buried prone, revealed a socketed iron arrowhead lodged against the spine. Does this indicate conflict between settlements of this period?

The preliminary look at the faunal remains from Noen U-Loke also provided some surprises. Wild animals were rare. There were few bones from the water buffalo, some pig remains, but the overwhelming majority of remains come from quite small domestic cattle. Fish bones were not nearly as abundant as in the Bronze Age settlement of Ban Lum Khao. It seems that the occupants of the site during the Iron Age concentrated on rice cultivation and cattle breeding.

During the course of research at Noen U-Loke, a detailed examination of the mound's surface was undertaken, in order to identify likely activity areas. Carl Heron and Gerry McDonnell from Bradford University were able to track down the remains of iron forging, where the implements we found in graves were fashioned. Iron smelting and forging requires a constant supply of fuelwood, and deforestation must have had a major impact on the environment. As you look across the landscape from Noen U-Loke and Non Muang Kao, you will see a number of small, steeply rising mounds. On close examination, these are coated with prehistoric pottery and concentrations of charcoal, and the majority, if not all of them, were formed as a result of salt processing.

There are no similarly extensive exposures of an Iron Age cemetery on the Khorat Plateau with which to compare these finds from Noen U-Loke, but the results from a series of small excavations in the area by Kanchanagama (1996) have shown that Noen U-Loke was one of many similar sites. At nearby Ban Ko Hong, for example, he uncovered an inhumation grave at a depth of two metres which, while not nearly as rich as burials 14 and 69 from Noen U-Loke, was found with one identical bronze belt. At Ban Dan Thong Lang, he found three burials in a 2 by 3 metre exposure, orientated north-south. Two individuals lay along side each other, the heads pointing in

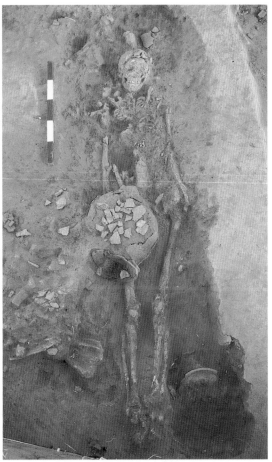

253

254

255

256

257

maximum width 16 cm.

258

maximum width 5.5 cm.

253-254: *With the last mortuary phase, we find an increase in iron implements. These include sickles, knives and with burial 6, a spearhead.*

255: *The last burials at Noen U-Loke were only 65 centimetres below the surface of the mound. Here, we find more agate beads and pendants.*

256: *The final phase of interments also included an infant burial at the head of an adult, within a large and elegant Phimai Black phase pottery vessel.*

257-258: *There were many examples of expertly forged iron implements at Noen U-Loke, and exotic agate jewellery.*

259: An unusual necklace, made of tiger's canine teeth from burial 27 at Noen U-Loke. Note the bored holes and the grooves, worn perhaps when the teeth were suspended round the man's neck. Height, 4.3 cm.

opposite directions and one wore a bronze ring round the neck which, while not identical, recalls the torcs found with burial 27 at Noen U-Loke. These people were also interred with many bronze toe, ear and finger rings, bangles and glass, agate and carnelian jewellery. Again, as at Noen U-Loke during phase 3, there is little evidence of interring pottery vessels with the dead. Many bronze rings and bangles were also found with a single burial encounterd in the 2 by 3 metre exposure at the appropriately named site of Ban Samrit (Bronze Village), near Phimai. A further burial belonging to the Iron Age in this area was found at Ban Tanot, associated with bronze bangles and toe rings.

Salt: a Vital Resource

The Khorat Plateau is rich in natural deposits of salt. During the dry season, there are areas where water rising to the surface evaporates, leaving a crust of white salt, a vital commodity in this region, because it is used to ferment fish, thus allowing wet season surpluses to be preserved for consumption during the dry. It can also be accumulated by its owners for exchange transactions, thus providing a route to wealth and status. Today, the salty soil is scraped up and brought to the processing centre. There, it is mixed with water and placed in a hollowed log at the bottom of which, rice straw acts as a filter. The water percolates down through the soil, becoming increasingly briny. It is then reticulated into a shallow metal tray placed over a fire. The brine is brought to boiling point, and continues to seeth until only salt is left. This procedure leads to an accumulation of soil as the hollowed tree trunks are emptied ahead of a fresh consignment.

There have been several excavations in these salt mounds, leading to common conclusions. The basal layers date back to, but not beyond, the Iron Age. The second is that the extraction technique has survived, virtually unaltered, since prehistoric times. Only the metal trays have replaced the large ceramic vessels for containing the brine for boiling. Nitta (1991, 1992, 1997) has examined, for example, salt working sites at Non Tung Pie Pone, a mound 5.5 metres in height. He found water storage tanks, and furnaces for boiling the brine, along with coarse industrial pottery and sherds of Phimai Black pottery. So there is no doubting the Iron Age context of this activity.

It may have been the growing wealth of these communities, linked with the strategic command of the route linking the plateau with the plains of Central Thailand, which accounts for the presence in this upper Mun Valley of some of the great bronze drums. That from Pak Thong Chai lies right on this arterial route (Nitta 1994).

The Middle Mun Valley

As one proceeds eastward down the Mun Valley, the Iron Age sites continue to lie thick on the ground, although Phimai Black pottery became scarce and then petered out, to be replaced by a local painted and cord-marked style. Yet the principal features of Iron Age settlement recurred here, as has been shown by Nitta's excavations at Ban Don Phlong (Nitta 1991). He actually revealed a specific iron smelting area, comprising 17 clay lined furnaces and a pit for raking out slag. The remains of tuyeres and slag, together with the fact that some furnaces were stratified on top of earlier ones, indicates that the area had been designated for smelting the local laterite ores over a significant time span. According to the radiocarbon dates, this fell towards the end of the first millennium BC. This facility overlay an inhumation cemetery in which individuals, grouped together in a cluster, had been laid out on a north to south axis. One in particular, that of an adult male, stands out: the grave was lined with clay walls, and the man's face was covered with a block of clay. He wore three large, ornate bronze bangles on each arm, and three bronze rings had been located respectively on the

260: Small mounds like Non Teeng Seeng, here seen during the 1981 excavation, were built up through salt processing. Here and elsewhere, it seems that intensive salt production began during the Iron Age.

261: Modern salt processing, as seen here, involves the accumulation of soil in groups of mounds.

260

261

262

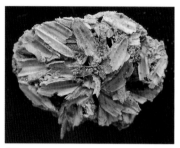

263

262: *Rice was the staff of life for the Iron Age people of Thailand. These carbonised grains were found in a pit at Noen U-Loke.*

263: *At Noen U-Loke, people were buried in beds of burnt rice. Here is some rice taken from such a grave.*

chest and the right hand. His necklace was made up of 10 agate and 31 glass beads. It also seems, to judge from surviving fragments of wood, that the whole had been contained within a split tree trunk coffin. Other burials also contained a profusion of bronze rings and glass ornaments and even a child had been interred in a clay-lined grave. This cemetery confirms hints already seen at Noen U-Loke and Non Muang Kao, that much more energy was devoted to burying the dead than during the preceding Bronze Age.

Several other large Iron Age sites in the middle Mun Valley have been excavated. Non Yang, which has been eroded by the river itself so that only a third remains, lies 50 km northeast of Ban Don Phlong and excavations by Eiji Nitta have produced some fascinating evidence for structures (Nitta 1991). This mound rises 10 metres above the surrounding rice fields and only the upper part of this sequence has been excavated. It seems that the building technique matched that seen at Non Muang Kao. All four structures uncovered were built at ground level: there is no evidence for their being raised on posts. Walls were built of clay over a timber framework, and the interior surfaces were smoothed, one wall still standing to a height of 30 cm. A further parallel with Non Muang Kao, was the deposition of whole pottery vessels, often associated with rice, under the foundations. These were not large structures, the best preserved measuring only 2.6 by 1.7 metres. It is conceivable that they were rice stores rather than habitations. Radiocarbon dates, obtained from the actual structural timbers, fall within the period 300-1 BC.

These buildings were destroyed by fire. In due course, two ditches were dug 70 cm deep and up to a metre wide, and significantly, an iron spade was found within the fill. After this event, the area excavated was used as a cemetery, but with a novel mortuary ritual which involved interring the dead in a row of lidded jars. Finally, a ditch up to 4.4 m wide and 2 m deep crossed the site, and Nitta has suggested that it might have been an enclosure ditch with a palisade for the settlement as it existed at this late period, dated by radiocarbon to 263 BC-79 AD. A problem with dating these structural timbers is that they might have inbuilt age, that is, old trees were employed. Hence, the actual date could be some centuries later. It is intriguing to speculate that such a large ditch and palisade fence could have been thrown up in times of stress or danger.

Ban Takhong is a small settlement site on the bank of the Lam Takhong Stream, which flows north ultimately to join the Mun River. It is interesting on several counts: there is an extension to the area occupied, suggesting the possibility of a growth in population during the course of its prehistoric occupation, and excavations by Elizabeth Moore have revealed a stratified sequence extending to a depth of 6 metres. A radiocarbon sample from a depth of a metre suggest that late occupation took place between 1-300 AD, just as seen at Non Muang Kao. Two other dates from depths of 1.7 and 2.5 metres likewise suggest occupation into the first millennium AD. Other finds confirm the pattern derived from other sites: structural remains of clay were encountered and iron tools and a bronze bracelet were found (Moore 1992).

264: Surviving by its proximity to iron, this spade (seen in detail) from Noen U-Loke was covered in rice grains when buried 2,000 years ago.

In 1988, Indrawooth *et al.* (1990) opened an area of 6 by 3 metres at Ban Krabuang Nok, Nakhon Ratchasima Province. This site lies near the present confluence of the Mun and the Lam Sa Thaet rivers, and their excavation reached the natural substrate at the amazing depth of 8.5 metres. The excavators have divided the sequence into three phases. The first belongs to the Iron Age, and dates between 300 BC-200 AD. There is much evidence for iron smelting in the form of slag, while bronze rings, bracelets and bells recall the repertoire at Noen U-Loke at the same period. The pottery, however, was different from the Phimai Black ware, being red slipped or buff with red painted designs. During the second phase, which dates from 200-900 AD, the occupants adopted the practice of interment in lidded jars. Iron smelting continued and the recovery of an enclosed kiln still containing pottery vessels points to technical improvements in the area of ceramic production. The final phase dates beyond the prehistoric period, from 900-1300 AD.

The Lower Mun Valley

Near Ubon Ratchathani, the Mun and Chi join before making their final journey to the Mekong. Ban Kan Luang is located in this region, and a series of investigations there have revealed an urnfield cemetery. These huge jars, 75-85 cm high, contain human remains, and sets of grave goods (Prishanchit 1991, 1992, Woods and Parry 1993). Among the latter, there are large and beautifully decorated bronze bracelets, rings and spearheads, socketed axes, arrowheads and the figurine of a man. Iron tools

265

266

265: The channels round Non Dua still retain water. The prehistoric mound rises beyond the water, and harbours a series of villages today.

266: Bo Phan Khan, an extensive deposit of salt, was exploited during the Iron Age, and remains a vital source of wealth to this day.

and smaller pots are also found as grave goods. No radiocarbon dates are available, but the presence of iron slag and the style of the bronzes places the site firmly within the Iron Age. The site can now be viewed as an open museum (Doyarsa 1992).

Further downstream and to the Mekong itself, there is much evidence for exchange in exotic goods. Don Tan is a remarkable site for, despite severe looting, there are reports of Chinese coinage and burials which incorporated bronze drums (Vallibhotama 1991). A further drum has been found at Ban Na Pho Tai at the confluence of the Mun and the Mekong and another at Ban Chi Tuan (Nitta 1994).

Up the Valley of the Chi

Let us now make an archaeological journey towards the north west from this nodal area, examining the pattern of Iron Age settlement as we proceed. Non Dua is a massive settlement site in the valley of the Lam Siao Yai River. In late 1969, a team led by Charles Higham began a site survey and series of small excavations in this remote part of Roi Et Province (Higham 1977). Viewed from the air, Non Dua appears as an elongated oval mound ringed by a broad channel. It is so large, that it now contains four or five distinct villages. The Lam Siao Yai can be seen entering the channel, but one can also detect a linking canal, and a possible second channel leading north into the present rice fields. The size of this settlement might be related to the extensive salt deposit, known as the Bo Phan Khan, which lies only 700 metres to the northeast. Today, the edge of this saltpan is crowded with temporary habitations, as the villagers process the salt which provides the wealth of the local communities. This demands so much wood that spent rubber trees are freighted in from hundreds of kilometres to the south.

Excavations were undertaken in three parts of this complex of prehistoric sites: in the central area of Non Dua site, on the mounds which ring the salt pan, and on a subsidiary mound called Don Taphan. The cultural deposits at Non Dua itself, which reach down 4.85 m from the mound's surface, have been divided into three ceramic phases. The lowest is dominated by red-slipped pottery vessels, and is dated from about 500-1 BC. The second (1-700 AD) has a characteristic pottery style called Roi Et ware, which was cord marked, then smoothed over and painted with red bands. The final phase (700-1000 AD) has a

thin white variety of pottery, and might just antedate the
construction of a Khmer temple sanctuary. No burials were
found – the excavation was small, but iron slag was present at
the bottom of the site. The ceramic sequence is clearly
structured, and allows us to integrate this settlement with the
industrial extraction of salt at Bo Phan Khan. While pottery at
this latter site is dominated by coarse industrial wares, there is
some Roi Et material at the very base of the excavation at a
depth of 5.3 m. It is associated with a radiocarbon date of 228-
597 AD. There was much structural evidence for salt processing,
along with masses of concentrated charcoal, presumably from
fuelling the furnaces. Don Taphan also revealed Roi Et pottery
at a depth of 5.85 metres, associated with a radiocarbon date of
250 BC-AD 341.

267: Excavations in progress at Don
Taphan in 1970.

There appears to have been an intense concentration of
human activity in this area with the Iron Age. No evidence has
been forthcoming for Bronze Age settlement at any of these
sites. Salt processing was established and its demands on timber
would doubtless have involved significant local deforestation.

Ten years after these excavations were complete, a team
from Silpakon University directed by Srisakara Vallibhotama
undertook a wide ranging survey in the lower valleys of the
Mun and Chi, and recovered the band-painted Roi Et pottery
from many more sites, including Nong Yang in Surin Province.
Moreover, they identified a considerable number of small
mounds, presumably resulting from salt working, and evidence
for iron smelting (Suchitta 1983).

In 1980, Higham and Kijngam (1984) conducted a site
survey and limited excavations just south of the Chi River and
west of Mahasarakham. Payom Chantaratiyakarn assisted in this
fieldwork and went on to study the material excavated for her
Master's degree (Chantaratiyakarn 1984). The area chosen for
survey had in its centre, the large settlement of Ban Chiang
Hian. The air view reveals a cross valley dam, two channels, a
small reservoir, and a series of canals issuing from the northern
edge of the site to the rice fields which now dominate the Chi
flood plain. These channels enclose a high mound which covers
just over 38 hectares. We have seen already that the lower layers
formed during the Bronze Age. The earliest evidence for iron
came with layer 7, just above the first presence of the water
buffalo of domestic size. These same layers, which belong to
phase 2 of the settlement sequence (600-1 BC), also furnished a
concentration of clay moulds which had been used to cast bells

268

269

268: One of the channels surrounding Ban Chiang Hian. The site lies on the opposite bank.

269: The historic structures of Muang Fa Daet cover an Iron Age settlement and cemetery.

and bracelets. These moulds provide unequivocal evidence for lost wax bronze castings and naturally, the copper and tin had to be imported. In this context, the pottery from later phase 2 is informative: it includes styles which match those from upstream, from contemporary Non Dua and the Phimai area. Taken in conjunction with the ubiquitous glass beads, it is hard to avoid the conclusion that riverine exchange between Iron Age communities flourished.

In her consideration of the settlement pattern in this area, Chantaratiyakarn has stressed the contrast between the single large site and the many smaller settlements which were strung along the edge of the Chi flood plain, and stretched up into the interior stream valleys. Since many of the latter were clearly occupied during the Iron Age, it is possible, she has argued, that Ban Chiang Hian was the seat of an elite group which exercised a form of political dominance over subsidiary settlements. She has proceeded to argue that, given a population in the order of 2,000 people at Ban Chiang Hian, there would have been sufficient accessible rice land to provide for the site's occupants.

By crossing the Chi opposite Ban Chiang Hian, one soon comes to Muang Fa Daet which at 171 hectares, is arguably the largest early site in Northeast Thailand. It was, however, a focus of intense activity after the end of the prehistoric Iron Age, and the several additions made to its area by enclosing progressively greater tracts within later moats make its size during the Iron Age impossible to estimate. However, Indrawooth has opened a small area in the interior village of Ban Muang Kao and revealed three inhumation graves (Indrawooth *et al.* 1991, Indrawooth 1994). These contained an iron harpoon and an axe, along with glass, carnelian and agate beads. In a second test pit, they also found a group of lidded jar burials. The prehistoric part of Muang Fa Daet needs a major excavation of the type carried out by Pisit Charoenwongsa at Non Chai, on the outskirts of Khon Kaen.

Pisit Charoenwongsa directed arguably the most significant excavation to date of an Iron Age site in this area when, in 1977-8, he worked at Non Chai. This site covered up to 38.5 ha and rose 15 metres above the surrounding area. Unfortunately, it has been removed for road fill, so no information beyond the excavation will become available (Bayard *et al.* 1986). Van Liere (1979) has mentioned a former moat or canal round the site. One most useful aspect of this site is that it was occupied only during the Iron Age, and therefore it is possible, given the deep stratigraphic buildup of cultural remains, to detect changes and developments over a relatively short passage of time. There are five phases. The first has been radiocarbon dated to about 400-300 BC, Phases II-III to 300-200 BC, Phase IV from 200-1 BC and phase V to 1-200 AD. Iron was already available from the initial occupation, the layers of which show clearly that the first settlers could exploit a low-lying marshy habitat rich in aquatic fauna. Many shellfish and the remains of crocodile and rhinoceros were found. The second phase saw the continuation of local bronze casting, evidenced by the presence of crucibles which, during phase III, certainly incorporated lost wax castings of bracelets and bells. It was also during phase II that the first blue glass beads were recovered. Phase IV saw a surge in the amount of iron slag. Throughout the period, a distinctive and attractive red-on-buff painted ware was made, richly tempered with the remains of rice (Rutnin 1979). If estimates of the former site size are accurate, the population may have comfortably exceeded a thousand people, considerably larger than any known Bronze Age settlement. Indeed, is there at Non Chai and its contemporary sites in the valley of the Chi, a hint that some settlements were assuming the role of regional centres?

This issue increases in relevance when one proceeds even further up the Chi catchment to Non Muang in Khon Kaen Province. This site comprises an enclosure 420 metres across, within a later addition which took the maximum diameter to 600 metres, giving an area of 36 hectares. Such additions are not unusual, they are also seen at Muang Fa Daet, Muang Sema and Sri Thep. Excavations of 14 squares there by the Fine Arts Department between 1982 and 1991 uncovered evidence for continuous occupation from the Iron Age to the period of Dvaravati (from the 7th century AD). It was abandoned probably in the 10th century. The excavations uncovered 17 Iron Age burials, four females, five males and four of unidentified gender aged between 20 to 45 years at death. Graves were oriented with the head to west, northwest or southwest. The dead were placed over sheets of broken pottery vessels, with complete pots beyond the feet.

Kaosaiyanon (1992) has divided the sequence into four periods. The first falls into the Iron Age, and one radiocarbon date falls within the period 800-400 BC. Burials include as grave goods, iron hoes, knives and sickles, and jewellery made of bronze and marine shell. Spindle whorls were also encountered.

270

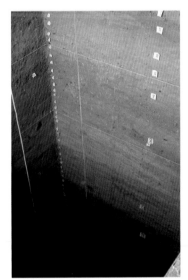

271

270: Pisit Charoenwongsa (in the white shirt) is seen here inspecting the edge of the quarried area of Non Chai. The depth of Iron Age deposits is clearly apparent.

271: The cultural deposits at Ban Chiang Hian are even deeper than at Non Chai.

272

272-273: Bronze casting during the Iron Age at Ban Na Di involved the construction of clay-lined furnaces (above) and clay moulds for casting decorated bangles using the lost wax method. (width 4 cm).

Phase 2 has yielded a radiocarbon date of 155 BC-AD 220. The mortuary ritual was relatively unchanged, but there were more grave offerings. Phase 3 belongs to the period of Dvaravati, and cultural remains are similar to the many contemporary sites in Central Thailand. The radiocarbon date for this context is AD 345-600. During this period, there was major dislocation with preceding behaviour. Clay images of the Buddha and *sema* stones reveal the adoption of Buddhism, and cremation succeeded inhumation as the preferred means of burial. There was also much evidence for local iron smelting. The last phase comprised a mixture of Dvaravati and Khmer influence in the range of ceramics. Occupation lasted into the 11th and 12th centuries before abandonment.

The continuation of settlement in smaller villages, however, is seen at Don Klang, located 50 km northeast of Non Muang (Buranrak 1994b). This site covers only two hectares, and reveals occupation dating to the last centuries BC (Schauffler 1976). The 17 graves uncovered in 1993 included iron ornaments and an axe, but perhaps the most interesting aspect of the material culture is the continuation into the Iron Age of the pottery vessels and bronze axe types seen at Non Nok Tha, which is only 20 km to the southeast.

The Sakon Nakhon Basin

Compared with the broad flood plains of the Mun and Chi, the Sakon Nakhon Basin has small rivers and was naturally better watered, for rainfall increases as one leaves behind the rain shadow imposed by the Phetchabun Range. Here, there are no large sites, and Iron Age culture represents a clear dislocation from the previous Bronze Age tradition. This is nowhere more clearly illustrated than in the upper layers of Ban Na Di. After the end of the life of the Bronze Age cemetery, the area excavated revealed a quite different pattern of use. A row of small clay-lined furnaces had been dug into the ground, and these were ringed by many fragments of bronze, crucibles and pieces of clay moulds for casting bells and bracelets by the lost wax technique. Already, we have seen that identical casting techniques had been in use at Non Chai. The technique was first to make a clay core and cover it with wax. This wax was often decorated before being coated with a fine clay, then a layer of coarser, rice-tempered clay. Again, the wax was melted out and bronze poured into the void thus formed. The intriguing point about this layer at Ban Na Di is the concentration of such furnaces, as if it had been a specialised industrial part of the settlement.

The layer immediately following this episode revealed a group of lidded jars. These contained the remains of infant humans, one of which was so tiny that it is thought to come from a foetus only six months old from conception. The tiny skeletons were accompanied by grave goods, which include blue glass beads and iron harvesting knives. The latter were covered in the remains of rice. This, allied with the blood red colour of the interior of each vessel, might be sending messages on the nature of the ritual of death during the Iron Age.

273   (width 4 cm)

A detailed examination of the artefacts from Bronze and Iron Age layers at Ban Na Di has suggested that there were deep-seated changes. The style of the pottery vessels changed, as did the technique employed in preparing the clay needed (Wichakana 1984, Vincent 1988). A similar change applied to the clay crucibles, while a new range of artefacts was encountered, such as cylinders of clay, pierced with a hole lengthwise, and decorated by excising designs on the exterior surfaces. A similar tradition of making pottery vessels has been found at the nearby Iron Age settlement of Ban Muang Phruk, while at Ban Chiang, just over 20 km to the north, excavations over a number of seasons have uncovered Iron Age graves which confirm a series of pervasive changes.

At Ban Chiang, the excavations by Nikhom Suthiragsa in 1973 near the centre of the mound, were followed two years later and a few metres away by a second excavation by Charoenwongsa and Gorman. The problem with both was that the area available was limited by modern houses, so the excavations were only 3.5 metres wide. This severely limits information on the spatial layout of graves, and therefore, our understanding of past social organisation. However, more room was available in the grounds of the Wat Pho Si Nai, and excavations there have revealed how large and exquisitely ornamented pottery vessels were commonly used in Iron Age burial rituals. The Wat Pho Si Nai excavation, which covers easily the largest area of any investigation at this site, has revealed orderly rows of inhumation graves on a northwest to southeast orientation (Bannanurag and Khemnak 1992). The pottery vessels which abound here and in the Iron Age contexts of the site as a whole are justifiably renowned for the vitality and

274

275

274: *The Iron Age layers at Ban Na Di contained a cemetery of infant jar burials.*

275: *When we opened the lidded jars at Ban Na Di, we found the skeletons of tiny infants. One was aged only 6 months from conception. They were buried with rice, iron sickles and glass beads.*

276: *These clay rollers are typical of the Iron Age in the Sakon Nakhon Basin, but their purpose is not known.*

276

(maximum height 8 cm)

range of red painted designs. There are swirling spirals, geometric designs, lizards, animal figures, and rarely, human outlines (Khemnak 1991, Rattanakun 1991). It is difficult to be precise on the context of many bronzes and pottery vessels ascribed to this Ban Chiang painted ware tradition, because the vast majority of available material results from indiscriminate looting, and virtually all known sites have been thus destroyed (Vallibhotama 1983). Properly excavated bronzes reveal a variety of ornamented bracelets, and a wire-like necklace made from the same high tin alloy as characterised the Ban Don Ta Phet bowls. Iron was used for implements rather than for ornaments, and the decorated clay rollers were often found, commonly in the graves of children. The remains of animals also recur. One child was interred under the skeleton of a dog, the skull of a cow lay beyond the head of an adult, but pig's jaw bones were preferred.

One characteristic of these Iron Age sites in the Sakon Nakhon Basin is that they remained relatively small. Setting aside the rich decorative element of the pottery vessels, the sprinkling of glass beads and the high tin bronze necklace, these

277

278

277: The open museum at Ban Chiang reveals the wealth of pottery vessels found with the dead.

278: This Ban Chiang painted vessel was uncovered during the 1975 excavations.

sites do not match the wealth seen at Ban Don Ta Phet, or contain the elaborate clay coffins of Ban Don Phlong or Non Muang Kao. Despite the glare of publicity which has illuminated Ban Chiang, dispassionate analysis reveals that it and its contemporary sites in the Sakon Nakhon Basin have a provincial feel when compared with the size and the energy evident in the centres to the south. The same may be said of the western margins of the Khorat Plateau in Loei Province, where Rutnin (1988) has shown that it was only during the Iron Age that the area came under continuous human settlement.

279

280

279-280: Clothing during the Iron Age was almost certainly an index of a person's status. Spindle whorls (above, width 3.5 cm) were used to create the fine filaments used to weave fabric, seen on an iron blade from Noen U-Loke burial 113, below.

The Iron Age of Thailand: Summary

The Iron Age was a period of rapid and fundamental change which set the stage for what was to follow. The evidence available at present suggests that Neolithic and Bronze Age communities were few and small. This probably reflects the late arrival of rice farmers into Thailand, and the time it took for settlement to extend over the riverine lowlands suited to agriculture. We know of no Neolithic site in the whole Mun Valley, and only a handful which belong to the Bronze Age. But the area is thickly studded with Iron Age settlements some of which reached a considerable size. Why should this be the case? A contributory factor may have been the impact of iron. We have emphasised above, the frequency with which individuals were interred with iron tools which could have been used in tilling the soil, clearing the forest, or harvesting rice. The potency of iron, with its more ready local availability, added weight and once steeled, its tensile strength, would have greatly assisted in expanding the area brought under cultivation, and made possible the forging of weapons for conflict.

But technical advances alone do not explain the social changes which we can detect in the Iron Age. While we have no unchallenged evidence, we feel that there are reasonable grounds for proposing the presence of social elites. By this, we mean a hereditary upper chiefly class which exercised authority over a political unit larger than a single settlement. The burials of Ongbah, the rich interments within the mortuary enclosure of Ban Don Ta Phet, and the social complexity we associate with sites up to 50 hectares containing clay-lined coffins and richly-endowed individuals, contrast sharply with what went before. In trying to understand how this change may have begun, we stress in particular the opening of Southeast Asia to exchange with distant states. There are many recent examples in human history, of the effect on simply-organized societies of exposure to members of a more complex state. New ideas are introduced, and new demands placed on local production. Exciting and exotic goods create fresh demands on the means to obtain and distribute them. Often, more powerful weaponry becomes available, allowing those fortunate to obtain them first to settle old scores. There is often a ferment to take advantage of the new opportunities, and an elite group will often emerge rapidly.

We know that marine shell, copper, tin and marble were exchanged between Bronze Age settlements, but with the opening of Southeast Asia to the products of India and beyond it to Rome, or in an easterly direction to the exotic goods of China, new opportunities were presented. And in taking them, there is a strong likelihood that emerging groups entered a competitive framework, first to gain access to exotic traders, and in the sequel, to outrank in power and status, other emerging chiefdoms. Hence, particularly in Central Thailand, the forging of iron weaponry.

The principle of social inequality which is axiomatic in the development of chiefdoms is a cornerstone of civilization. The first states of Thailand developed from the Iron Age chiefdoms, and we will now explore their origins and history.

282

281

283

281: Excavations at Noen U-Loke in 1998 revealed a 'mortuary landscape' of Iron Age burials and the post holes which may represent a structure over them.

282-283: Iron tools from Noen U-Loke have changed little over 2,000 years.

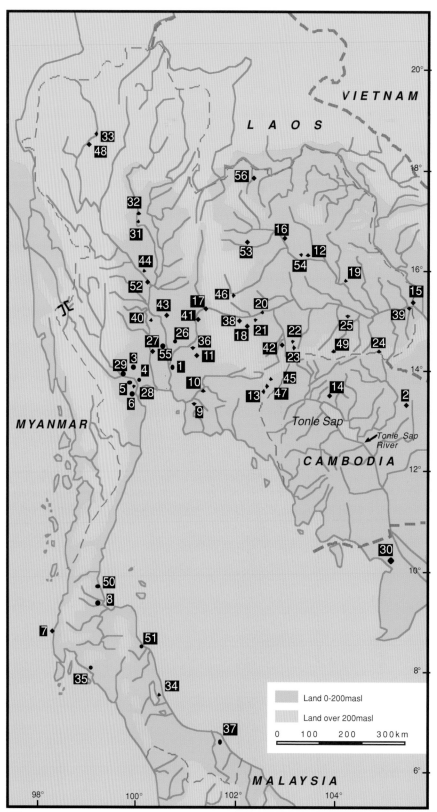

Land 0-200masl

Land over 200masl

0   100   200   300km

Tonle Sap

Tonle Sap
River

VIETNAM

LAOS

MYANMAR

CAMBODIA

MALAYSIA

20°

18°

16°

14°

12°

10°

8°

6°

98°   100°   102°   104°

284

Chapter Six
Early Civilizations of Thailand

All taxes must, at last, fall upon agriculture
(**E. Gibbon**, *The Decline and Fall of the Roman Empire*)

The rise of civilization is one of the most popular and intriguing topics for anyone interested in the past, for in studying ancient states, we can recognize many aspects of behaviour that recall our own experience. The visitor to Pompeii, for example, can walk down streets, enter homes and visit shops not dissimilar to those found in Italy today. The ruins of Sukhothai and Phimai are a poignant reminder of former magnificence, and the transience of all societies. What is it that sets a state apart from its predecessors? There is a nexus of key behavioural changes, centred on the structure of society. Until the rise of early states, most people found their place in the community and world around them by means of a kinship web. In a segmentary village, everyone knew their relationship with others, and social obligations between kin, immediate and more distant, cemented group solidarity. Kin relations and duties remained an essential bonding mechanism in a chiefdom. Even the humblest participants could identify their relationship to the chief through a shared ancestry. In a state, however, we encounter a new system of relationships co-existing with kinship, and this involves the idea of social class.

Social classes make up a hierarchy. There are elite individuals at the top of a social pyramid in which other classes descend in order of their status. The presence of a supreme ruler of a polity that now extends over a much larger area and incorporates more people than a chiefdom, requires organization calling on specialists in many fields. One entails administration:

285

284: The location of sites mentioned in chapter VI. 1. Ayutthaya, 2. Isanapura, 3. U-Thong, 4. Nakhon Pathom, 5. Pong Tuk, 6. Ku Bua, 7. Ko Kho Khao, 8. Laem Pho, 9. Muang Phra Rot, 10. Dong Si Mahosod; Sa Morakod, 11. Dong Lakon, 12. Muang Fa Daet, 13. Prasat Khao Noi, 14. Angkor, 15. Khan Thevada; Tham Pu Manai, 16. Sri Muang Aem, 17. Sri Thep, 18. Hin Khon, 19. Wat Ban Song Puay, 20. Phimai, 21. Phanom Wan, 22. Phanom Rung, 23. Muang Tam, 24. Phra Viharn, 25. Prasat Kamphaeng Yai, 26. Lopburi; Tha Kae, 27. Suphanburi, 28. Ratchaburi, 29. Prasat Muang Singh, 30. Oc Eo, 31. Sukhothai, 32. Sri Satchanalai, 33. Chiang Mai, 34. Satingpra, 35. Khuan Lukphad, 36. U-Taphao, 37. Yarang, 38. Muang Sema, 39. Pak Dom Noi, 40. Muang Dongkorn, 41. Sab Champa, 42. Tham Ped Thong, 43. Chansen, 44. Dong Maenang Muang, 45. Chong Srajaeng, 46. Muang Ham Hork, 47. Khao Rang, 48. Haripunchai, 49. Prasat Phum Phon, 50. Chaiya, 51. Nakhon Sri Thammarat, 52. Nakhon Sawan, 53. Non Muang, 54. Kantara-wichai, 55. Ban Khu Muang, (Inburi), 56. Phu Phrabat.

285: Vessel with fish, from Sri Satchanalai. (Photo: Michael Freeman)

286: Carved stone lintels provide us with a glimpse of the enthusiasm with which the Hindu religion was followed in Thailand a thousand years ago. This example from Prasat Ban Prasat in Buriram Province, shows Indra seated on the head of an elephant. The figure of Indra stands 10 cm in height.

taking central orders and implementing them in a region removed from the capital. Since the ruler and such bureaucrats do not involve themselves in primary production, they must be sustained through taxation. So administrators must ensure that a proportion of surplus production finds its way to the central authority. It is then the elites' task to deploy this surplus to their best advantage. While service to the overlord might involve free labour used, for example, to work on the construction of elite buildings, other surpluses must sustain the upper classes. A central court society must also be able to maintain itself through self defence, or expand its territory by force of arms. Warfare is therefore a widespread feature of state societies. We also find that the galvanizing power of a state religion bonds individuals together, and impressive religious structures are an outer manifestation of inner beliefs.

Many new aspects of human behaviour reflect this social transformation. We find that settlements often become much bigger not only in view of larger numbers of people, but also because of the many new forms of structure: temples, palaces, warehouses, military quarters. With so many people living in one urban centre, regulation through a legal system becomes necessary. As the amount and range of taxable goods grow, so it is necessary to record transactions, and we find the development of systems of writing. A state religion brings with it the need for specialised, full time priests. A ruling elite will normally have the resources to maintain specialist craft workshops, so we find a whole new range of elite goods employed as symbols of status. Communication helps maintain cohesion and the rule of law against marauders or usurpers, or on occasion truculent peasantry. So rapid means of transport often characterise early states. The straight Roman road, or the roads that radiated from Angkor to the provinces, were sinews which held together the body politic.

The Origin of Early Civilizations in Thailand

The roots of civilization in Thailand were firmly anchored in the prehistoric past, but were nourished by contact with exotic societies. We have seen that the Iron Age in Central and Northeast Thailand involved large settlements within which certain individuals were interred with impressive wealth. These were the people who encountered a new range of goods and ideas as Indian traders reached the shores of Southeast Asia. In the India of the day, Southeast Asia was described as the land of gold. Bringing with them trade goods – jewellery of agate, carnelian and glass, and keenly interested in acquiring spices, bronze vessels and gold, Indians provided local leaders with the opportunity of cornering a new source of valuables. They also provided an outlet for increased local production.

There was also an increasing Chinese interest in Southeast Asia. Already by 100 BC, the Han Chinese were expanding their empire to the south, not only seeking out sources of exotic trade goods, such as rhino horn and plumage, but also carving off new territories and imposing imperial rule. By the time they reached the uplands of northern Laos and the Truong Son Cordillera beyond the Mekong, the energy driving this expansion waned, and the Chinese called the latter range, "the Fortress of the Sky". While they never penetrated it in a colonial sense, trade goods and ideas filtered across the passes. The Historian Pan Gu, for example, writing in about 100 BC, noted that "Officials and volunteers put out to sea to buy lustrous pearls, glass, rare stones and strange products in exchange for gold and various silks". Chinese pilgrims during the 7th century also described a state called Duoluobodi, located west of a place called Isanapura and east of Sriksetra. The former was a large centre in Cambodia, while the latter refers to Myanmar. We are thus informed of a state probably located in Central Thailand.

Yet there is no rule which says that exchange with exotic traders leads automatically to civilization. There must be an existing level of social complexity, and a suitable social framework for the necessary changes to take place. In many respects, it seems highly likely that it was the local leaders who pursued an interesting opportunity to advance their status, and took it (Wolters 1979). For example, the religious ideas brought by Indians, which incorporated Buddhism and Hinduism, involved a system of beliefs wherein individuals could aspire to divine status. By dedicated worship of Siva, for example, an overlord could become godlike. The Sanskrit and Pali languages likewise provided an esoteric means of communication sure to command respect and awe among the uninitiated, just as the stone or brick temples that began to mushroom in emerging court centres were the foci of a new form of worship. In the case of Hinduism, this involved the erection of a large stone *linga*, or phallus, which represented the power of the state and its ruler, and which was the focus of new and powerful rituals. Impressive

287: The central figure on this lintel shows a deity riding on the head of Kirtimukha. It comes from Prasat Muang Tam, and dates to the 13th century. The deity is 13 cm in height.

288: This photograph of a large stone Buddha image in the Dvaravati style was taken by King Chulalongkorn. It is haused in Wat Na Phra Men, Ayutthaya. (RBC)

stone inscriptions were raised, extolling the virtues of the overlord now bearing an exotic Sanskrit name. Priests intoned prayers dedicated to a pantheon of gods protective of the state and its ruler. And at the base of the social pyramid, the peasantry in the rice fields was called upon to provide for this new order.

Archaeological confirmation that Central Thailand, the heart of the kingdom, was also home of the earliest state came with the discovery of two coins at Nakhon Pathom inscribed *"sridvaravatisvarapunya"* that reads "meritorious deeds of the King of Dvaravati" (Diffloth 1981). This is the Sanskrit name of Thailand's first civilization (Boisselier 1991), and the word means "which has gates". More recent discoveries have confirmed this name. A silver coin in private hands has a brimming jar motif and the same Sanskrit inscription. It is unique in Thailand for its use of the Kharosthi script (Kaewglai 1991). Another inscribed coin comes from Ban Khu Muang (Inburi).

Our knowledge of this civilization draws on excavations at a series of large moated sites located along the margins of the Central Plain. The sea level was higher then, and settlements were accessible by sea (Vanasin and Supajanya 1981). Most sites were also located so that a stream or river supplied water to an encircling moat. Large religious structures dominated within and beyond the moated perimeter. Excavations are needed to see whether or not there were domestic structures as well, for at present we do not know the size of the population. If evidence for intensive occupation is found, then we could call them urban centres. But if the population was thin, then perhaps elite or ceremonial centres would be a better description. In either case, there is no doubting that they were the base of overlords. At U-Thong, for example, a mid 7th century AD copper inscription records that "Sri Harsavarman, grandson of Isanavarman, having expanded the sphere of his glory, obtained the Lion Throne through regular succession". It then recounts gifts of a jewelled litter, a parasol and musical instruments to the *linga* Amratakesvara.

This is a fascinating and revealing document, because it shows how the overlords had adopted Sanskrit names. *Varman* means protector or shield, while Isana refers to the god Siva. The gift of a parasol to the *linga* suggests the worship of Siva, the parasol being an emblem of high status individuals.

Harsavarman stressed in his inscription that he was descended from royalty and it was his ancestry that gave him the right to the throne. Two remarkable stone objects confirm this evidence for royal status. Their surfaces are decorated with symbols of royalty, including fly-whisks, parasols, elephant goads and conch shells. Lyons (1979) has suggested that they were used in investiture ceremonies.

Dvaravati coinage confirms the importance of royalty. The minting of silver coins appears to have been a royal prerogative, and counterfeiting was punished by the removal of the offender's arm. The symbolism on Dvaravati coins derives from Indian precedents of the 1st-4th centuries AD, and includes the conch, the *srivatsa* motif, and the rising sun. The conch shell symbolises water, and therefore fertility and was used in royal lustration ceremonies. *Srivatsa* derives from *Sri,* the mother goddess representing fertility and kingship. At initiation ceremonies, the essence of *sri* was supposed to enter the king. The rising sun motif reflects how the royal line originated with the solar dynasty (Gutman 1978).

U-Thong must have been an impressive site at that period. The moats enclose an area 1,690 by 840 metres in extent, and excavations have uncovered the foundations of a series of Buddhist monuments, including an ordination hall and brick *stupas* (Boisselier 1968). These buildings were ornamented with stucco mythical animals, such as the *naga* snake and the *makara* marine monster, along with lions. Nakhon Pathom was even larger, covering an area of 3,700 by 2,000 metres dominated in the centre by the Phra Pathom *Caitya.* This was an impressive structure which was modified several times during the life of the centre. It incorporated access steps flanked by lion statues while wall niches above contained statues of the Buddha (Dupont 1959).

Indrawooth (1984) has expanded our knowledge of this site by excavating in the occupation area. She has identified many artefacts which recall prehistoric activities: there are tin and bronze ornaments, iron spears and spindle whorls. The occupation layer is relatively shallow at 40 cm, and settlement appears to have taken place in the 8th and 9th centuries. The site was probably abandoned when the river moved its course.

The foundations for Buddhist religious monuments were recognized early at the site of Pong Tuk, located northwest of Nakhon Pathom and beyond the Mae Khlong River. Here, the

289: Plaque from Chedi Chunla Pathon, Nakhon Pathom. Eighth century. Bronze. Bangkok National Museum.

remains of a Buddha statue in bronze dated later than about 550 AD was found, along with the remains of buildings which were probably a *stupa* and a *vihara* or meeting house. A Byzantine lamp of a style popular during the 5th and 6th centuries was also found in the vicinity of this site (Brown and MacDonnell 1989, Krairiksh 1990).

Ku Bua is a moated site 200 by 800 metres in extent, found in Ratchaburi Province and excavated in 1961 (Rattanakun 1992). The finds were soon to be cited as evidence for Thailand's participation in an exchange network which included large parts of the Old World on the basis of a series of stucco figures (Lyons 1965). One group depicts Semitic traders with distinctive high-peaked hats. This should be considered with the abundant evidence for exchange goods in Dvaravati sites and contemporary settlements, particularly in peninsula Thailand. The stuccos from Ku Bua also illuminate social relations. There are royal figures and bound prisoners being kicked by their guard. We can also admire a group of musicians, one of whom is playing a stringed instrument. The women have elaborate hairstyles, large ear ornaments and elegant clothing which bring home to us the sophistication of court life in these centres. Fragments of a wheel of the law at Wat Khlong Suwan Kiri, together with numerous representations of the Buddha, emphasise the early importance of Buddhism. Indeed there are 11 religious structures inside the moats, and 33 beyond.

This is matched at Lopburi, with the discovery of a *Thammachakra*, or wheel of the law, representing that set in motion by the Buddha himself during a sermon in the Benares deer park. An inscription in Sanskrit dating to the 8th or 9th century from the base of a statue of the Buddha, names a certain Arshva, the Director of the Muang Tankura, and son of the King of Sampuka. A second inscription found in 1981 at Ban Bhramatin is in Pali, and mentions the doctrine of Buddhism. While the modern town of Lopburi makes it difficult to establish the extent of the Dvaravati centre, the Wat Nakhon Kosa, excavated in 1987, revealed a typical *stupa* and Dvaravati style stucco ornamentation. The excavators also recovered four votive tablets in typical Dvaravati style depicting the Buddha (Jermsawatdi and Charuphananon 1989).

The Bang Pakong Valley also incorporates a number of large Dvaravati centres. Muang Phra Rot measures 1,350 by 700 metres, and has furnished a stone relief of the Buddha together with Brahma and Indra. Excavations by Sulaksananont (1987)

revealed ceramics belonging to the Dvaravati tradition, dating
from the 6th to the 11th centuries, followed by dominance of
Khmer wares. Dvaravati style potsherds found during
excavations are also known from a number of smaller
settlements within a 10 km radius of the site, suggesting that it
was a focus for dependent communities in its orbit.

Dong Si Mahosod is similar in size and intensive
investigations by Pisnupong (1992) have identified four phases
of occupation. The earliest is dated to the late prehistoric
through to the 6th century AD, and includes in the ceramics
recovered, some parallels with Iron Age pottery in the upper
Mun Valley. There are also items, such as the design of the
sivalinga which strongly recall those from the Funan polity
located above the Mekong and Bassac deltas. Just beyond the
southwest corner of the moated site, there lies a water tank cut
into the laterite which is surrounded by an extraordinary
decorated laterite wall. The motifs include *makaras,* lions and a
frieze of elephants which have been dated stylistically to the 5th
or 6th centuries AD (Pisnupong 1993b).

The sequence then proceeds smoothly into phase 2, which
belongs to the Dvaravati culture of the 6th to 8th centuries.
During the third phase, which is represented by thick layers in
the stratigraphic build up, there is evidence for much exchange,
including imported Chinese ceramics of the Tang (618-906 AD)
and Song (960-1279 AD) dynasties. It was during the fourth
and last phase, however, that there appears to have been strong
Khmer influence, if not intrusive settlement. Monument 11, a
rectangular building measuring 7 by 15 metres, included a cache
of inscribed bronzes. The Khmer language inscription on the
base of a bronze mirror records that Jayavarman VII donated
this object to a hospital at Sri Vatsapura (Avatayapura). A bronze
candle holder also has a Khmer inscription which notes that
Jayavarman VII gave the object to the hospital at Sangvok. A
bronze bowl in the same cache mentioned the name
Virendradhipativarman (Pisnupong 1992). The uncovering of
brick foundations of many religious monuments inside and
outside the moated enclosure, evidence for extensive water
control and wealth of exchange goods recovered, not to mention
the long sequence identified, make this one of the most
significant investigations into a Dvaravati site.

Sra Morakod lies only three kilometres southeast of Dong
Si Mahosod (Pisnupong 1991). It is so close that it might be
part of the same complex. There are two phases: in the first, the

*290: This charming stucco from Ku Bua
gives us an impression of the sophistication
of a Dvaravati court centre.*

ceramics match those from many Dvaravati sites of Central Thailand dating to the 6th-11th centuries. There are also Persian and Chinese Tang trade wares, both dated in the 9th-10 centuries.

The second phase (11-13th centuries) includes Song Dynasty (960-1279 AD) trade wares. This site is well known for the recovery of two Buddha footprints which comprise the focal point of an impressive ceremonial complex. In the middle of each footprint, there is a wheel of the law with a diameter of just over a metre. A hole cut in the centre, 40 cm across and 1.5 m deep, is associated with further cut lines in the form of a swastika, which could have been the base for a parasol over the complex. Pisnupong suggests that this monument is earlier than the 9th century, but it also has two phases: a brick wall covers part of it, as if to afford shelter. As an indication of the wealth attracted to the worship of the Buddha at this sacred centre, Pisnupong recovered a copper box at the base of a column in monument 11, containing three gold finger rings and gold sheet.

Dong Lakhon is a further moated site, located between the Bang Pakong and Chao Phraya catchments in Nakhon Nayok Province. Excavations there by Sukawasana (1996) have shown that there was continuity of occupation from the late prehistoric Iron Age into the period of Dvaravati. Among the exotic items, she has described Chinese porcelain, Persian glass and Indian beads.

Further to the north, at Sri Thep, there is another large moated site which, to judge from the two moats, was considerably enlarged during the historic occupation until it

291: Sri Thep seen from the air, showing clearly the earlier moated area and the later extension. (Courtesy Wichai Tankittikorn)

covered 4.7 km². It was discovered by H.R.H. Prince Damrong in 1904, and later research has shown that the historic occupation covers the 6th until the 13th centuries (Tankittikorn 1991). During the earlier part of this sequence, there is clear evidence for Hinduism, linked with a fragmentary Sanskrit inscription. A second inscription, also in Sanskrit and dated stylistically in the 7th century, reads "In the year (missing), a king who is nephew of the great king, who is the son of Pruthiveenadravarman, and who is as great as Bhavavarman, who has renowned moral principles, who is powerful and the terror of his enemies, erects this inscription on the occasion of his ascending to the throne" (Weeraprajak 1986a). It would seem that asserting the royal genealogy, proclaiming high moral principles and success in war were desirable ingredients for kingship.

The Khao Klang Nai monument, built in the 6th to 7th centuries and located in the centre of the city, is particularly interesting, as it bears stucco ornamentation, including a row of crouching dwarves each with large earrings and some with lion's or cow's heads. These recall similar representations at monument 18, Wat Khlong Suwan Kiri, at Ku Bua. A wheel of the law was also found within the moats, bronze Buddha images and votive tablets. Khao Klang Nork, located outside the moats, probably dates to the 8th and 9th centuries. It indicates the adoption of Mahayana Buddhism. From the mid 10th century, the art style of the Baphuon and later Khmer styles manifest themselves. Prang Song Phi Nong is a large brick temple complex located in the centre of the older moated enclosure, and is dated to this period. Recent excavations have unearthed a lintel depicting Siva

292: Khao Klang Nai monument, built in the 6th to 7th centuries and located in the centre of Sri Thep incorporates a row of crouching dwarves each with large earrings and some with lion's or cow's heads. (Courtesy Wichai Tankittikorn)

Inscriptions

Inscriptions are a vital source of historic information in Thailand. Most are inscribed in stone, there is a famous copper inscription from U-Thong, while inscribed coins are widespread in Central Thailand. The earliest evidence for writing, however, comes from seals and rings found in Southern Thailand and Oc Eo in Vietnam, where the Indian *Brahmi* script, stylistically dated from the 2nd-5th centuries AD, was employed (De Casparis 1979). Most stone inscriptions were put in place to record an event, such as the foundation of a temple, or a meritorious gift by an overlord. Until the late 8th century, most of these inscriptions employed the *Pallava* script of southern India. Some record the names of individual leaders, and even the date of the event being celebrated. The language employed is of great interest. In Thailand, it was often Pali, and sometimes Sanskrit. Both are Indo-European languages introduced into Southeast Asia together with the Buddhist and Hindu religions. The Thai landscape today is dotted with Sanskrit place names. Chaiyaphum means "land of victory", Suwannaphum is "land of gold", Nakhon Sawan is "holy heavenly city". But some inscriptions also contain passages in local languages and in Thailand, most are in Mon, and a few are in Khmer. The former concentrate in Central Thailand, and the latter are found more often in the Mun Valley. These passages are vital clues on the languages spoken at the dawn of Thai history. Later, we find the first inscriptions in Thai and these, naturally, appear first in the region of Sukhothai before spreading to the south.

The most complete reference on Thai inscriptions is Weeraprajak (1986a and b). See also Jacques (1989) for an example of historic detective work based on a study of inscriptions and De Casparis (1979) for a review of the scripts employed.

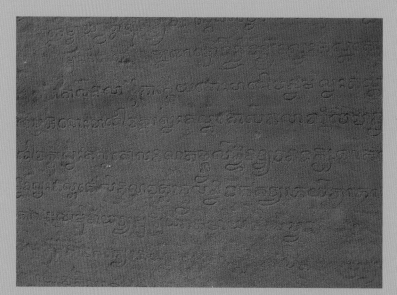

293: Inscriptions are a vital source of information on the history of early kingdoms in Southeast Asia. This sandstone inscription from Phimai is a Khmer text, which describes the career of Jayavarman VI.

and his wife on Nandin. Prang Sri Thep lies just to the east, and is part of the same complex. It is a large brick temple lying on a laterite base. Excavations found a lintel dating to the 11th and 12th centuries, and Hindu statues of the same date. There is also evidence for reconstruction during the 13th century. It is apparent that the city had a long life originating in the Iron Age, and that it was the seat of a royal line.

We have seen that Iron Age settlement preceded the establishment of U-Taphao as a major Dvaravati centre. This site was ringed by a moat and a rampart standing up to 10 metres high. In 1963, Manit Vallibhotama undertook a survey of this region, and found numerous Dvaravati ceramics and silver coins of the period, stamped with conch shell, fish and the *srivatsa* motif. Wilaikaeo (1991a, b) has undertaken two excavations, one within the moated area and the other on the site of a wheel of the law 1.8 km beyond the ramparts. A particular feature of the former was the abundant evidence for local iron smelting, a reflection perhaps of the availability of good quality ore which sustained an iron industry until recently. The circular foundation for the wheel of the law found beyond the confines of the site includes a Pali inscription in the Pallava script recording Buddhist doctrine.

Ban Khu Muang in Amphoe Inburi, Singburi Province, has been the focus of three seasons of excavations undertaken by Silpakon University (Silpakon University 1980). It is a large settlement covering an area of 650 by 750 metres, currently a kilometre west of the Chao Phraya River. Many brick temple foundations cluster round the moated area. In a stratigraphic sequence up to 4 metres in depth, four phases were identified. The first contains jewellery of tin and bronze, as well as pottery which recalls that of Oc Eo in southern Vietnam. This implies a date in the vicinity of 300-550 AD. The second and third phases belong to early and late Dvaravati, and include religious structures, together with material culture which includes stamp-decorated pottery, spindle whorls, iron knives and spears, and clay anvils. An infant burial in a jar represents a rare Dvaravati inhumation burial. Finally, the site was occupied during the period of Sukhothai, for Ming Dynasty and Khmer ceramics were found.

Sab Champa is a moated settlement which lies up the Pasak Valley from U-Taphao. It was first investigated in 1971 by Maleipan (1979), who noted that it covers an area of 834 by

294: At Muang Fa Daet there are several Dvaravati-style monuments.

700 metres, and is girt by a rampart wall 10 metres high and a moat cut into the limestone substrate. Brick temple foundations and the remains of religious statuary indicate a 6th to 8th century occupation. Five fragmentary inscriptions in both Pali and Sanskrit have been recovered, confirming the practice of Buddhism (Weeraprajak 1986a, Bhumadhon n.d.).

Muang Dongkorn has not been excavated, but this large moated Dvaravati site, measuring 755 by 555 metres, holds much promise. There are brick temple foundations inside and beyond the moats, including Khok Prasat, a large *stupa*. The discovery of three polished stone adzes also hints at a prehistoric period prior to the Dvaravati establishment by the 7th century. Among the surface finds, Bhumadhon (1987) has reported a fragment of a stone ritual tray similar to that from Nakhon Pathom, a stone relief of the Buddha with a wheel of the law and a parasol, and bivalve stone moulds for casting ear and finger rings. The most interesting of all the surface finds, however, are the 11 coins bearing the conch, *srivatsa,* rising sun and cow with calf motifs. Six also bear inscriptions referring to the King of Dvaravati, of which one also mentions the royal consort. Two coins have also come from the excavations at Tha Kae, one having an elephant with a frond in its trunk, the other a throne (Hanwong 1985).

The development of unusually large settlements which provide evidence for Indian-inspired religions was not restricted to the Central Plains. One of the most remarkable of sites on the Khorat Plateau is located in Kalasin Province, a few kilometres from the junction of the Chi and Pao rivers. Muang Fa Daet incorporates a series of possible moats which Indrawooth *et al.* (1991) have interpreted as representing successive stages of enlargement. There is a large rectangular enclosure to the northeast of the site which might have been a *baray* or reservoir. M.C. Subhadradis Diskul (1956) has published a description of the many Buddhist *sema* stones which form such a striking feature of this site, one of which showed a city wall with defenders. The sequence of events was then enigmatic due to the lack of excavations, but in 1968, the Fine Arts Department uncovered the foundations of 14 brick or laterite monuments including *stupas* and *viharas.* Associated stucco ornaments suggested strong stylistic affinities with Dvaravati sites in Central Thailand (FAD 1968).

In 1991, Indrawooth directed excavations aimed at identifying the nature of the occupation rather than the style of the monuments (Indrawooth *et al.* 1991, Indrawooth 1994). By opening a series of squares four by four metres in extent, she was able to define the presence of a pottery kiln, suggesting industrial activity. This should be considered in conjunction with the presence on the surface of iron slag which indicates smelting as well. Furthermore, the recovery of inhumation burials revealed that the site was occupied from at least the prehistoric Iron Age. Some of the graves included red on buff pottery, while later burials, stratified over the Iron Age material, incorporated iron artefacts, as well as bronze, carnelian and agate jewellery. One small test square also contained lidded jar burials. Confirmation of occupation between the 7th and 11th centuries AD, a period corresponding in part to the Dvaravati sites in Central Thailand, is seen in the style of pottery as well as in the *sema* stones and many Buddhist votive tablets. Muang Fa Daet is clearly a site of great significance due to the way in which it bridges the prehistoric and Dvaravati contexts.

A few kilometres to the southwest lies a further moated settlement, Kantarawichai. Excavations in 1972 in the foundations of a religious structure, probably a Buddhist ordination hall, uncovered a ceramic vessel containing 66 decorated silver plaques each about 10 by 5 cm. In his description of this unique find, H.S.H. Prince Subhadradis Diskul (1979) has noted the presence, in repoussé style, of images of the Buddha, wheels of the law and *stupa* structures. The presence too of a royal figure wearing a profusion of ornaments, including a jewelled necklace and earrings informs us on the social hierarchy consistent with such large settlements. The particularly imaginative might also identify a belt on this figure, similar to those found with burial 14 and 69 at Iron Age Noen U-Loke to the south.

New techniques have also been deployed recently to expand our knowledge of similar sites in the Northeast. The analysis of Landsat images by Punee Wara-Aswapati, for example, has led to the recognition of the site of Muang Ham Hork in Chaiyaphum Province (Wara-Aswapati 1997). The extent of Dvavarati art and, presumably, adoption of Buddhism in the northeast has recently been extended to include the *sema* stones and ceramics at Non Muang, and the extraordinary series of monuments at Phu Phrabat. In the latter area, we find that an unusual stone stack was ringed by *sema* stones. Stone surfaces were also carved into the form of standing and sitting Buddha images, as, for example, at Tham Phra. Subsequently, some of the Buddha images were converted into Hindu gods wearing Khmer style garments. The former date on stylistic grounds to the 9th century, the latter from the 10th-13th centuries (Wichakana 1994).

Northern Thailand

We have seen at Ban Wang Hi, that there was a vigorous Iron Age presence in northern Thailand, so it comes as no surprise that the Lamphun Chronicles refer to the foundation of a local polity when the Rishi Warsuthep invited a Princess from Lopburi to rule there within the period of the 7th–9th centuries. The surviving monuments at Lamphun, ancient Haripunchai, as well as the available inscriptions in Mon, are considerably later. But this does not rule out an earlier foundation (Prapathong 1986, Phommanodch 1991b). This issue has recently been tested through excavations in front of the Lamphun city hall (Rungrugee *et al.* n.d.). He found clear evidence for Dvaravati settlement in the lowest layer, including typical pottery forms paralleled at Ban Khu Muang (Amphoe Inburi), querns, pestles, clay lamps and red-slipped human figurines. Song Dynasty ceramics date this occupation to the 10th–12th centuries. Overlying it is a further layer containing ceramics from the Samkamphaeng kilns dated by the excavator to the 13th century.

A further series of excavations have refined our knowledge of the occupation of Lamphun (Indrawooth *et al.* 1994). Initial settlement at the City Hall and Wat Prathat Haripunchai sites involved a ceramic assemblage with strong parallels in the Dvaravati sites to the south, associated with a radiocarbon date of 570-760 AD. This Dvaravati relationship continued into the second phase, seen at Wat Phrathat Haripunchai and Wat Sanghkaram, but now with clear evidence for cultural contacts with Myanmar in the 10th-11th centuries. With the third phase, we also encounter Khmer Bayon Period and Chinese Song Dynasty influence in the pottery vessels found, associated with a radiocarbon date in the 13th century AD.

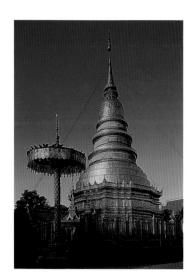

295: Wat Phra That Haripunchai, Lamphun. (Photo: Michael Freeman)

Southern Thailand

The establishment of an international exchange network linking Rome and India with China during the early centuries AD had a profound impact in Southern Thailand. This is largely due to its strategic location linking the Andaman Sea with the Gulf of Thailand and beyond to the South China Sea. As an alternative to the Melaka Strait, it was possible to trans-ship trade goods across the narrow Kra Isthmus or, not far to the south, between Songhkla and Trang.

Already by the 1st to the 5th centuries AD, Khao Sam Kaeo became established as a manufacturing centre for glass beads, as well as one in which etched carnelian and onyx beads were produced. This site has also provided undoubted evidence for contact with India in the form of items inscribed in the *Brahmi* script. Of even further significance is the recovery from this area, of two bronze Dong Son drums recalling those found at Ongbah to the north. The smaller has a diameter of 15.6 cm, the larger is almost 69 cm in diameter (Thepchai 1988). Both are decorated with birds and the rayed sun, and their presence in Peninsular Thailand emphasises its nodal position in maritime exchange, for the distribution of these drums is found across island Southeast Asia as far as New Guinea.

One of the earliest excavations in Thailand was undertaken at Ko Kho Khao by Crown Prince Vajiravudh in 1909. This site lies on an island off the Takuapa River, and when taken in conjunction with the site of Laem Pho on the opposite side of the isthmus, provides compelling evidence for the intensity of the entrepot trade which came to be established by the 9th century AD. As Bronson and Charoenwongsa have stressed, an extraordinary variety of Middle Eastern and Chinese ceramics have been recovered, the latter originating from ten different sources (Ho *et al.* 1990, Bronson 1996). This trade has left more Tang Dynasty pottery than any other site outside China. Bronson (1996) suggest that, while probably in the hands of locals, a Tamil inscription discovered in 1902 near Takuapa records the construction of a reservoir by an association of Indian merchants, and how it had Indian guards. Bronson and Charoenwongsa have identified this structure, which measures 800 by 200 metres, at Ko Kho Khao. Laem Pho has been excavated by Thepchai and a team led by Bronson and Charoenwongsa (Thepchai 1983, 1988, 1989, Bronson 1996), and in both cases, the research emphasises the wealth of 9th century Chinese imported ceramics.

296: The Bodhisattva Lokesvara dates to the Srivijaya period.

297: Wat Phra Boromathat, Nakhon Sri Thammarat. (Photo: Muang Boran)

Khuan Lukpad is a second site in which local production of glass and stone jewellery was established. We find evidence for quartz, chalcedony and carnelian ornaments being transformed into beads. Not only are bead blanks found, but also the remains of the dropping wax which was used to affix them to a firm surface during the manufacturing process. Lead ingots have been found, and as Bronson (1990) has noted, tin was also locally smelted and cast into ingots or converted to a range of ornaments. The geographical scale of the trade links of which this site was part, is to be seen in the carnelian seals bearing Greek and Roman motifs. There is Perseus, and the goddess Tyche, as well as inscriptions in the *Pallava* script dating between the 6th and 9th centuries. One such text reads "permission granted; those who dare can pass through", suggesting that trade may have involved some form of permit (Weeraprajak 1985).

Glass, however, seems to have been the principal focus of local manufacturing. Excavations by Veraprasert in 1983 produced an extraordinary range of colours and forms of glass bead have been found, as well as the bulk glass used in their formation (Veraprasert 1992). Bronson (1990) has outlined a range of possibilities to account for this intensity of industrial activity. Was it involved in import substitution, that is the local manufacture of desirable exotic imports? Was there an enclave of Indian entrepreneurs along the lines of those mentioned in the Takuapa inscription? Or could there have been a local organizational hierarchy which took advantage of the location facing the Andaman Sea and ultimately India, which imported bulk glass for the local industry? This evidence for early exchange contact with India comprises the first of four periods proposed by Krairiksh (1980) for southern Thailand, periods based principally on art history.

The social context within which international exchange and local specialised workshops developed, has been examined by Stargardt (1983) in her excavations of the centre of Satingpra. It is evident from Chinese texts that Southeast Asia during the first millennium AD was an important stepping stone in a southern "Silk Route", but identifying the trading centres on the ground is difficult short of the recovery of inscriptions. At Satingpra, however, Stargardt has focussed her research on a moated centre 1,600 by 900 metres in extent, within which lies a central citadel with brick walls 3 metres thick, and three substantial water tanks. Her excavations in the area of the citadel reached the underlying natural sand at a depth of 1.6 metres, and revealed four cultural phases. The earliest, which probably dates between 300 BC to 200 AD, was characterised by exotic glass and onyx jewellery already seen at the sites further to the north. From the 6th century AD, Stargardt argues, the site took on the form of an urban centre linked with the development of impressive hydraulic works, including canals and storage tanks which would have facilitated exchange and the cultivation of rice on the extensive alluvial soils to the north of the settlement. The bricks employed in the construction of the religious monuments were liberally tempered with rice chaff. One temple built in the 6th century was dedicated to Visnu, as was a second constructed two centuries later. Among the pottery are forms with clear parallels at the contemporary port of Oc Eo, 600 km to the northeast, and Isanapura, seat of one of the leading overlords of Zhenla in Cambodia. Two radiocarbon dates in the 9th century AD are linked with evidence for a burning phase, possibly involving a raid or warfare, after which the style of the artefacts suggest the establishment of links with the Srivijayan kingdom centred on the island of Sumatra to the south.

During the period of Srivijayan ascendancy (7th-13th centuries), which corresponds to Krairiksh's third period, southern Thailand continued to prosper due, at least in part, to its control of trans-isthmian exchange routes. Chaiya was one of the major centres and at the Phra Boromathat and Wat Kaew there, one can appreciate the splendour and energy of this polity. Again, the Phra Boromathat at Nakhon Sri Thammarat identifies this site as a second centre (Wongthes 1988). Yarang was also occupied during this period of Srivijaya. It is situated in the valley of the Pattani River, and from its position it dominates the coastal plain to the north. The moated settlement has attracted much interest over the years (Youkongdee and Phantukovid 1992), and there are numerous brick temple foundations, exposed during excavations in 1989. Sawanglerdrit and Welch in 1986, used an augur to recover evidence for the sequence, and identified three phases of occupation. The Early Period saw a small moated settlement. The Middle Period involved expansion into a bigger settlement, the construction of a brick wall and of religious monuments beyond the walled area. This period dates from the 8th to the 10th centuries AD, and saw much evidence for widespread trade. Finally, during the 14th to the 18th centuries, forts were constructed in each corner of the main site.

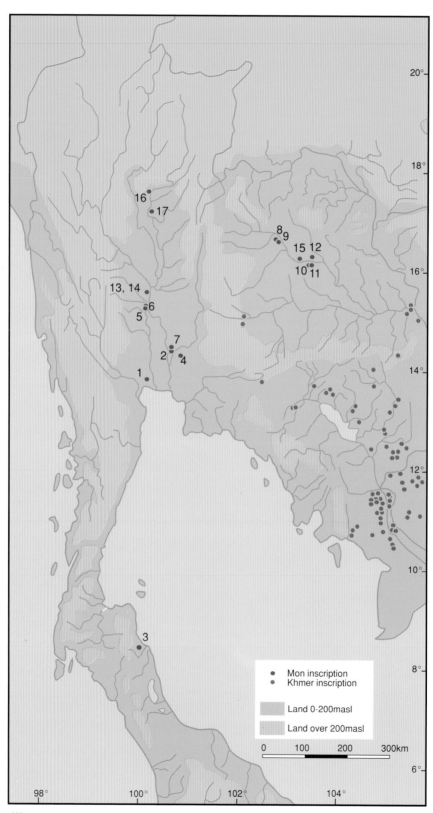

Mon inscription
Khmer inscription

Land 0-200masl
Land over 200masl

0   100   200   300km

Zhenla and Angkor

In order to appreciate the sequence of events in Central and Northeast Thailand from about 550 AD onwards, it is necessary to describe briefly, certain developments in Cambodia. In many respects, the present boundary between Thailand and Cambodia along the Dang Raek Range had no meaning in prehistory or during the period of early civilizations. It is not high, and there are many crossing points. Even today there are many Khmer-speaking citizens of Thailand in the border provinces and relatives or traders regularly cross the border. When they do so, they have before them the broad and flat expanse of Northwest Cambodia, which gives way to the Tonle Sap, the Great Lake. The Tonle Sap River drains the lake, linking its waters with the Mekong River. This region, from the Mekong up to the Great Lake, saw the development of a series of small states which culminated, in the early 9th Century, with the energetic conquests of Jayavarman II, the overlord who more than any other laid the foundations for the empire of Angkor. These developments involved the communities of the Mun Valley and ultimately, much of Thailand.

The clearest picture of the states which preceded Jayavarman's reforms can be gained by considering the available inscriptions in conjunction with the remains of Isanapura, modern Sambor Prei Kuk. This centre was the seat of a powerful overlord, Isanavarman, who ruled in the 620s AD. His capital was girt by a double wall measuring 2 by 2 km, and within, there are three walled precincts each containing a series of brick temples round a main central sanctuary. The outer wall of one precinct enclosed an area of 300 by 270 metres (Parmentier 1927). Inscriptions associated with these structures leave us in no doubt that Isanavarman was responsible for their construction, nor that they were dedicated to the worship of Siva, the god after whom this overlord was named. Beyond the outer wall, there is a *baray,* and the location of this site in the valley of the Stung Sen, above the level of wet season flooding, would have been favourable for rice cultivation (van Liere 1980).

Isanavarman was one of a handful of overlords whose names have survived. He was probably the son of Mahendravarman, who was the brother of Bhavavarman. Jayavarman 1, who ruled at least in 657, claimed descent from this line. According to the available inscriptions, this period saw much friction between rival overlords. But we can also obtain

299

298: The distribution of inscriptions in Mon and Khmer. 1. Nakhon Pathom, 2. Ban Sao, Lopburi, 3. Nakhon Sri Thammarat, 4. Amphoe Phra Buddhabhat, Saraburi, 5-6. Amphoe Swang Arom, Lopburi, 7. Amphoe Muang, Lopburi, 8-9. Amphoe Chumphae, Khon Kaen, 10-11. Amphoe Nadune, Mahasarakham, 12. Muang Fa Daet, 13-14. Amphoe Muang, Nakhon Sawan, 15. Kumalasai, Kalasin, 16. Amphoe Sanpatong, Chiang Mai, 17. Lamphun.

299: This drawing of a temple at Isanapura, which first appeared in 1927, illustrates the sort of brick structure the foundations of which have been found at Phimai, Phanom Wan and Phanom Rung. (Courtesy Ecole Française d'Extrême Orient)

glimpses from the inscriptions of other aspects of daily life, of rice field boundaries, water storage facilities, paths, orchards and temples (Jacob 1979). Doubtless, the seasonal agricultural round, which saw surplus production going to support the central court, was punctuated with military campaigns in which rival overlords sought regional hegemony.

As has been shown by H.S.H. Prince Subhadradis Diskul (1990a), sites belonging to this period are also found in Thailand. An inscription at Khao Rang is dated to 639 AD, and mentions a list of slaves who were given to the temple. Altogether, there were 32 slaves, both adults and children, and gardeners for the temple, and their duties included both work in the temple and the orchards. One comprised 105 betel nut trees and 20 coconut trees and a second orchard near the temple comprised 123 betel nut and 120 coconut trees.

Excavations by Pisnupong at Prasat Khao Noi have unearthed a row of three temples which incorporate exquisite lintels. These are dated stylistically to the 7th century AD and incorporate a scene popular in eastern Thailand at this period, a *makara* or sea monster associated with a swan. Most intriguingly, an inhumation burial behind temple 1 included as

300: This row of three brick temples from Prasat Khao Noi date, according to the style of the lintels, to the 7th century AD. (Photo: Michael Freeman)

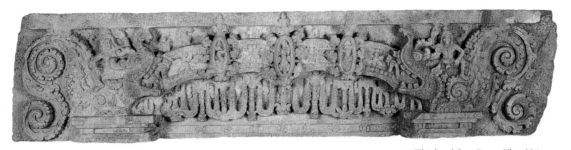

301: This lintel from Prasat Khao Noi shows the makara, *or sea monster, at each end, and is typically found at the Cambodian site of Isanapura. (Photo: Michael Freeman)*

grave goods, 13 burnished and incised vessels which might well indicate late prehistoric occupation of this site prior to temple construction (Pisnupong and Thawiphon 1989).

Other finds, including an inscription from this site dated to 637 AD in Sanskrit and Khmer notes: "Let Visnu win, so that he can protect and keep the country completely . . . ." Here, the name of the king is sadly missing, but there remains the likelihood that a highly ranked person with Hindu leanings ruled here. The Khmer text provides the name of the highly ranked officer, Jyesthapura, and also the names of a number of officials and slaves (Kaewglai and Saenanon 1990). Jacques (1989) has drawn attention to an inscription from Prachinburi Province which mentions a ruler Sivadatta, son of Isanavarman who ruled over the state of Jyesthapura as vassal of his father. In Laos, just over the Mekong from Thailand, lies the large, early Zhenla period site of Wat Phu. Its very presence there emphasises the significance of the lower Mun Valley in the transition to state societies (Musigakama 1993).

Chinese writings refer to a land and a water Zhenla as if they were two separate states. In her consideration of Northeast Thailand at this period, Saraya (1992a) has proposed that the former lay on the Khorat Plateau and the latter, south of the Daeng Raek Range in Cambodia. It is, however, always difficult to take Chinese records at face value, and it is possible that there were many small and transient polities. It is beyond doubt that the late prehistoric societies of Cambodia and the Mun Valley shared a common culture, and therefore it is not surprising to find inscriptions and early temple complexes of Zhenla in both regions.

The incorporation of such regional polities under central authority began to be realised in the early ninth century by Jayavarman II. Through a series of military victories, he turned potential rival polities into provinces under central rule, gave the exclusive right of consecrating a new ruler to the successive

302: This splendidly vigorous scene on a lintel from Surin shows Visnu riding on Garuda, king of the birds. Visnu's head is 5 cm in height.

members of one high ranking family, and established a series of central capitals in the region between the Tonle Sap and Kulen Hills to the north. These reforms were followed by a long succession of overlords one of whom, Yasovarman 1st (889-910), established Angkor as his capital.

The communities of the Mun Valley were active participants in all these developments. Several inscriptions describe the military exploits of Mahendravarman during the early years of the 7th century. Three come from the vicinity of the strategic confluence between the Mun and Mekong rivers. The Khan Thevada stela records both the illustrious ancestry of Mahendravarman and boasts of a victory. The language in these inscriptions is most revealing. After recounting his royal credentials, he asserts that "his name was renowned for good morals since he was young, and that he received his name in a royal lustration ceremony". When he conquered this land, he raised a *sivalinga* on the mountain to symbolise his victory. The inscription from the cave of Tham Pu Manai described the raising of a stone statue of a bull, symbol of Siva, while a foundation for another inscription from Pak Dom Noi belongs to the same style and could also belong to this episode (Weeraprajak 1986a, Prishanchit 1992). But these ventures were not confined to the Mun Valley. At Tham Ped Thong in Buriram, we pick up the trail of Mahendravarman, and even as far north as Sri Muang Aem, about 40 km north of Khon Kaen, we encounter epigraphic evidence for the construction of a monument to celebrate a victory by this overlord (Jacques 1989). To the south, in Prachinburi at Chong Srajaeng, an inscription in Sanskrit describes Mahendravarman as being responsible for the construction of a water tank.

There is also a concentration of inscriptions carved sometimes in Mon or Khmer, and on occasion with Sanskrit texts, in Nakhon Ratchasima and Chaiyaphum Provinces which stylistically belong in the 7th to the 9th centuries. These must be considered in relation to the recent excavations at Muang Sema (Hanwong 1991). This is a critical large site covering an area of 755 by 1845 metres, which reveals through its two moated enclosures, a considerable expansion in size. Excavations showed that occupation began with a 3-metre-thick deposit in which the ceramics, such as the carinated and incised bowls, reveal close similarities with the Dvaravati material from Central Thailand. This was followed by a 40-cm-thick layer in which Khmer material appeared, to be followed in the uppermost 1.1

metres, by Khmer ceramics dating from the 10th century onwards. The initial Dvaravati occupation provides strong evidence, in the form of bronze Buddha images, a part of the wheel of the law, stone statues of deer and tablets of Boddhisatvas, that Buddhism was the dominant religion at this site. It is also to this period, that an enormous reclining Buddha, the largest in Thailand, belongs.

The Bor E-ka is a 10th century temple sanctuary located in the middle of the moated enclosure. An inscription, stylistically belonging to the 9th century, in Sanskrit and Khmer, records a gift of 20 fat and healthy water buffalo cows, 50 cows with full udders and healthy calves, with ten male and female slaves to a Buddhist community by the overlord of a polity named Sri Canasa in order to gain merit. An inscription of 937 AD found at Ayutthaya records that a Mangalavarman ruled over Sri Canasa. Hanwong (1991) has suggested that at this period, Muang Sema was the centre of the polity of Sri Canasa. Saraya (1989, 1992b), however, has preferred Sri Thep as the capital. Perhaps only the discovery of more inscriptions will resolve issues such as this but in either case, Muang Sema illustrates first, the size and scale of early Dvaravati centres in the Mun Valley before strong influence from the Khmer manifested itself. Again, by more extensive excavations, preferably in the older of the two moated areas at Muang Sema, prehistoric origins to settlement may well be found.

There is a small corpus of other inscriptions which tell the same story, of local rulers with Sanskrit names, ruling over groups who probably spoke Khmer. At Hin Khon, 35 km south of Nakhon Ratchasima, an overlord called Nripendradhipativarman, who ruled in a city called Sro Vraah, erected four *sema* stones during the 8th century, and made the meritorious gift of rice fields, slaves, flowers, fruit, cattle, gold and silver utensils, and an elephant and betel trees to a Buddhist temple (Weeraprajak 1986a). Two further inscriptions also records actual names of rulers: Indravarman, Soryavarman and Jayasinhavarman, and a capital called Tamran. Further to the east, there is an inscription from Wat Ban Song Puay in Yasothon which mentions King Pravarasena and his capital Sankhapura. Jacques (1989) has hinted at a potential link between such 7th and 8th century polities and the large Iron Age settlements described above.

303: Krishna looks down, an elegant scene from a 12th century lintel from Phimai. The face of the deity is 6 cm in height.

304

305

304: *Phimai, the central sanctuary, from the air.*

305: *Excavations in 1998 beside the main temple at Phimai revealed its foundations, part of an earlier brick structure, and a layer containing Iron Age pottery.*

We do not have any information on the nature of warfare at this juncture, perhaps these were little more than raiding expeditions from Cambodia. But several of the large late Iron Age sites of the Mun Valley were later chosen for the construction of Angkorean temples, and it is particularly intriguing to note at Phanom Wan, that Iron Age burials underlay the central temple. During the reconstruction of Phimai, a small brick temple was found directly under the main sanctuary tower (Pichard 1976). Further parts of this early structure were uncovered by excavations in 1998. Taken in conjunction with the presence of Iron Age pottery at Ban Suai within the precinct of Phimai, It seems highly likely that there was cultural continuity between the late prehistoric period and the inception of temple construction.

Northeast Thailand may have been the object of early raids, but there is no doubt that it became an important part of the civilization of Angkor. The landscape reveals abundant evidence for many Khmer cities, *barays*, hospitals, temples, quarries and roads. Prasat Phumphon is the oldest known Khmer temple in Thailand, being located in Surin Province. The style of a

306

surviving lintel places this brick complex in the 7th century. The largest and best known centre is Phimai, the modern name for the Khmer city of Vimayapura. It is located where the Mun River has its confluence with two tributaries. Its size and grandeur might seem to represent a major break with the late prehistoric period, as if there had been an intrusive movement into the region from Cambodia. But this is not the case. Phimai had been settled during the Iron Age. Jayavarman VI (1080-1107) was responsible for the major additions, a matter of considerable interest. Until his accession, Angkor had been ruled for almost three centuries by members of the dynasty founded by Jayavarman II. But Jayavarman VI was a usurper who, according the available inscriptions, hailed from the vicinity of Phimai and belonged to the dynasty of Mahidharapura. This noble Mun Valley family's successful bid for power naturally led them to Angkor, but Phimai remained their ancestral base, and later members of the dynasty embellished it with new buildings until it reached its present form.

307

306: Phimai, a view of the central temple and its surrounds, taken during the restoration in 1970.

307: The central temple of Phimai today.

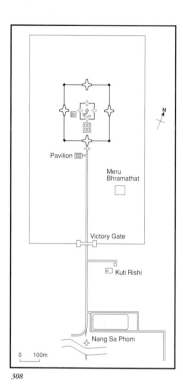

308

308: Plan of the Khmer city of Phimai, ancient Vimayapura.

309: Plan of the central precinct of Phimai, ancient Vimayapura.

This layout is best appreciated from the Nang Sa Phom, a laterite landing stage to the south of the city walls. It borders the Khem stream, and lies adjacent to the road with linked Phimai over a distance of 225 km to Angkor. It would have been used to facilitate the transport of goods by water. Looking south, there lies a large but now dry *baray*. The ancient route then follows the modern road to the *Pratu Chai* or Victory Gate, which gives access to the city of Vimayapura. But on the right hand side, before reaching the gateway, lies a *Kuti Rishi* or hospital built during the reign of Jayavarman VII. The present town of Phimai is laid out on a grid pattern which might relate to the town plan of the ancient city, and within the walled precinct, which to the north and west still retains part of the moat, there is a walled sanctuary housing a series of temples devoted to the worship of the Buddha. We can imagine that a successful bid for the throne at Angkor might well have given Jayavarman VI reason and opportunity to tear down the old brick temple of his ancestors and replace it with the present magnificent structure.

Access to this sacred precinct was gained first by means of a raised *naga* bridge, and then a monumental *gopura*, or entrance building. An inscription on the wall of a second *gopura* which divides the inner and outer courtyards tells us that the overlord, Virendradhipativarman, dedicated a statue of a *Trailokyavijaya* in the year 1108 AD. It is highly likely that this overlord was a close kinsman of the supreme sovereign in Angkor. Indeed, he is depicted, riding a massive war elephant, in one of the murals at Angkor Wat. 1112 AD, the date when the inscription was raised, was the year before Suryvarman II became the king at Angkor, and it was he who was ultimately to have Angkor Wat built as his temple mausoleum, The fact that the architects of Angkor Wat employed innovations seen at Phimai, such as the contour of the central tower, stresses the links between the two and the importance of the latter (Freeman 1996).

Jayavarman VII, who also made Buddhism his religion, likewise turned his attention to his ancestral temple at Phimai, adding the Prang Brohmadat and Prang Hin Daeng, two further temples the former housing a statue of the king himself.

Phanom Wan is a second major sanctuary, and is situated about 50 km southwest of Phimai and further up the Mun Valley. It reveals, as does Phimai, a continuity back to the Iron Age, for not only is there the foundation of a structure within the precinct made of bricks which predates the main sanctuary,

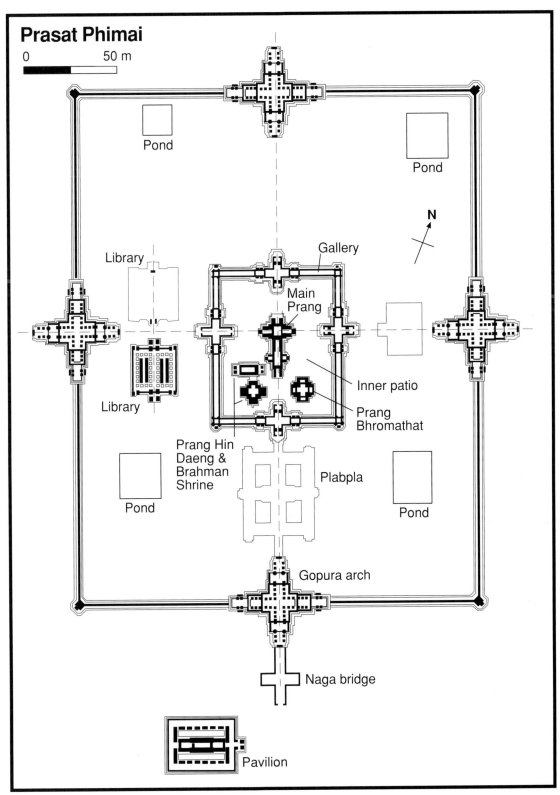

Prasat Phimai

0   50 m

Pond

Pond

N

Library

Gallery

Main
Prang

Inner patio

Library

Prang
Bhromathat

Prang Hin
Daeng &
Brahman
Shrine

Plabpla

Pond

Pond

Gopura arch

Naga bridge

Pavilion

309

310

310: A view of the Iron Age burial at Phanom Wan, laid out on the same orientation and only a metre from the foundations of the later Khmer temple. The foundation for the Khmer temple is seen as light fill on the right of picture, cut into the darker soil.

311: Phanom Rung is one of the most beautiful Khmer sites in Thailand. (RBC)

312: There are many examples of Khmer expertise in decorating sandstone monuments at Phanom Rung.

313: Looking to the south from Phanom Rung, one sees the Dang Raek range and Cambodia to the south, and in the middle foreground, the baray of Prasat Muang Tam.

but there is also an Iron Age cemetery hard up against the central temple. A grave within a metre or so of the foundations lies on the same east to west orientation as the building. Phanom Wan comprises this central temple surrounded by a walled enclosure. Three inscriptions reveal that it was embellished over at least two centuries between 891 and 1082. The latest inscription mentions Jayavarman VI who, as we have seen, came from this area. It also refers to the site as Ratnapura and instructs priests to maintain the temple.

The temple is surrounded by a moat, north of which is a huge *baray* while a smaller reservoir is located to the east. The whole complex, which was dedicated first to Siva and later saw the worship of Visnu and the Buddha, represents Mt Meru, home of the gods, and the surrounding oceans.

Phanom Rung, a third major temple in the northeast, is spectacularly located on the summit of an extinct volcanic cone in Buriram Province. On a clear day, the view to south reveals the full sweep of the Dang Raek range only 30 km distant, beyond which lies the plain of northern Cambodia. The present structure overlies a series of earlier brick temples which, to judge from the earliest of the eleven inscriptions found at Phanom Rung, go back at least to the 7th or 8th centuries. One cannot fail but be impressed by the sweeping contours of the central tower and its approaches, which incorporate two *naga* bridges, steep flights of steps and a processual way 160 m long, flanked by stone columns in the form of lotus buds. The temple was a centre for the worship of Siva, and the latest of the inscriptions, in Sanskrit, reveals that this was the centre of a highly-ranked lineage of the Mahidharapura Dynasty, that which ruled at Phimai and provided a long line of kings at Angkor. The most notable feature of this inscription is the manner in which it stresses that Narendraditya, the overlord of Phanom Rung, successfully defeated the enemies of his kinsman Suryavarman II. This provides an insight into the relationships which existed between the centre at Angkor and the outlying provinces: the latter were personal fiefdoms of high ranking overlords whose support of the central authority was essential for the king's survival. On one decorative relief at Phanom Rung we can see a leader, probably Narendraditya himself, astride his war elephant and defeating his enemy. Such reliefs anticipate the imminent raising of Angkor Wat.

311

312

313

A lintel depicting the reclining Visnu from Phanom Rung
has particular significance to the people of Thailand. As H.S.H.
Prince Subhadradis Diskul (1989) has described, the two pieces
of this lintel were stolen from the site, and one he later
recognised on exhibit in the Art Institute of Chicago. After long
negotiations between 1972 and 1988, the cherished lintel was
finally returned to its rightful place.

If you look down at the broad plain to the south of Phanom Rung, you can make out a huge rectangular *baray*. This is part of the sanctuary of Prasat Muang Tam which on stylistic grounds belongs to the 10th and 11th centuries. It comprises an outer enclosure with four gateways, leading past four ponds to the inner precinct. The latter contains five most impressive temple towers. The temples represent the five peaks of Mt. Meru, while the four ponds symbolise the encircling oceans. The outer wall is the boundary of the universe. There are two *barays* outside the temple area, the larger measuring 1150 by 400 metres. According to air photographs, this *baray* was a focus for a series of canals which might, according to Siribhadra and Moore (1992), have augmented the supply of water to rice fields in time of draught.

Khao Phra Viharn lies on the crest of the Dang Raek Range in what is often described as one of the most magnificent settings of all Angkorian temples. It dates to the early 11th century and was, it is thought, the inspiration of King Suryavarman I (1002-1050). Later additions have been dated to the reign of Suryavarman II. Due to the constraints of its ridge top location, its form resembles Phanom Rung in having a long series of causeways broken by *gopuras* leading ever higher to the main temple building. At Phra Viharn, one has to cover 850 metres of such processional ways, rise 120 metres and pass through five *gopuras* before reaching the summit temple. Due to its frontier location, this site has not received the same reconstruction as have the main temples in Thailand.

315: The south gopura of the third court Khao Phra Viharn. (RBC)

One of the most significant finds of recent years in terms of Angkorian art in Thailand comes from Prasat Kamphaeng Yai in Sisaket. In 1989, during the reconstruction of this 11th century foundation to Siva, a superb bronze statue of a *dvarapala* or door guardian 1.84 metres in height was recovered near the southern gate (Boisselier 1989, Subhadradis 1990b, 1991). To judge from the surviving traces of gold, the whole figure was formerly gilded. There can be little doubt that the traditional skill of the northeasten bronze casters found new heights during this period. The guardian wore anklets, armlets and a complex necklace. Again, an inscription from this site in Khmer notes that a Vra Kamraten An Sivadesa and three other aristocrats purchased land in 1042 AD which they dedicated to Siva.

Central Thailand

The Northeast was part of the heartland of the Angkor polity, but Central Thailand was, as we have seen, home of the Mon polities of Dvaravati. An inscription from Preah Khan dating from the reign of Indravarman II (1219-1243) recorded that his father, Jayavarman VII, ordered the placement of statues to the Buddha in 23 regional centres. Of these, six are thought to have been located in Central Thailand. Subhadradis (1978) has suggested correlations between the names on the stela, and modern locations. Lavodayapura, for example, is probably Lopburi. He suggests that Suvarnapura is modern Suphanburi and Jayarajapuri is probably Ratchaburi. Clearly, during the 12th and 13th centuries the Khmer pushed into Central Thailand, and at Lopburi, one can see at Prang Som Yod the familiar architectural features of the temple towers but here, during the reign of Jayavarman VII, they were constructed of laterite and decorated with stucco. The most westerly of all Khmer centres in Thailand is today known as Prasat Muang Singh (meaning Temple of the Lion City). Most intriguingly, this modern name corresponds to one of the locations in the Preah Khan inscription, Srijayasinghapuri. This city, measuring 1,400 by 880 metres, lies on the northern bank of a bend in the Khwae Noi River, near the modern centre of Kanchanaburi. It probably owes its size and location to the strategic need to control the Three Pagodas Pass to the west. The laterite outer wall survives to a height of five metres, and was associated with multiple moats. Within, there lay a central temple precinct as at Phimai, dedicated to the Buddha and stylistically belonging to the Bayon style current during the reign of Jayavarman VII. This is a telling confirmation of the power of this overlord and the extent of his domain.

316: The bronze statue from Kamphaeng Yai shows how a long tradition of prehistoric bronze casting reached new heights of expertise. Dating to the 11th century, this statue stands 1.84 m in height including the base. (Photo: Michael Freeman)

Beyond the Great Centres

Naturally, much energy has been devoted to the reconstruction and analysis of the major Khmer centres, such as Phimai and Phanom Rung. Far less is known of the pattern of settlement in the surrounding countryside, or how the centres integrated economically and socially with their sustaining areas. Recently, however, Welch (1997) has outlined the results of fieldwork undertaken in the vicinity of Phimai, and the picture he provides is one of the most significant contributions towards a fuller understanding of the Angkorian period in Thailand. He began his review by referring to a description of Angkor by Zhou Daguan, an emissary of Timur Khan who visited the court of King Indravarman III in 1296-7. Having spent a year in the country, Zhou Daguan's description is both authoritative, and covered many topics (Zhou Daguan 1993). Among the points emphasised by Welch was the description of provinces, each with a ruler, a temple and a fortified centre. According to the many inscriptions set up during the Angkorian state, such temples were maintained by gifts of goods and services from dependent communities. Welch argues for three tiers of temples,

317: Prasat Muang Singh is the most westerly of all Khmer centres in Thailand. This view shows the central enclosure. (Photo: Michael Freeman)

the central, regional and those at the level of the village. It is vital to appreciate that the temples formed an economic and political as well as a religious function, allowing through the donations made, for the economic integration of communities within province and state. Following a successful military campaign or appropriation of new territory, a ruler would commonly make a grant of land to his followers, as we have already seen in the case of Narendraditya at Phanom Rung. This temple would then be the focus for the exploitation of the land around through new settlement and opening of land to agriculture, mining or, in the case of the Mun Valley, the extraction of salt. Welch has undertaken field work in the Phimai area in order to define the regional pattern of Khmer settlement. Within the broad alluvial plain of the Mun and its major tributaries, he identified just the two major centres, Phimai and Phanom Wan. But he also noted a series of small temple structures set in land marginal for extensive rice cultivation, each surrounded by Khmer settlements or evidence for such activities as iron smelting or salt working. These, he suggested, represent the economic development associated with new temple foundations. While settlement on the plain varied little from that he documented for the late prehistoric period, the number of sites in the marginal uplands virtually doubled with the period we associate with the heyday of sites like Phimai.

That was not all, for Zhou Daguan (1993) also mentioned roads and rest houses which linked Angkor with the provinces. The route of the road linking Angkor with Phimai is known over most of its length, and several virtually identical buildings located at intervals are thought to have been rest houses for travellers. These would have included government officials, perhaps pilgrims and certainly those involved in the transport of goods to and from Angkor.

318: The inscription from Tham Pu Manai records the raising of a stone statue of a bull, which symbolises Siva. It provides evidence for a war expedition in the Mun Valley led by King Mahendravarman in the early 7th century AD. (Courtesy Fine Arts Department)

The Coming of the Thai

"The Thai people had probably originally lived in southeastern China. They might have migrated into present-day Thailand in separate small groups a long time ago, even before the conquest of Kublai Khan over China in the early thirteenth century" H.S.H. Prince Subhadradis Diskul 1996:7

Who are the Thai? when and how did they reach the land which bears their name? We can be confident, based on inscriptions, that prior to 1200 AD, most people living in Thailand spoke either Mon or Khmer. An inscription dated to 1167 from Nakhon Sawan is said to be the earliest evidence for the use of Thai in Thailand, as it includes two words, *Phra* (cleric or royal prefix) and *nam* (bring) (Weeraprajak 1986b). It is in such evidence of language that we can pinpoint possible homelands for the Thai. There are numerous peoples occupying Yunnan, Guizhou, Guangxi and Guangdong provinces in southern China, as well as the island of Hainan, the northern uplands in Vietnam, parts of Myanmar and northeast India in addition to Thailand and Laos, who speak languages which belong to the so-called Austro-Tai family (Liangwen 1992). Na Nakhon (1991) has stressed the considerable diversity of Tai languages spoken in Guangxi Province, and has suggested this area as a likely homeland for the Thai. Another possible centre of origin lies in the Wushui River valley of Guizhou Province. But we can go even further back in time than this, according to Blust (1996). There are some vague similarities between Austro-Tai and Austronesian languages which open the possibility that the earliest speakers of Austro-Tai were linked into the Austric superfamily with a homeland in the middle to upper Yangzi Valley. Blust would then envisage the speakers of languages remotely ancestral to Thai expanding slowly to the south and with time, occupying much of southern China.

Such a dispersal would help us account for the many distinct languages which nevertheless have a common origin, which are found over so much of Southeast Asia.

If the homeland of the Thais is, then, in southern China, how did they reach Thailand? Imagine Southeast Asia in the year 1200 AD. King Jayavarman VII ruled much of what is now Thailand from his capital at Angkor. As one proceeded away from the centre, so one would encounter regional overlords who offered tribute and acknowledged the supremacy of Jayavarman. This king placed almost impossible demands on his followers. He had built roads, hospitals, reservoirs and temples on an unprecedented scale. This policy exhausted the populace and weakened their dedication to the sovereign. Along the northern fringes of this empire, in the upland valleys of Laos, northern Thailand and Yunnan, there developed a swarm of small but young, vigorous and expansive groups which the Thai called *muang* (Wyatt 1984). In English, we could use the word principality perhaps, but the essence of the *muang* was the charisma of the overlord and establishment of a central settlement, usually walled and girt with moats. A great leader, and there have been many in the history of the Thai down to the present, could expand his domain by accepting the homage of his contemporary rulers and thus, through kinship relationships or receipt of tribute, magnify his influence and prestige. But any sign of weakness or loss of character, could equally see his domain contract or collapse.

319: *The famous inscription 1 from Sukhothai was raised during the reign of king Ramkhamhaeng. (Courtesy Bangkok National Museum)*

To such rulers as Mangrai and Ramkhamhaeng, the sprawling and flaccid Khmer empire stood in the way of expansion over the rich riverine plains bordering the upland valleys which had been home to the Thai for numberless generations. The former ruler was born in 1239, and by a series of alliances and military campaigns, he absorbed much territory including the old Mon centre of Lamphun in 1281. In 1292, he founded his new capital at Chiang Mai, from which base he established a rich and prosperous polity which, in effect, acted as a bulwark against the predatory policy of the Mongol rulers of China. Ramkhamhaeng, or Rama the Bold, was a contemporary of Mangrai and they formed an alliance which saw Rama establish a realm from the capital at Sukhothai which in short order, incorporated much of present Thailand. He confirmed Therevada Buddhism as the preferred religion and even shared his throne with religious leaders, thus bonding religion and politics into an unbreakable unity. If we take his famous inscription of 1292 at face value, Ramkhamhaeng ensured the wise administration of law, encouraged prosperity through trade and saw that there was an abundance of food for his followers. Among these, he included not only artists of a growing Thai school of expression, but also Chinese skilled in the production of ceramics. His capital at Sukhothai and its associated centres now stand as testimony to his achievement, at his death in

1298, he was a sovereign who ruled over a genuinely Thai kingdom in Thailand (Gosling 1991).

Although it is not possible, short of major excavations, to ascribe particular monuments or building phases at Sukhothai to individual rulers, nevertheless the extent and splendour of the physical remains speak eloquently of their power. If this is self evident today to the visitor to the Historic Park, it must have been more so to King Rama IV in his visit of 1833, and to King Rama VI when he saw Sukhothai, shrouded in the pervading forest, in 1908. Both future sovereigns were to impress on their subjects, the role of Sukhothai in the foundations of Thai nationhood. The heart of Sukhothai lay within a walled enclosure measuring 1.7 by 1.3 kilometres. There are broad triple walls separated by moats about 18 metres wide. Like its Dvaravati predecessors, it incorporates a series of religious monuments, but many more are also found beyond the walls. Among these is the Wat Phra Phai Luang, which is thought to represent the location of a Khmer centre dating at least to the reign of Jayavarman VII.

The centre of Sukhothai is dominated by the remains of the Wat Mahathat, a Buddhist complex defined by a brick wall, which was first mentioned during the reign of King Mahathammaracha I who ruled during the middle of the 14th Century. No visitor could fail but be impressed by the energy which must have been involved in the construction of so many

320: Crown Prince Maha Vajiravudh, who later become H.M. King Rama VI, opened public awareness to the significance, of Sukhothai in the history of the Thai people. (Courtesy The National Archives, Bangkok)

321: Wat Phra Phai Luang lies north of the moated central enclosure of Sukhothai, and is often seen as evidence for a Khmer ccupation of the area during the reign of Jayavarman VII. (RBC)

320

321

322

323

structures, including chedis and a large building to house the image of the Buddha (*viharn*). Noen Prasat is a square mound just east of the Wat Mahathat, and excavations by the Fine Arts Department have revealed the brick foundations of a structure which may have been a royal pavilion. It was here that King Rama IV recovered a large stone seat, known as the *Manangsilabat,* and the famous inscription of King Ramkhamhaeng. The throne is now housed in the Temple of the Emerald Buddha in Bangkok (Moore *et al.* 1996).

Numerous temples are to be found within the walls, together with over 150 ponds or reservoirs. Some such reservoirs are associated with temples: Wat Srasri is found on a small island in the middle of the Tra Phang Tra Kuan reservoir, while the Tra Phang Ngoen reservoir is surrounded by religious buildings. Beyond the walled precinct, the landscape is dotted with further Buddhist temples. Of these, Wat Si Chum is best known since it was here that King Naresuan the Great of Ayutthaya had his army swear allegiance in 1567, during a military expedition against Sawankhalok and Phichai. The temple is also noted for its subterranean tunnel lined with slate

322-323: Wat Mahathat is the large temple in the centre of Sukhothai, and is probably that described in the famous incription of King Ramkhamhaeng. (RBC)

324: Noen Prasat is thought to be the base of a royal pavilion. It was here that King Mongkut, then a monk, found the inscription of King Ramkhamhaeng and the Manangsilabat throne. (Courtesy Paisarn Piemmettawat)

slabs on which are engraved scenes which enact the history of the Buddha. These are accompanied by inscriptions in the Sukhothai period Thai script. Inscriptions in some of these extramural temples also assist in dating their construction. Wat Hin Tang, for example, contains a dedicatory inscription of King Thammaraja.

Between 1977-1982, no fewer than 82 squares were excavated within the moated area, through the walls and in the moats beyond (Rungrugee *et al.* n.d., Supyen *et al.* 1988). Rungrugee identified six principal occupation phases inside the walls, all falling within the historic period. The first included substantial postholes with whole stoneware vessels at the base, possibly as votive offerings associated with the construction of a monument. Phases 1b and 1c also provide evidence for Khmer style ceramics dating from the 8th and 13th centuries. A radiocarbon date of about 1280 AD comes from this first occupation phase. The second period saw a marked change in the material culture, the construction of the city wall and the surrounding moats. Through the excavations, we obtain a rare glimpse of domestic activity: houses were made of wood joined by nails and covered by roof tiles. There was much hunting of deer, but also domestic cattle, pig and dog bones were found. Rice was recovered, and glazed local ceramic wares were encountered together with imported Chinese ceramics dated from the 14th century.

Sri Satchanalai

Wat Chom Chuen lies on the northern bank of the Yom River, about 1.5 km east of the city walls of Sri Satchanalai. Excavations there have uncovered late prehistoric burials at a depth of 6-7 metres, with glass beads as grave goods (Hein *et al.* 1988, FAD n.d.). Further excavations under the *viharn* of Wat Phra Sri Ratanamahathat have revealed early brick structures which indicate a long preceding history to Sri Satchanalai before the establishment of the Kingdom of Sukhothai. Traditionally, Sri Satchanalai was a dependent city to Sukhothai, and it lies only 75 km to the north. It shares many features in common with Sukhothai. The city proper is ringed by laterite walls and moats on three sides and the Yom River to the northeast. The southwestern wall attains a length of just over a kilometre. During his visit to this site, King Rama VI identified an area near the northeastern town wall as being a possible location for the royal palace. While nothing is visible on the present surface, recent excavations have indeed revealed substantial brick foundations and a rectangular reservoir. Again, the energy devoted to the construction of Buddhist monuments is clearly seen in the 39 larger than life standing elephants which adorn the exterior of the Wat Chang Lom temple. This stands in the

325: Wat Phra Sri Ratanamahathat at Sri Satchanalai has a long history, beginning with early brick structures and ending with additions during the Ayutthaya period. (RBC)

326

327

326: Wat Chang Lom at Sri Satchanalai was, according to an inscription, constructed over a period of six years at the command of King Ramkhamhaeng. It incorporated 39 huge elephants and is centrally located in the city.

327-328: One of the Sri Satchanalai kilns still retains the fired vessels within. (Photo: Michael Freeman)

middle of the ancient city. There are no fewer than 33 subsidiary *chedis* in the Wat Chedi Jet Thaew. To remind us of the endemic warfare which characterised the period, the gates leading into the city are associated with forts but beyond, in the surrounding countryside, we find numerous temples and evidence for industrial activity on a grand scale.

Sri Satchanalai is famous for its ceramic industry. Over several centuries, the age-old skills of the prehistoric potters found a new expression in the outstanding glazed wares revealed at the Ban Ko Noi and Ban Pa Yang kilns located just north of the Sri Satchanalai. Excavations by Hein have revealed how technical improvements in kiln types, from the early underground form to the sophisticated up and cross-draft kilns was accompanied by progressive techniques in decoration and glazing culminating in the 13th century white clay celadons of Pa Yang. There are literally hundreds of kilns along the right bank of the Yom River, and not only export wares, but also the roofing tiles needed in the construction of the temples and palaces were produced. The call on timber for firing must have caused serious deforestation, but the industry was clearly a central part of the local economy and some superb ceramics were produced. So successful were these increasingly specialised

328

producers, that a satellite industry was established at Sukhothai
by about 1200 AD which, while not as extensive nor as long
lived as the Sri Satchanalai centre, nevertheless employed the
same techniques in the production of export wares (Hein *et al.*
1985).

*329: A lidded vessel. As one might expect in a
country with at least a 4,500 year tradition of
making pottery vessels, the products of the Sri
Satchanalai kilns were of outstanding quality.
(Photo: Michael Freeman)*

330

Chapter Seven
Conclusions

With the establishment of Sukhothai and the dynasty of which Ramkamhaeng was a member, we encounter a society within which any modern Thai would have felt at ease. The state was ruled by a wise and able monarch who respected the law and honoured the Buddhist religion. The fields beyond the city walls were emerald green with rice in the wet season, while skilled artisans added to the wealth of the community at large in the manufacture of ceramics. The inscriptions were written in Thai.

One of the commonest questions we are asked by visitors to our excavations is "were these ancient people Thai?". At Sukhothai, the answer would be straightforward: "yes". But for earlier periods, our answer would be longer. Thailand occupies a strategic position in Southeast Asia and the world. For 2,000 years, it has been a vital stepping stone in east-west international trade. It also straddles several major rivers flowing from north to south. Even for the earliest humans in their expansion into the east from Africa, it would have been hard to avoid the land of Thailand. Today, it is home to many different peoples, who speak their own languages and have their own religions, traditions and customs. And so it was in the past.

One of the most rewarding aspects of prehistoric research in Thailand over the past 20 years has been the new images revealed with every major excavation. Until the 1960s, the Thai authorities quite rightly concentrated on the monuments of the historic past, all in need of conservation and restoration. Prehistoric people and their remains were left underground. So the really major advances in our understanding of the complete picture of Thailand's past have been made among the people who preceded the historic kingdoms. As we have stressed more

330: Seated Buddha image, Sukhothai style. (Courtesy The A.B. Griswold collection, The Walters Art Gallery)

215

than once, the discovery of a new prehistoric sequence often involves problems of interpretation, and in retrospect, mistakes have been made from which we are not exempt. But this must not detract from the fact that we are continually refining and improving our understanding through more excavations, radiocarbon dates and information. We are keenly aware that any synthesis of Thai prehistory has a short shelf life, and this is as it should be. At present, the following general structure seems to fit the available data.

We have only fleeting glimpses of the earliest humans. They are named *Homo erectus*, and originated in Africa. Hunter-gatherers were found in small, scattered groups in the inland by 40,000 years ago. Life on the rich coast is unknown to us because the sea level was lower then, and any settlements are now covered by the oceans. Only when the sea rose and formed raised beaches behind the present shore, is it possible to appreciate the sophistication of coastal hunters and gatherers at Nong Nor and Khok Phanom Di. These are the only two early coastal sites so far excavated. The splendid pottery they made, the wealth of their mortuary ritual and personal ornaments provide us with a new image of hunting and gathering societies. They were not just collectors of shellfish: people of Nong Nor took dolphins and three metre sharks. In contrast, the small inland rock shelters like Spirit Cave or Lang Rongrien depict small, mobile groups with a less impressive material culture. It must, however, be recalled that occupation of such sites could have contrasted with life in the open, beside rivers or lakes. Sadly, the destructive mobility of rivers means that settlements beside them would have been particularly vulnerable.

The pervasive heat, luxuriance of the vegetation during the monsoon, the predictable and abundant sources of fish, shellfish and game sustained hunters and gatherers for tens of thousands of years. We must ask why should such people show any interest in cultivating rice, or domesticating animals? Current thinking world-wide suggests that agriculture began among sedentary hunters and gatherers who experienced some form of environmental stress which encouraged innovation (Price and Gebauer 1995). This occurred with a climatic deterioration in the Yangzi Valley, and the archaeological record there includes early farming villages. But there is no evidence for a transition to agriculture in the hot fecund lands of Southeast Asia. So, we suggest that early farmers, who ultimately originated in the

Yangzi Valley, gradually expanded their numbers and area of settlement. By the late third millennium BC, on present evidence in the vicinity of 2300 BC, they began to move into Thailand. We can see evidence for this at sites like Ban Kao and Tha Kae. Such a process of expansion might help us understand how it came to be that people speaking distantly related languages are found from Vietnam to India.

We are aware that this proposal is relatively new and might spark controversy. In response, we say that in our view, it best fits the information now available. It might be wrong. Perhaps one day, someone will find 5000 BC rice-growing sites in the Northeast, for White (1997) has shown excitement at the possibility that burning episodes of that date revealed in the sediments of Lake Kumphawapi relate to a very early Ban Chiang agricultural tradition. We are sceptical, and will remain so until the archaeological evidence is identified.

The expansionary movement we are suggesting would have brought southern Mongoloid people into Thailand, a pre-or proto-Mon language and the dog, as well as a sedentary farming economy. The prehistoric dog is interesting, for it is descended from a wolf. The nearest wolves live in China.

There are two ways in which the Bronze Age could have begun in Thailand. It may have been through local innovation, after all Thailand is rich in sources of copper and tin. Alternatively, the idea might have reached Thailand and the rest of Southeast Asia through exchange routes linking our area with the Shang state of the Yellow River valley in China. We favour the latter, because from Thailand through Vietnam to Hong Kong, similar bronzes were cast in the same way, and the growing number of radiocarbon dates indicate that these bronzes are later than the importation of Chinese jades which originated in the wealthy Bronze Age Shang civilisation. Trade links also involve the communication of ideas. The possibility of obtaining copper by heating green rocks could have reached Southeast Asia on the coat tails of the jade trade. Yet again, we are not sure. If someone were to discover a Bronze Age site in Thailand, dated without doubt in the region of 2000 BC, we would be surprised, but more than prepared to accept a local origin for metallurgy.

There is virtually universal agreement among archaeologists that iron smelting was underway in Thailand from about 500 BC, and that this innovation was one of several which encouraged rapid population growth and the development of social elites. It was these Iron Age chiefs whose descendants, in due course, were to establish the first kingdoms, of Dvaravati in the Mon speaking part of Thailand, and of Zhenla in the Mun Valley and Prachinburi, where old Khmer was spoken. These two rich and splendid civilizations developed in tandem until the coming of the Thai, by which time they were growing tired, and were unable to withstand the young and vibrant Thai leaders.

So, when Thai-speaking peoples first expanded south into the present country of Thailand, they would have encountered highly sophisticated people who spoke Mon, or Khmer. What happened to the former, those responsible for monumental civilization of Dvaravati? Many would have been assimilated into the new Thai states. But there are also, to this day or in living memory, isolated villages in Nakhon Ratchasima, Chaiyaphum and Phetchabun provinces where people still speak Mon. They call themselves the Nyah-Kur, meaning mountain people, the Thai call them the *Chao Bon*. Diffloth (1981) has pointed out some fascinating aspects of these people and their language. First, their present location, concentrating in the uplands bordering the Pasak River, places them in "a sort of cultural 'no man's land between the North-East and the Central Plain. This is the sort of area where one could expect to meet remnants of earlier populations, squeezed, so to speak" (Diffloth 1981:223). Diffloth, in his close examination of the Nyah-Kur language, has concluded that it separated, that is began to differentiate, during the period when the Dvavarati Old Mon language was being spoken in Central Thailand.

But the lowland Mon people, over the generations, have been incorporated by intermarriage into Thai society, and adopted the increasingly dominant Thai language as their own. In just the same way more recent settlers, the Portuguese and Chinese for example, have been absorbed into Thai society. This issue has been well summarised by Rasmibhuti (1993) when he noted the common cultural heritage and southern Mongoloid stock of the peoples of Thailand, Laos and Cambodia. So the answer to the question "are these people Thai" is yes, the Neolithic, Bronze and Iron Age peoples' genes flow within the present population of Thailand, and each contributed to the development of the country as we know it today.

Every healthy society takes pride in its cultural heritage and Thailand is no exception. It is a world leader in education through the restoration of historic centres. Phimai, Sukhothai, Ayutthaya and numerous other great sites have been sensitively and expertly restored, and the visitor can now savour their former splendour. But beyond these states there lies an unfolding vista of prehistory, of anonymous societies returned from oblivion by the archaeologist. We can follow in the footsteps of the earliest farmers, expanding into the river valleys of Thailand during the course of the third millennium BC. It is possible to appreciate the skill of the casters of bronzes as metallurgy took hold from about 1500 BC, and to open their mines, explore their workshops and handle the very bangles and spears they so expertly fashioned. During the ensuing Iron Age, we can perceive through cemeteries such as Noen U-Loke and Ban Don Ta Phet, the rise of social elites, ancestors physically and metaphorically of the overlords of Dvaravati and Angkor. And then we can trace the pattern of the early civilisations, their origins, peaks and troughs.

By preserving its independence when states all round it fell under the yoke of colonialism, Thailand developed its own tradition of archaeological enquiry. Under royal inspiration, the civilisations represented at Sukhothai and Lopburi, no less than the prehistoric heritage, have come under increasingly close scrutiny. Again, the welcome given to foreign archaeologists has made it possible for *farangs* to share in the excitement of discovery, and work together, as in the writing of this book, to reveal the pattern of Thailand's past.

This study will, then, have served its purpose if it brings a swell of pride to the Thai reader, and a sense of respect and understanding for the nation's heritage to the visitor.

References

Abbreviations

BIPPA: Bulletin of the Indo-Pacific
            Prehistory Association
EFEO: Ecole Française d'Extrême
            Orient
FAD: Fine Arts Department
PEFEO: Publications of the Ecole
            Française d'Extrême Orient

Ahn, S-M. 1990. *Origin and Differentiation of Domesticated Rice in Asia.*
Ph.D. thesis, University of London.

Anderson, D.D. 1990. *Lang Rongrien Rockshelter: a Pleistocene-Early Holocene Archaeological Site from Krabi, Southwestern Thailand.*
University Museum Monograph No. 71, Philadelphia.

Aymonier, E. 1901. *La Cambodge II: Les Provinces Siamoises.*
Leroux, Paris.

Bannanurag, R. 1988. Evidence for ancient woodworking: a microwear study of Hoabinhian stone tools. In Charoenwongsa, P. and Bronson, B. editors, *Prehistoric Studies: The Stone and Metal Ages in Thailand,* pages 61-79.
Thai Antiquity Working Group, Bangkok.

Bannanurag, R. and Khemnak, P. 1992. *Prehistoric burials at Wat Pho Si Nai, Ban Chiang* (in Thai).
FAD, Bangkok.

Bayard, D.T. 1980. *The Pa Mong Archaeological Survey Programme, 1973-1975.*
University of Otago Studies in Prehistoric Anthropology 13, Dunedin.

Bayard, D.T. 1984. A tentative regional phase chronology for Northeast Thailand. In Bayard, D.T. editor, *Southeast Asian Archaeology at the XV Pacific Science Congress,* pages 161-8.
Otago University Studies in Prehistoric Anthropology 16, Dunedin.

Bayard, D.T., Charoenwongsa, P. and Rutnin, S. 1986. Excavations at Non Chai, Northeastern Thailand. *Asian Perspectives,* 25:13-62.

Bellwood, P. 1989. The colonisation of the Pacific: some current hypotheses. In Hill, A.V.S. and Serjeantson, S.W. editors, *The Colonisation of the Pacific. A Genetic Trail,* pages 1-59.
Oxford University Press, Oxford.

Bellwood, P. 1992. Southeast Asia before history. In Tarling, N. editor, *The Cambridge History of Southeast Asia,* pages 55-136.
Cambridge University Press, Cambridge.

Bellwood, P. 1993. Cultural and biological differentiation in peninsular Malaysia: the last 10,000 years. *Asian Perspectives,* 32:37-60.

Bennett, A. 1988. Prehistoric copper smelting in Central Thailand. In Charoenwongsa, P. and Bronson, B. editors, *Prehistoric Studies: the Stone and Metal Ages in Thailand,* pages 125-135.
Thai Antiquity Working Group, Bangkok.

Bennett, A. 1989. The contribution of metallurgical studies to Southeast Asian archaeology.
World Archaeology, 20:329-51.

Bhumadhon, B. 1987. *The Archaeology of Muang Dongkorn* (in Thai).
Amarin Printing Group, Bangkok.

Bhumadhon, B. n.d. *Muang Sab Champa* (in Thai).
Pakpreawkarnchang 2, Saraburi.

Blust, R. 1996. Beyond the Austronesian homeland: the Austric hypothesis and its implications for archaeology. In Goodenough, W. editor, *Prehistoric Settlement of the Pacific. Transactions of the American Philosophical Society,* 86 part 5, Philadelphia.

Boisselier, J. 1968. *Nouvelles Connaissances Archaéologique de la Ville d'U-Tong.*
Bangkok.

Boisselier, J. 1989. Notes on the bronze sculpture discovered at Prasat Sa Kamphaeng Yai.
Silpakon Journal, 33:4-6.

Boisselier, J. 1991. Comments on Dvaravati art in Thailand.
Spafa Journal, 1:319.

Bronson, B. 1979. The late prehistory and early history of Central Thailand with special reference to Chansen. In Smith, R.B. and Watson, W. editors, *Early Southeast Asia,* pages 315-36.
Oxford University Press, Oxford.

Bronson, B. 1990. Glass beads at Khuan Lukpad, Southern Thailand. In Glover, I.C. and Glover E. editors, *Southeast Asian Archaeology, 1986.*
British Archaeological Reports, (International Series), 561:213-29.

Bronson, B. 1996. Chinese and Middle Eastern Trade in Southern Thailand during the 9th century A.D. In Srisuchat, A. editor, *Ancient Trades and Cultural Contacts in Southeast Asia,* pages 181-200. National Culture Commission, Bangkok.

Brown, R.L. and MacDonnell, A.M. 1989. The Pong Tuk lamp: a reconsideration. *Journal of the Siam Society,* 77(2):9-20.

Buchan, R. 1973. *The Three-dimensional Jigsaw Puzzle: a Ceramic Sequence from Northeast Thailand.* M.A. dissertation, University of Otago.

Buranrak, 1994a. *Report on the Excavation of Non Praw* (in Thai). FAD, Bangkok.

Buranrak, 1994b. *Report on the Excavation of Don Klang* (in Thai). FAD, Bangkok.

Chaimongkol, S. 1988. Prehistoric culture on the Andaman east coast. *Spafa Digest,* IX(2):28-33.

Chaimongkol, S. 1991. The history of the study of Ban Chiang and some thoughts concerning it (in Thai). *Silpakon Journal,* 34(5):7-18.

Chang, T.T. and Loresto, E. 1984. The rice remains. In Higham, C.F.W. and Kijngam, A. editors, *Prehistoric Investigations in Northeast Thailand,* pages 384-5. British Archaeological Reports, (International Series), 231, Oxford.

Chantaratiyakarn, P. 1984. The research programme in the Upper Chi. In Higham, C.F.W. and Kijngam, A. editors, *Prehistoric Investigations in Northeast Thailand,* pages 565-643. British Archaeological Reports, (International Series), 231, Oxford.

Charoenwongsa, P. 1982. *Communities of the Prehistoric Period. Laksana Thai* Volume 1: *Background* (in Thai). Thai Wattana Phanich, Bangkok.

Charoenwongsa, P., Khemnak, P. and Kwanyuen, S. 1985. *An Inventory of Rock Art Sites in Northeastern Thailand.* Seameo Projects in Archaeology and Fine Arts, Bangkok.

Ciarla, R. 1992. The Thai-Italian Lopburi regional archaeological project, a preliminary report. In Glover, I.C. editor, *Southeast Asian Archaeology 1990.* pages 111-28. Centre for Southeast Asian Studies, University of Hull.

Cremaschi, M., Ciarla, R. and Pigott, V.C. 1992. Palaeoenvironment and late prehistoric sites in the Lopburi region of Central Thailand. In Glover, I.C. editor, *Southeast Asian Archaeology 1990,* pages 129-42. Centre for Southeast Asian Studies, University of Hull.

Daeng-iet, S. 1978. Khok Phlap: a newly discovered prehistoric site (in Thai). *Muang Boran,* 4:17-26.

Damrong, H.R.H. Prince, 1995. *Visitations in Monton Nakhon Rajasima and Monton Udon Isarn in Rattanakosin 125 and B.E. 2449* (in Thai). Diskul Foundation, Bangkok.

De Casparis, J.G. 1979. Palaeography as an auxiliary discipline in research on early Southeast Asia. In Smith, R.B. and Watson, W. editors, *Early Southeast Asia,* pages 380-94. Oxford University Press, Oxford.

Diffloth, G. 1981. Reconstructing Dvaravati-Old-Mon. In Bhumadon, P. and Na Nakhon Phanom, S. editors, *The Earliest Inscriptions Found in Lopburi and*

Nearby (in Thai). FAD, Bangkok.

Diffloth, G. 1991. Austro-Asiatic languages. *Encylopaedia Britannica Macropaedia,* 22:719-21.

Donner, W. 1982. *The Five Faces of Thailand.* University of Queensland Press, St. Lucia, Queensland.

Douglas, M.T. 1997. A preliminary discussion of trauma in the human skeletons from Ban Chiang, Northeast Thailand. *BIPPA,* 16:111-8.

Doyarsa, T. 1992. Ban Kan Luang. The late prehistoric site (in Thai). *Silpakon Journal,* 35(6):48-67.

Dupont, P. 1959. *L'Archéologie Mone de Dvaravati. EFEO,* Paris.

Freeman, M. 1996. *A Guide to Khmer Temples in Thailand and Laos.* River Books, Bangkok.

FAD, 1968. *The Survey and Excavation at Muang Fa Daed Song Yang, Ban Sema, Tambon Nong Pan, Amphoe Kamalasai, Changwat Kalasin, 1967-8.* FAD, Bangkok.

FAD, 1991. *80 Years of Thai Cultural Heritage Preservation* (in Thai). FAD, Bangkok.

FAD, n.d.. *The World Heritage Sukhothai, Sri Satchanalai and Khampaeng Phet Historic Parks.* FAD, Bangkok.

Glover, I.C. 1989. *Early Trade Between India and Southeast Asia: a Link in the Development of a World Trading System.* The University of Hull Centre for Southeast Asian Studies, Occasional Paper No. 16, Hull.

Glover, I.C. 1990. Ban Don Ta Phet: the 1984-5 excavation. In Glover, I.C. and Glover, E. editors, *Southeast Asian Archaeology 1986. Proceedings of the First Conference of the Association of Southeast Asian Archaeologists in Western Europe,* pages 139-83.
British Archaeological Reports, (International Series), 561. Oxford.

Glover, I.C. 1996. The southern Silk Road: archaeological evidence for early trade between India and Southeast Asia. In Srisuchat, A. editor, *Ancient Trades and Cultural Contacts in Southeast Asia,* pages 57-94.
National Culture Commission, Bangkok

Gorman, C.F. 1977. *A priori* models and Thai prehistory: a reconsideration of the beginnings of agriculture in Southeast Asia. In Reed, C. editor, *Origins of Agriculture,* pages 322-55.
Mouton, The Hague.

Gorman, C.F. and Charoenwongsa, P. 1976. Ban Chiang: a mosaic of impressions from the first two years. *Expedition,* 8:14-26.

Gosling, B. 1991. *Sukhothai. Its History, Culture and Art.*
Oxford University Press, Oxford and Singapore.

Groslier, B.P. 1979. La cité hydraulique Angkorienne. Exploitation ou surexploitation du sol?
BEFEO, 66:161-202.

Gutman, P. 1978. The ancient coinage of Southeast Asia.
Journal of the Siam Society, 66:8-21.

Hall, D.M. 1993. Aspects of the pottery decoration. In Higham, C.F.W. and Thosarat, R., editors *The Excavation of Khok Phanom Di.* Volume 3 (part 1): *The Material Culture,* pages 239-74.

Society of Antiquaries of London, Research Report no. L, London.

Hanks, L.M. 1972, *Rice and Man. Agricultural Ecology in Southeast Asia.* Aldine, Chicago and New York.

Hanwong, T. 1985. *Artefacts Analysis from the Excavation at Ban Thakae Amphor Muang Changwat Lopburi* (in Thai).
Master's Disseration, Silpakon University.

Hanwong, T. 1991. Reclining Buddha at Wat Thammachak Semaram (in Thai). *Silpakon Journal,* 34(6):61-77.

Hein, D., Barbetti, M. and Bishop, P. 1988. Inhumation burials found at Sisatchanalai.
Siam Society Newsletter, 4(2):12-15.

Hein, D., Burns, P. and Richards, D. 1985. An alternative view on the origins of ceramic production at Si Satchanalai and Sukhothai, central northern Thailand.
Spafa Digest, VII(1):22-33.

Higham, C.F.W. 1977. The Prehistory of the southern Khorat Plateau, Northeast Thailand, with particular reference to Roi Et Province. *In Modern Quaternary Research in Southeast Asia* Volume III. Balkema, Rotterdam.

Higham, C.F.W. 1989. *The Archaeology of Mainland Southeast Asia.* Cambridge University Press, Cambridge.

Higham, C.F.W. 1996. *The Bronze Age of Southeast Asia.* Cambridge University Press, Cambridge.

Higham, C.F.W. and Bannanurag, R. 1990. *The Excavation of Khok Phanom Di, a Prehistoric Site in Central Thailand.* Volume I: *The Excavation, Chronology and Human Burials.*

Society of Antiquaries of London, Research Report no. XLVII, London.

Higham, C.F.W. and Kijngam, A. editors, 1984. *Prehistoric Investigations in Northeast Thailand.* British Archaeological Reports, (International Series), 231, Oxford.

Higham, C.F.W. and Thosarat, R. 1994. *Khok Phanom Di: Prehistoric Adaptation to the World's Richest Habitat.* Harcourt Brace, Fort Worth.

Higham, T.F.G. 1993. The shell knives. In Higham, C.F.W. and Thosarat, R., editors *The Excavation of Khok Phanom Di.* Volume III (part 1): *The Material Culture,* pages 177-212.
Society of Antiquaries of London, Research Report no. L, London.

Ho, C-M, Charoenwongsa, P., Bronson, B., Srisuchat, A. and Srisuchat, T. 1990. Newly identified Chinese ceramic wares from ninth century trading ports in Southern Thailand.
Spafa Digest, XI:12-17.

Ho, C-M. 1984. *The Pottery of Kok Charoen and its Farther Context.* PhD thesis, University of London.

Houghton, P. and Wiriyaromp, W. 1984. The people of Ban Na Di. In Higham, C.F.W. and Kijngam, A. editors, *Prehistoric Investigations in Northeast Thailand,* pages 391-412.
British Archaeological Reports, (International Series), 231, Oxford.

Huai-jen, Y. and Zhiren, X. 1984. Sea level changes in East China over the past 20,000 years. In Whyte, R.O. editor *The Evolution of the East Asian Environment.* Volume I. *Geology and Palaeoclimatology,* pages 288-308.
Centre for Asian Studies, University of Hong Kong.

Indrawooth, P. 1984. Results from the excavation within the ancient town of Nakhon Phathom, Tambon Phra Praton, Amphoe Muang, Changwat Nakhon Phathom (in Thai).
Journal of Silpakon University, Special Issue to Commemorate its 40th Anniversary, 148-68.

Indrawooth, P. 1994. Dvaravati culture in the Chi Valley. A study on Muang Fa Daet Song Yang.
Muang Boran, 20(1):99-120.

Indrawooth, P., Krabuansang, S. and Narkwake, P. 1990. Archaeological study of Ban Krabuang Nok. *Spafa Digest,* XI:12-20.

Indrawooth, P., Krabuansang, S. and Narkwake, P. 1991. Muang Fa Daed Song Yang: new archaeological discoveries. In Université Silpakon, editor, *Récentes Recherches en Archéologie en Thailande: Deuxieme Symposium Franco-Thai,* pages 98-111. Silpakon University, Bangkok.

Indrawooth, P., Krabuansang, S. and Narkwake, P. 1994. The study of ancient civilisation from archaeological evidence in Lamphun before the 19th century B.E. (in Thai).
Archaeology Journal, Special Issue to Commemorate its 40th Anniversary 7-44.

Jacob, J. 1979. Pre-Angkor Cambodia: evidence from the inscriptions in Khmer concerning the common people and their environment. In Smith, R.B. and Watson, W. editors, *Early Southeast Asia,* pages 406-26.
Oxford University Press, Oxford.

Jacques, C. 1989. The Khmers in Thailand: what the inscriptions inform us.
Spafa Digest, 16-24.

Jérémie, S. and Vacher, S. 1992. Le Hoabinhien en Thailande: un example d'approche experimentale. *BEFEO,* 79:173-209.

Jermsawatdi, P. and Charuphananon, C. 1989. Votive tablets from excavation at Wat Nakhon Kosa, Lopburi (in Thai).
Silpakon Journal, 32(6):40-55.

Jiejun, H. 1986. The Neolithic culture of the Lake Dongting area (In Chinese).
Kaogu Xuebao, 1986 (4):385-408.

Kaewglai, C. 1991. Inscription on a Dvaravati silver coin: recent evidence.
Silpakon Journal, 34(2):21-7.

Kaewglai, C. and Saenanon, B. 1990. Stone inscriptions from Khao Noi (in Thai). in *Prasat Khao Noi.*
FAD, Bangkok.

Kanchanagama, P. 1996. *Archaeological Excavation at the late Metal Age Sites in Changwat Nakhon Rachasima* (in Thai). Department of Archaeology, Silpakon University.

Kaosaiyanon, K. 1992. Archaeological site at Non Muang.
Muang Boran, 18(3):172-86.

Kealhofer, L. 1996. The human environment during the terminal Pleistocene and Holocene in Northeastern Thailand: preliminary phytolith evidence from Lake Kumphawapi.
Asian Perspectives, 35(2):229-54.

Kerr, A.F.G. 1924. Notes on some rock paintings in Eastern Siam.
Journal of the Siam Society, 18(2):144-6.

Khemnak, P. 1991. The design motifs on Ban Chiang pots (in Thai).
Silpakon Journal, 34(5):61-95.

Krairiksh, P. 1980. *Art in the South Before the 14th Century AD* (in Thai).
FAD, Bangkok.

Krairiksh, P. 1990. *Art History and Archaeology in Thailand* (in Thai). Amarin Printing Group, Bangkok.

Leong, S.H. 1991. Jenderam Hilir and the Mid-Holocene prehistory of the west coast plain of Peninsular Malaysia.
BIPPA, 10:150-60.

Liangwen, Z. 1992. *The Dai, or the Tai and their Architecture and Customs in South China.*
D.D. Books, Bangkok.

Loofs, H.H.E. 1970. A brief account of the Thai-British archaeological expedition, 1965-70.
Archaeology and Physical Anthropology in Oceania, 5(3):177-84.

Loofs, H.H.E. 1979. Problems of continuity beween the pre-Buddhist and Buddhist periods in Central Thailand, with special reference to U-Thong. In Smith, R.B. and Watson, W. editors, *Early Southeast Asia,* pages 342-51. Oxford University Press, Oxford.

Loofs-Wissowa, H.H.E. 1983. The development and spread of metallurgy in Southeast Asia: a review of the present evidence.
Journal of Southeast Asian Studies, 14(1):1-11, 26-31.

Loofs-Wissowa, H.H.E. 1997. 'Hill of Prosperity': state-of-the-art of the publication of Khok Charoen site, Lopburi Province, Thailand.
BIPPA, 16:199-211.

Loubère, S. de la, 1693. *A New Historical Relation of the Kingdom of Siam.* London.

Lunet de Lajonquière, E.E. 1907. Inventaire Descriptif de Monuments de Cambodge. *PEFEO* 4, Paris.

Lunet de Lajonquière, E.E. 1912. Essai d'Inventaire Archéologique du Siam. *Bulletin de la Commission Archéologique de l'Indochine,* Paris.

Lyons, E. 1965. The traders of Ku Bua. *Archives of the Chinese Art Society of America,* XIX:52-6.

Lyons, E. 1979. Dvaravati; a consideration of its formative period. In Smith, R.B. and Watson, W. editors, *Early Southeast Asia,* pages 352-9. Oxford University Press, Oxford.

Maleipan, V. 1972. Old Stone Age tools at Chiang Saen (in Thai). *Archaeology Journal,* 4:35-43.

Maleipan, V. 1979. The excavation at Sab Champa. In Smith, R.B. and Watson, W. editors, *Early Southeast Asia,* pages 337-41. Oxford University Press, New York.

Maloney, B.K. 1991. Palaeoenvironments of Khok Phanom Di: the pollen, pteridophyte and microscopic charcoal record. In Higham, C.F.W. and Bannanurag, R. editors, *The Excavation of Khok Phanom Di.* Volume II (part 1): *the Biological Remains,* pages 249-314. Society of Antiquaries of London, Research Report no. XLVIII, London.

Mankong, S. 1989. *Noen Ma Kok* (in Thai). FAD, Bangkok.

Mason, G.M. 1991. The molluscan remains. In Higham, C.F.W. and Bannanurag, R. editors, *The Excavation of Khok Phanom Di.* Volume II (part 1): *the Biological Remains,* pages 249-319.

Society of Antiquaries of London, Research Report no. XLVIII, London.

Mason, G.M. 1996. The micromolluscs. In G. B. Thompson, *The Excavation of Khok Phanom Di, a Prehistoric Site in Central Thailand.* Volume IV: *Subsistence and Environment: the Botanical Evidence. The Biological Remains* (Part II), Higham, C.F.W. and Thosarat, R. editors, pages 239-64. Research Report of the Society of Antiquaries of London LIII. London.

Mason, G.M. 1998. The shellfish, crab and fish remains. In Higham, C.F.W. and Thosarat, R. editors, Nong Nor. A Prehistoric Site in Central Thailand, pages 173-211. Anthropoogy Department, University of Otago.

McKenzie, K. G. 1991. The Ostracodes and Forams. In Higham, C.F.W. and Bannanurag, R. editors, *The Excavation of Khok Phanom Di.* Volume II (part 1): *The Biological Remains,* pages 139-46. Society of Antiquaries of London, Research Report no. XLVIII, London.

McNeill, J.R.1997. Muang Phet: Quaritch Wales's moated site excavations re-appraised. *BIPPA,* 16:167-76.

Monkhonkamnuanket, N. 1992. *Ban Prasat. An Archaeological Site* (in Thai). FAD, Bangkok.

Moore, E. 1989. Water management in early Cambodia: evidence from aerial photography. *The Geographical Journal,* 155:204-14.

Moore, E. 1992. Ancient habitation on the Angkor Plain: Ban Takhong to Phum Reul. Unpublished draft paper.

Moore, E., Stott, P. and Sukhasvasti, S. 1996. *Ancient Capitals of Thailand.* River Books, Bangkok.

Moore, M. 1993. The burnishing stones. In Higham, C.F.W. and Thosarat, R., editors *The Excavation of Khok Phanom Di.* Volume III (part 1): *The Material Culture,* pages 105-118. Society of Antiquaries of London, Research Report no. L, London.

Musigakama, N. 1993. *History and Archaeology of Cambodia* (in Thai). FAD, Bangkok.

Na Nakhon, P. 1991. The investigation of Thai language in China (in Thai). *Inscriptions and Historical Work of Professor Dr. Prasert Na Nakhon,* pages 173-80. Kasetsart Universty, Nakhon Pathom.

Nai Pan Hla, 1994. Ngia Kua, or Chao Bon. Who are descended directly from Dvaravati? (in Thai) *Siam Arya,* 2(23):13-16.

Natapintu, S. 1988a. Current research on ancient copper-base metallurgy in Thailand. In Charoenwongsa, P. and Bronson, B. editors, *Prehistoric Studies: The Stone and Metal Ages in Thailand,* pages 107-24. Thai Antiquity Working Group, Bangkok.

Natapintu, S. 1988b. *Ban Lum Khao* (in Thai). FAD, Bangkok.

Natapintu, S. 1991. Archaeometallurgical studies in the Khao Wong Prachan Valley, Central Thailand. *BIPPA,* 11:153-9.

Natapintu, S. and Phommanodch, S., 1990. *Archaeology of Chiang Rai* (in Thai). FAD, Bangkok.

Nitta, E. 1991. Archaeological study on the ancient iron-smelting and salt-making industries in the northeast of Thailand. Preliminary report on the excavations of Non Yang and Ban Don Phlong. *Journal of Southeast Asian Archaeology,* 11:1-46.

Nitta, E. 1992. Ancient industries, ecosystem and environment. *Historical Science Reports, Kagoshima University,* 39:61-80.

Nitta, E. 1994. Archaeological meanings of Heger 1 drums newly found in the Mekhong Basin. *Historical Science Reports, Kagoshima University,* 41:9-23.

Nitta, E. 1997. Iron-smelting and salt-making industries in Northeast Thailand. *BIPPA,* 16:153-160.

Noksakul, D. 1983. *A Study of the Culture and the Environment of an Ancient Community at Khok Phanom Di, Changwat Chonburi.* (in Thai) Master's Thesis, Silpakon University.

O'Reilly, D.J.W. 1995. *An Archaeological Analysis of the Initial Occupation Phase at Nong Nor.* Master's Thesis, Department of Anthropology, University of Otago.

Parmentier, M.H. 1927. *L'Art Khmer Primitif.* PEFEO, XXI-XXII. Paris.

Parry, J.T. 1992, The investigative role of Landsat-TM in the examination of pre- and proto-historic water management sites in Northeast Thailand. *Geocarto International,* 4:5-24.

Pautreau, J-P., Matringhem, A. and Mornais, P. 1997. Thailande, la fin des temps préhistoriques. *Archéologia,* 330:60-6.

Penny, D., Grindrod, J. and Bishop, P. 1996. Preliminary microfossil analysis of a lake sediment core: Nong Han Kumphawapi, Udon Thani, Northeast Thailand. *Asian Perspectives,* 35:209-29.

Phommanodch, S. 1991a. The past at Thung Samrit at Ban Prasat (in Thai). *Silpakon Journal,* 34:6-21.

Phommanodch, S. 1991b. *Archaeology of the Upper Ping Valley* (in Thai). FAD, Bangkok.

Pichard, P. 1976. *Pimay. Etude Architecturale du Temple.* EFEO, Paris.

Pietrusewsky, M. 1997. The people of Ban Chiang: an early Bronze Age site in Northeast Thailand. *BIPPA,* 16:119-48.

Pigott, V.C. and Natapintu, S. 1988. Archaeological investigations into prehistoric copper production: the Thailand Archaeometallurgy Project 1984-6. In Maddin, R. editor, *The Beginnings of the Use of Metals and Alloys,* pages 156-62. M.I.T. Press, Cambridge, Mass.

Pilditch, J.M. 1984. The insect wax. In Higham, C.F.W. and Kijngam A. editors, *Prehistoric Investigations in Northeast Thailand,* pages 124-5. British Archaeological Reports, (International Series), 231, Oxford.

Pilditch, J.M. 1992. The glass beads of Ban Bon Noen, Central Thailand. *Asian Perspectives,* 31(2):171-82.

Pilditch, J.M. 1993. The personal ornaments. In Higham, C.F.W. and Thosarat, R., editors *The Excavation of Khok Phanom Di.* Volume III (part 1): *The Material Culture,* pages 119-76.

Society of Antiquaries of London, Research Report no. L, London.

Pisnupong, P. 1984. *Preliminary Report on the 1982 Excavation at Khok Phanom Di* (in Thai). FAD, Bangkok.

Pisnupong, P., editor, 1991. *Report on the Excavation of the Sra Morakod Monuments* (in Thai). FAD, Bangkok.

Pisnupong, P. 1992. *History and Archaeology of Si Mahosod* (in Thai). FAD, Bangkok.

Pisnupong, P. 1993a. The industrial stone technology. In Higham, C.F.W. and Thosarat, R., editors *The Excavation of Khok Phanom Di.* Volume III (part 1): *The Material Culture,* pages 45-104. Society of Antiquaries of London, Research Report no. L, London.

Pisnupong, P., editor, 1993b. *History and Archaeology of Si Mahosod: Two* (in Thai). FAD, Bangkok.

Pisnupong, P. 1997. Khamphaeng Phet in the pre-Sukhothai period (in Thai). *Muang Boran,* 23(1): 57-65.

Pisnupong, P. and Thawiphon, S. 1989. Archaeological works at Khao Noi (in Thai). *Silpakon Journal,* 32(6):24-39.

Pookajorn, S. 1981. *The Hoabinhian of Mainland Southeast Asia: New Data from the Recent Thai Excavation in the Ban Kao Area.* M.Sc. dissertation, University of Pennsylvania.

Pookajorn, S. 1992. Recent evidences of a Late Pleistocene to a Middle Holocene archaeological site at Moh Khiew Cave

Krabi Province, Thailand. *Silpakon Journal,* 35(3):93-119.

Pope, G.G. 1985. Evidence of early Pleistocene hominid activity from Lampang, northern Thailand. *BIPPA,* 6:2-9.

Pope, G.G., Frayer, D.W., Liangcharoen, M., Kulasing, P. and Nakabanang, S. 1978. Palaeoanthropological Investigations of the Thai-American expedition to Northern Thailand (1978-1980): an interim report. *Asian Perspectives,* XXI:147-63.

Pope, G.G., Barr, S., MacDonald, A. and Nakabanlang, S. 1986. Earliest radiometrically dated artifacts from Southeast Asia. *Current Anthropology,* 27:275-8.

Praprathong, K. 1986. *Historic Archaeology* (in Thai). *FAD,* Bangkok.

Price, T.D. and Gebauer, A.B. 1995. New perspectives on the transition to agriculture. In Price, T.D. and Gebauer, A.B. editors, *Last Hunters-First Farmers,* pages 3-20. School of American Research, Santa Fe.

Prishanchit, S. 1986. Ban Yang Thong Tai (in Thai). In Charoenwongsa, P. editor, *Muang Mae Moh Ob Luang and Ban Yang Thong Tai,* pages 69-115, FAD, Bangkok.

Prishanchit, S. 1991. New prehistoric evidence of the lower Mun Valley (in Thai). *Silpakorn Journal,* 34(6):22-35.

Prishanchit, S., editor, 1992. *Archaeology of Pak Mun* (in Thai). FAD, Bangkok.

Prishanchit, S., Santoni, M. and Pautreau, J-P. 1988. Ob Luang. Report

on survey and excavation in 1985 (in Thai). In Charoenwongsa, P. editor, *Muang Mae Moh Ob Luang and Ban Yaang Thong Tai,* pages 36-68. FAD, Bangkok.

Rajpitak, W. and Seeley, N.J. 1979. The bronze bowls from Ban Don Ta Phet: an enigma of prehistoric metallurgy. *World Archaeology,* 11(1):26-31.

Rasmibhuti, S. 1993. Forward in Musigakama, N., *History and Archaeology of Cambodia* (in Thai). FAD, Bangkok.

Rattanakun, S., editor, 1991. *Ban Chiang Heritage* (in Thai). FAD, *Archaeology Division Publication No. 8,* Bangkok.

Rattanakun, S. 1992. *The Archaeology of Muang Ku Bua* (in Thai). FAD, Bangkok.

Reid, L.A. 1993. Morphological evidence for Austric. *Oceanic Linguistics,* 33:323-44.

Reinecke, A. 1996. Ohrringe mit tierkopfenden in Sudostasian. *Beitrage zur Allgemeinen und Vergleichenden Archaeologie,* 16:5-51.

Renfrew, C. 1987. *Archaeology and Language: the Puzzle of Indo-European Origins.* Penguin, London.

Renfrew, C. and Bahn, P. 1996. *Archaeology. Theories, Methods and Practice.* Thames and Hudson, London.

Reynolds, T.E.G. 1992. Excavations at Banyan Valley Cave, Northern Thailand: a report on the 1972 season. *Asian Perspectives,* 31:77-98.

Rispoli, F. 1992. Preliminary report on the pottery from Tha Kae, Lopburi, Central Thailand. In Glover, I.C. editor, *Southeast Asian Archaeology 1990,* pages 129-42, Centre for Southeast Asian Studies, University of Hull.

Rostoker, W. and Dvorak, J.R. 1989. Direct reduction of copper ore by oxide-sulfide mineral interaction. *Archaeomaterials,* 3:69-87.

Rungrugee, B., Disyadech, P. and Prishanchit, S. n.d. *Fieldwork of the Archaeological Project (Northern Thailand). Fieldwork in 2525-2528 B.E.* (in Thai).

Rungrugee, B., Tassanasrit, P., Prishanchit, S., Vutrnuchit, T., Klinkajorn, S., Pradavsuk, C., Youkongdi, P., Khengsarikit, A., Pumsiri, C. and Preechapichkupt, N. n.d. *Sukhothai Historic Park. Report of the Excavation in 2520-2525 B.E.* (in Thai).

Rutnin, S. 1979. *The Pottery from Non Chai, Northeast Thailand.* Master's thesis, University of Otago.

Rutnin, S. 1988. *The Prehistory of Western Udon Thani and Loei Provinces, Northeastern Thailand.* PhD dissertation, Australian National University, Canberra.

Santoni, M., Pautreau J-P. and Prishanchit, S., 1986. Excavations at Obluang, Province of Chiang Mai, Thailand. In Glover, I.C. and Glover, E. editors, *Southeast Asian Archaeology, 1986.* British Archaeological Reports, (International Series), 561:37-54.

Saraya, D. 1989. *Sri Dvaravati: the Initial Phase of Siam's History* (in Thai). *Muang Boran,* Bangkok.

Saraya, D. 1992a. *The Kingdom of Chenla, Part of the History of Northeast Siam* (in Thai). *Silpawattanatham* Special Issue, Bangkok.

Saraya, D. 1992b. The hinterland state of Sri Thep Sri Deva: A reconstruction. in Glover, I., Suchitta, P. and Villiers, J. editors, *Early Metallurgy, Trade and Urban Centres in Thailand and Southeast Asia,* pages 131-47. White Lotus, Bangkok.

Saraya, D. 1997. *Rethinking the historical evolution of Sukhothai* (in Thai). *Muang Boran,* 23(1): 27-48.

Sarasin, F. 1933. Prehistoric research in Siam. *Journal of the Siam Society,* 26(2):171-202.

Schauffler, W. 1976. Archaeological survey and excavation of Ban Chiang culture sites, Northeast Thailand. *Expedition,* 18:27-37.

Schmidt, W. 1906. *Die Mon-Khmer Volker: ein Bindeglied Zwischen Volkern Zentralasiens und Austronesiens.* Braunschweig.

Shoocondej, R. 1996a. Working towards an anthropological perspective on Thai prehistory: current research on the post-Pleistocene. *BIPPA,* 14:119-32.

Shoocondej, R. 1996b. Rethinking the development of sedentary villages in western Thailand. *BIPPA,* 14:203-15.

Silpakon University, 1980. *Report and a Study of Ancient Culture at Ban Khu Muang, Amphoe Inburi, Changwat Singburi* (in Thai). Department of Archaeology, Silpakon University, Bangkok.

Siribhadra, S. and Moore, E. 1992. *Palaces of the Gods.* River Books, Bangkok.

Siripanish, S. 1985. *An Analytical Study on Pottery from the Excavation of Ban Tha Kae, Muang District, Lopburi Province* (in Thai). Master's thesis, Silpakon University.

Solheim W.G. II 1968. Early bronze in Northeastern Thailand. *Current Anthropology,* 9(1):59-62.

Solheim W.G. II 1972. An earlier agricultural revolution. *Scientific American,* CCVI (4):34-41.

Songsiri, W. 1997. Iron-producing communities at the headwaters of the Lamphang River (In Thai). *Muang Boran,* 23(1):17-26.

Sørensen, P. 1963. North-south indications of a prehistoric migration into Thailand. *East and West,* 14:211-7.

Sørensen, P. 1973. Prehistoric iron implements from Thailand. *Asian Perspectives,* 16:134-73.

Sørensen, P. 1979. The Ongbah cave and its fifth drum. In Smith, R.B. and Watson, W. editors, *Early Southeast Asia,* pages 78-97. Oxford University Press, Oxford.

Sørensen, P. 1988. The kettledrums from Ongbah cave, Kanchanaburi Province. In Sørensen, P. editor, *Archaeological Excavations in Thailand. Surface Finds and Minor Excavations,* pages 95-156. Scandinavian Institute of Asian Studies Occasional Paper No. 1, Copenhagen.

Sørensen, P. and Hatting, T. 1967. *Archaeological Investigations in Thailand.* Volume II, *Ban Kao,* Part 1: *The Archaeological Materials from the Burials.* Munksgaard, Copenhagen.

Srivichit, T., editor, 1991. *Thailand in the 90s.* National Identity Office of the Prime Minister, Bangkok.

Stargardt, J. 1983. *Satingpra I. The Environmental and Economic Archaeology of South Thailand.* British Archaeological Reports, (International Series), 158. Oxford.

Subhadradis Diskul, M.C. 1956. Muang Fa Daet. An ancient town in Northeast Thailand. *Artibus Asiae,* XIX:362-7.

Subhadradis Diskul, M.C. 1979. The development of Dvaravati sculpture and a recent find from North-east Thailand. In Smith, R.B. and Watson, W. editors, *Early Southeast Asia,* pages 360-70. Oxford University Press, Oxford.

Subhadradis Diskul, M.C. 1978. Notes on recent excavations at Prasat Muang Singh. *Journal of the Siam Society,* 66:109-11.

Subhadradis Diskul, M.C. 1989. Stolen art objects returned to Thailand. *Spafa Digest,* X:8-12.

Subhadradis Diskul, M.C. 1990a. Pre-Angkorian discoveries in Thailand. *Spafa Digest,* XI:18-22.

Subhadradis Diskul, M.C. 1990b. Thailand: recent discoveries at the sanctuary of Kamphaeng Yai. *Spafa Digest,* XI:2-6.

Subhadradis Diskul, M.C. 1991. Prasat Kamphaeng Yai in Northeastern Thailand. *Spafa Digest,* 1:4-12.

Subhadradis Diskul, M.C. 1996. Foreward to Moore, E., Stott, P.

Suchitta, P. and Noksakul, D. 1979. Khok Phanom Di. A Neolithic shell mound (in Thai). *Muang Boran,* 5(3):71-9.

Suchitta, P. 1980. *Past and Present Use of the Khok Phanom Di Mound, Thailand. An Archaeological Assessment.* Thai Khadi Research Institute Research Series 3, Thammasat University, Bangkok.

Suchitta, P. 1983. Archaeological projects 1980-1983: Department of Anthropology, Silpakorn University, Bangkok. *Spafa Digest,* IV:37-41.

Suksawasana, Y. 1996. Recent excavation at Dong Lakon: early moated marine chiefdom in eastern coast of Thailand. Paper read at the 6th International Conference of the European Association of Southeast Asian Archaeologists, Leiden, The Netherlands, September 2-6th 1996.

Sulaksananont, A. 1987. *The Study of Muang Phra Rot, Amphoe Phanat Nikhom, Chonburi, from Material Culture and Stratigraphy* (in Thai). Master's thesis, Silpakon University, Bangkok.

Supyen, S., Pumpongpaet, P. and Rungrugee, B. 1988. *The Excavation in Sukhothai Historic Park* (in Thai). FAD, Bangkok.

Suthiragsa, N. 1979. The Ban Chieng culture. In Smith, R.B. and Watson, W. editors, *Early Southeast Asia,* pages 42-52. Oxford University Press, Oxford.

Tankittikorn, W. 1987. *The Archaeological Site of Ban Wang Hi* (in Thai). FAD, Bangkok.

Tankittikorn, W. 1991. *The Settlement Before Muang Sri Thep* (in Thai). FAD, Bankgok.

Tayles, N G. 1998. *The People of Khok Phanom Di.* Research Report of the Society of Antiquaries of London in press.

Thepchai, K. 1983. Excavations at Laem Pho: a Srivijaya Entrepot? *Spafa,* Bangkok.

Thepchai, K. 1988. Laem Pho. The Economic Site of Srivijaya (in Thai). FAD, Bangkok.

Thepchai, K. 1989. Excavations at Laem Pho. FAD, Bangkok

Thompson, G.B. 1996. *The Excavation of Khok Phanom Di. A Prehistoric Site in Central Thailand.* Volume IV. *Subsistence and Environment: the Botanical Evidence (The Biological Remains, Part II).* Society of Antiquaries of London Research Report LIII, London.

Vallibhotama, S. 1983. Ban Chiang culture and destruction of cultural heritage in Northeast Thailand (in Thai). *Muang Boran,* 9:20-38.

Vallibhotama, S. 1991. Bronze-Iron Age foundations for the origin of the state of Chenla. Unpublished paper read at the Conference on the High Bronze Age, Hua Hin, Thailand.

Vallibhotama, S. 1996. *Syam Prathet. Background of Thailand from Primeval Times to Ayutthaya* (in Thai). Matichon, Bangkok.

van Heekeren, H.R. and Knuth, E. 1967. *Archaeological Excavations in Thailand. Sai Yok.* Munksgaard, Copenhagen.

van Liere, W.J. 1979. The environmental archaeology of the prehistoric site of Non Chai. Unpublished report.

van Liere, W.J. 1980. Traditional water management in the lower Mekong Basin. *World Archaeology,* 11:265-80.

Vanasin and Supajanya 1981. *Ancient Cities on the Former Shoreline in the Central Plain of Thailand* (in Thai). Chulalongkorn University Press: Bangkok Research Report no. 1. Bangkok.

Veraprasert, M. 1992. Ancient bead-manufacturing at Khlong Thom. in Glover, I., Suchutta P. and Villiers, J. editors, Early Metallurgy, *Trade and Urban Centres in Thailand and Southeast Asia,* pages 149-62. White Lotus, Bangkok.

Vincent, B.A. 1988. *Prehistoric Ceramics of Northeast Thailand.* British Archaeological Reports (International Series) 461. Oxford.

Vongjaturapat, M. 1991. *Archaeology of Don Noi, Changwat Kanchanaburi* (in Thai). FAD, Bangkok.

Wara-Aswapati, P. 1997. Unearthing ancient Thailand from space. *GIS User,* 24:28-9.

Weeraprajak, K. 1985. *Inscriptions from South Thailand.* Spafa Consultative Workshop on Archaeological and Environmental Studies on Srivijaya. Bangkok.

Weeraprajak, K. 1986a. *Inscriptions in Thailand.* Volume 1. (in Thai). FAD, Bangkok.

Weeraprajak 1986b. *Inscriptions in Thailand.* Volume IV (in Thai). FAD, Bangkok.

Weiss, A.D.1992. The social context of copper production in Central Thailand: evidence from mortuary and industrial data. Paper read at the 4th International Conference of the European Association of Southeast Asian Archaeologists, Rome, 28th September-October 4th 1992.

Welch, D.J. 1997. Archaeological evidence of Khmer state political and economic organisation. *BIPPA*, 16:69-78.

Welch, D.J. and McNeill, J.R. 1991. Settlement, agriculture and population changes in the Phimai region, Thailand. *BIPPA*, 11:210-28.

White, J.C. 1997. A brief note on new dates for the Ban Chiang cultural tradition. *BIPPA*, 16:103-6.

White, J.C. and Pigott, V.C. 1996. From community craft to regional specialization: intensification of copper production in pre-state Thailand. In Wailes, B. editor, *Craft Specialization and Social Evolution: in Memory of V. Gordon Childe*, pages 151-76. University Museum Monograph 93, Philadelphia.

Wichakana, M. 1991. Prehistoric sacrifices at Noen U-Loke (in Thai). *Muang Boran*, 16:69-79.

Wichakana, M., editor, 1994. *Phu Phra Bat Historic Park* (in Thai). 2nd edition. FAD, Bangkok.

Wilaikaeo, J. 1991a. *The Archaeology of Muang U-Taphao* (in Thai). FAD, Bangkok.

Wilaikaeo, J. 1991b. Archaeological work at U-Ta Pao, Chainat Province (in Thai). *Silpakon Journal*, 34(2):1-20.

Wilaikaeo, J. 1997. The origin of Sukhothai people (in Thai). *Muang Boran*, 23(1):49-56.

Wilen, R.N. 1989. *Excavations at Non Pa Kluay, Northeast Thailand*. British Archaeological Reports, (International Series), 517. Oxford.

Williams-Hunt, P. 1950. Irregular earthworks in Eastern Siam: an air survey. *Antiquity*, 24:30-37.

Wolters, O.W. 1979. Khmer 'Hinduism' in the seventh century. In, Smith, R.B. and Watson, W. editors, *Early South East Asia*, pages 427-42. Oxford University Press, Oxford.

Wongthes, S. 1988. *Srivijaya* (in Thai). FAD, Bangkok.

Woods, M. and Parry, S. 1993. An archaeological assessment at Don Dong Muang, Northeast Thailand *Spafa Journal*, 3(2):10-17.

Wyatt, D.K. 1984. *Thailand. A Short History*. Yale University Press, New Haven.

Yen, D. E. 1977. Hoabinhian horticulture? the evidence and the questions from Northwest Thailand. In Allen, J. Golson, J. and Jones, R. editors, *Sunda and Sahul. Prehistoric Studies in Southeast Asia, Melanesia and Australia*, pages 567-99. Academic Press, London.

You-di, C. 1957. Stone tools in Thailand (in Thai). *Silpakon Journal*, 1(1) :48-58

You-di, C. 1976. *Ban Don Ta Phet: Preliminary Excavation Report, 1975-6* (in Thai). National Museum, Bangkok.

You-di, C. 1986. *Prehistory of Thailand* (in Thai). FAD, Bangkok.

Youkongdee P. and Phantukovid, P. 1992. *Surveys of Historic Monuments in Yarang* (in Thai). FAD, Bangkok.

Zhou Daguan, 1993. *The Customs of Cambodia*. Siam Society, Bangkok.

Zide, A. R. K. and Zide, N. H. 1976. Proto-Munda cultural vocabulary: evidence for early agriculture. In Jenner, P. N. Thompson, L. C. and Starosta, S. editors, *Austro-Asiatic Studies part II*, pages 1295-334. Oceanic Linguistics Special Publication 13, Honolulu.

Index